AN INTRODUCTION
TO CRITICAL DISCOURSE
ANALYSIS IN EDUCATION

AN INTRODUCTION
TO CRITICAL DISCOURSE
ANALYSIS IN EDUCATION

Edited by

Rebecca Rogers
Washington University in St. Louis

LEA LAWRENCE ERLBAUM ASSOCIATES, PUBLISHERS
2004   Mahwah, New Jersey   London

Lawrence Erlbaum Associates, Inc., Publishers
10 Industrial Avenue
Mahwah, New Jersey 07430

Cover design by Kathryn Houghtaling Lacey

Library of Congress Cataloging-in-Publication Data

An introduction to critical discourse analysis in education / edited by Rebecca Rogers.
     p.   cm.
  Includes bibliographical references and index.
  ISBN 0-8058-4817-7 (cloth : alk. paper) — ISBN 0-8058-4818-5 (pbk. : alk. paper)
  1. Interaction analysis in education.   2. Critical discourse analysis.   3. Learning.
I. Rogers, Rebecca.

LB1034.I49   2003
371.102'2—dc22   2003049327
                                                                          CIP

Books published by Lawrence Erlbaum Associates are printed on acid-free paper,
and their bindings are chosen for strength and durability.

Printed in the United States of America
10 9 8 7 6 5 4 3 2

For
our grandparents, especially
Doris and Leonard Rogers
and Edward Winne

Contents

Preface

OVERVIEW

The focus of this book is on the relationship between processes of learning in communicative interactions and Critical Discourse Analysis (CDA). Theoretically, the book seeks to conceptualize the relationship between language form and function in educational settings and merge CDA with theories of learning. Methodologically, the book demonstrates the ways in which CDA is put to work in critical ethnographic and interpretive research in education. The chapters draw on the contributors' empirical research in a variety of educational contexts, including teacher-research groups, an adolescent boy in an English classroom, a science museum, educational policy documents, adult literacy education, and a science teacher's talk about instructional practices. This is a timely book because there are few books that introduce and explore the myriad of concepts associated with CDA, especially in relation to educational research.

BACKGROUND OF THIS BOOK

This book represents a new synthesis of theoretical and empirical work in CDA in education. We bring together the work of new literacy studies (Barton, Hamilton, & Ivanič, 2000; Cope & Kalantzis, 2000; Gee, 2000), situated literacies (Barton & Hamilton, 1998; Cole, 1996; Lave & Wenger, 1991), and critical discourse theory and analysis (Chouliaraki & Fairclough,

1999; Fairclough, 1995) with theories of learning (Engestrom, 1996; Tomasello, 1999; Wenger, 1998). Although many discourse analytic accounts have produced useful accounts of discourse as it appears in classrooms and other settings, few have tried to go further and identify ways in which these forms of language are connected to theories of learning.

The agenda for CDA that runs through the chapters in this book surfaced from 3 days of discussions that occurred at Washington University in St. Louis in June 2001, a symposium at the American Educational Research Association, and the subsequent theorizing and analyses conducted by each of the participants (IDEA, 2001). It is rare for scholars working in separate universities and disciplines (policy, linguistics, anthropology, literacy) to sustain conversations over 3 days as we were able to do. The working group meeting originated out of the perceived need for critical discourse work in the United States to pay credence to its sociolinguistic and ethnomethodological roots and at the same time pursue how such theoretical frames and concurrent methods of analysis might contribute to education. After an initial set of electronic discussions, participants sent a set of articles that included their own work and the work of others doing important work in the critical analysis of discourse. We also established, as a group, five guiding questions for our discussions, readings, and subsequent work:

- What are the intersections of (critical) literacy and (critical) linguistics particularly in terms of theorizing linguistic models?
- How do we define context in our work?
- If one of the central goals of a politically and socially grounded analysis of discourse is to expose and undermine social injustice, how does the role of the public intellectual help achieve this goal?
- How do we theorize our own (researchers/analysts) production, consumption, distribution, and representations of language within a critical framework?
- How might we discuss the variation of approaches in analyses?

From this set of meetings, we articulated two directions that we see as important for approaches to CDA in education if it is to take hold in the American context. The first is the need to formulate an empirical basis for the relation between form and function in conducting critical analysis of discourse. The second is the need for a theory of learning in relation to critical discourse studies. Our main purpose in this book is to ground CDA in educational research in the direction of attention to linguistic structure and learning.

The chapters in this volume draw from a wide range of formal and informal learning sites. They are, however, united by (at least) three aspects:

1. The data are naturally occurring rather than being conducted in a lab setting or extracted from other studies of talk in interaction.
2. There is a focus on the socially organized process through which people orient themselves, and are oriented, through talk in context.
3. The studies are characterized by rigorously empirical methods that are motivated by the desire to head off common critiques of CDA: (a) theory driven, (b) extracted from context, and (c) lack of attention to learning.

A key problem for educators using CDA, as Terry Threadgold pointed out in an interview with Barbara Kamler (1997), is that educators are not often trained as linguists and thus, "when you do really detailed linguistic work on a text, you disable many of your readers. There are lots of readers who need to know about the power of critical discourse analysis, but if you do detailed linguistic work it means that only linguists have that text accessible to them" (p. 445). This is a dilemma, and it means careful approaches to the teaching of CDA that includes attention to its intellectual lineage, including ethnomethodology, narrative analysis, and linguistic anthropology. Lack of attention to linguistic predecessors[1] does not allow students of CDA to understand the relationships between microlinguistic aspects of texts, including modality (the nature of the producer's commitment to the message in a clause), transitivity (types of processes and participants in the clause), nominalization of processes (turning actions into nouns or states of being), and ways of representing knowledge and ways of being positioned as social beings within such knowledge arrangements.

NOTES TO THE READER ABOUT THE ORGANIZATION OF THE BOOK

The question of how learning is mediated through discourse has become a subject of debate and inquiry. We conceived the present volume as an effort to bring together separate, yet related, threads of theoretical and empirical work in CDA in a way that would lend new perspectives to the questions of critical discourse analysis and learning. The collection of chapters highlights the complexity of analytic and pedagogical decisions within a CDA framework. At the same time, the chapters begin to articulate a theory and method that analyzes both linguistic structure within and across contexts that can account for, and indeed make visible, the practices of social change, transformation, and learning.

---

[1]Linguistic predecessors of CDA include discourse analysis, conversation analysis, interactional sociolinguistics, and systemic functional grammar.

Each chapter addresses issues of form, function, and learning. To reflexively address matters of learning, we structured our chapters as if we were teaching them in a graduate seminar. At the beginning of each chapter, we pulled out key concepts from the chapter. In the bookend chapters by Gee (chap. 2) and Fairclough (chap. 10), I summarized the central argument of their chapter, which includes key terms. This is somewhat different from the other *central concepts* primarily because both Gee's and Fairclough's chapters focus on central concepts. We imagine that these are the ideas and terms that would be introduced and previewed before, during, and after reading the chapter. You will notice that different authors have different interpretations of key terms. You will also notice that various authors use CDA in different manners. Remember that this is a group of people who spent 3 days working together to sort through CDA and then collaborated for a national symposium. The variation in the chapters that follow reflects the variation embedded in what it means to conduct CDA.

Within each of the chapters (and sometimes at the end of each chapter), the authors have also added reflection/action questions. Our intention with adding these questions was twofold. First, the questions would make the book more interactive with the reader. Second, the questions would move the CDA toward action. As you read each of the chapters, think about the form–function relationships, the relationship between context and discourse, and the author's attention to learning. Also pay attention to how each of the authors uses CDA. In the final chapter, I come back to each of these points and guide the readers through a synthesis of each of the chapters.

CHAPTER OVERVIEWS

"Chapter 2: Discourse Analysis: What Makes It Critical?" by James Paul Gee

In this chapter, Gee discusses features common to many approaches to discourse analysis, at least those with one foot in the field of linguistics, before moving on to what is distinctive about CDA. His basic argument is this: All discourse analysis that intends to make empirical claims is rooted in specific viewpoints about the relationship between form and function in language, although these are rarely spelled out in discourse analytic work in education. Further, empirically motivated work in discourse is ultimately based, in part, on specific analytic techniques for relating form and function in oral and/or written texts. Different approaches to discourse analysis differ in their viewpoints and techniques in regard to form and function in language, although often in ways that do not necessarily make their various analyses incompatible. None of this, however, renders an approach to discourse analysis critical. He argues that CDA involves, beyond relating form and function in language, specific empirical analyses of how such form–function correlations correlate with specific social practices such as to help constitute the nature of such practices. Because social practices inherently involve social relationships, where issues of solidarity, status, and power are at stake, they flow bottom–up from work in CDA and are empirical claims. It is in terms of this claim that Gee treats a common and incorrect criticism of work in CDA—namely, that such work imposes its (usually leftist) politics top–down on the data from the start. Finally, he argues that work on both CDA and sociocultural approaches to language and literacy (the so-called "New Literacy Studies") needs to adopt a particular perspective on learning if such work is to make substantive contributions to education and the work of social transformation. Gee argues that learning (especially in the "new capitalism" of our "new times") is best seen not as a mental thing, but a type of social interaction in which knowledge is distributed across people and their tools and technologies, dispersed at various sites, and stored in links among people, their minds and bodies, and specific affinity groups (one type of which is a community of practice). Such a view of learning, he argues, allows an integration of work in CDA, situated cognition, sociocultural approaches to language and literacy, and particular forms of social theory.

"Chapter 3: A Critical Discourse Analysis of Literate Identities Across Contexts: Alignment and Conflict" by Rebecca Rogers

In this chapter, I (Rogers) theorize about the alignment and conflict among linguistic markers, discourses, and social languages (Gee, 1999) or styles (Fairclough, 2000) with adult literacy students to contribute to theoretical models of learning and critical linguistic analysis. The chapter draws on a research project where I conducted in-depth, oral history interviews with 20 adult literacy students enrolled in the St. Louis Public School system. Each interview consisted of three discursive contexts: (a) history with schooling, (b) present-day experiences with schooling, and (c) participation in their children's education. To develop a theoretical argument about the relationship between linguistic markers and social languages, I draw on a series of analytic moves, each of which is intertextual in nature (Chouliaraki & Fairclough, 1999; Fairclough, 1992, 1995). Specifically, I analyzed both across and within domains of practice (i.e., history with schooling, present-day experiences with schooling, experiences with children's schooling) and orders of discourse (i.e., genres, discourses, styles; Fairclough, 2000).

This was done to demonstrate the ways in which changes in social identity styles or social languages are transformed within domains between the form and function of language—moving from linguistic resources to social languages (Gee, 2000) and styles (Fairclough, 1999, 2000).

Taking up the form–function argument presented in Gee (2001; chap. 2, this volume), I demonstrate how shifts in linguistic resources and social languages comprise social practices. Further, I argue that any discussion involving the ideological nature of language (e.g., Kress, 1993; Pecheux, 1975; Volosinov, 1973) similarly extends to theories of learning (e.g., Wenger, 1998). This argument confronts critiques of CDA as being overly deterministic (e.g., Widdowson, 1998) by first offering empirical evidence for the form–function relationship between linguistic resources and social languages. Second, it confronts critique by contributing to the development of a theoretical model of learning that assumes the ideological and self-extending nature of language in the transformation of social life and self.

"Chapter 4: Discourse in Activity and Activity as Discourse" by Shawn Rowe

Set within a museum, Rowe sets out to accomplish two goals in this chapter. The first is to describe a particular learning theory that adds significantly to accounts of how discourse works to reproduce or transform social relations. The second is to explore through specific examples the possibility of using CDA techniques and concepts to analyze the intersections of linguistic and nonlinguistic semiotic systems in learning activity. Rowe begins with a description of learning as the appropriation of mediational means as part of participation in distributed, mediated activity. Accounts of learning as distributed, mediated activity are well established, but most often deal with learning in classrooms or everyday family (or peer) activities. One goal of this work is to move such studies into the in-between space of the science museum, where families and peer groups attend as natural groups and where learning is one goal of activity, but not perhaps the dominant mediated activity. Rowe then situates the empirical study of group activity, in a science museum, within that framework and suggests how a CDA may add to that account. Finally, using a new transcription system that accounts for activity, Rowe discusses the possibilities opened up by addressing nonlinguistic semiotic systems in a critical study of learning. The chapter concludes with a brief discussion of how analyzing both linguistic and nonlinguistic aspects of activity helps us better understand how the privileging of particular discourses is reproduced in local interaction.

**"Chapter 5: Reframing for Decisions:
Transforming Talk About Literacy Assessment
Among Teachers and Researchers"
by Loukia K. Sarroub**

In this chapter, Sarroub examines the decision-making process of a group
of teachers and researchers engaged in a literacy research project in an elementary school setting. Her aim is to explore, through microlinguistic and
empirical analysis, how one group meeting served to transform the actors
in the group, reconstitute previously agreed-on agendas, and shift authority
in the group. She does this by using several discourse analysis perspectives
ranging from Goffman's (1959, 1981) explication of footing, Davies and
Harré's (1990) and Harré and Van Langenhove's (1991) work on positioning, Gee's (1992, 1996) conceptualization of social discourses, and Fairclough's orders of discourse (i.e., ways of acting, ways of representing, and
ways of being; Fairclough, chap. 10, this volume). Sarroub focuses on one
discursive pattern that she calls "reframing," within which sharing and topic
shifting occur subsequently as co-patterns.

Part of being critical, Sarroub argues, lies in the questions one asks. She
argues that CDA offers educators insights into learning by providing a lens
or frame from which to view change at the personal and institutional levels. Sarroub offers an ethnographic description and analysis of teacher–
researcher talk and the transformation inherent in the social practice of
professional development in a school setting. Her findings reveal that
people interact and represent themselves and others in ways that subvert
and transform power relations at a local level. Hence, they inadvertently
question and reframe how professional development might be enacted.
Such transformation or learning might be missed without the type of analysis Sarroub provides.

**"Chapter 6: Learning as Social Interaction:
Interdiscursivity in a Teacher and Researcher Study Group"
by Cynthia Lewis and Jean Ketter**

This chapter analyzes discussions of young adult multicultural literature
among White middle-school teachers in a rural setting. The authors ask the
following overarching question: What is the nature of learning among the
participating teachers over a 4-year period of time? Related to this question,
how do interaction patterns in the group sustain or disrupt fixed discourses
in ways that shape the group's learning? Using CDA, the authors examined
how participants took up aspects of each others' worldviews, patterns of
talk, and systems of thought as they related to multicultural literature and,

more generally, to the meaning and purposes of multicultural education. These interdiscursive moments have implications for a theory of learning as social interaction and for the professional development of teachers in long-term informal settings.

**"Chapter 7: Cultural Models and Discourses
of Masculinity: Being a Boy in a Literacy Classroom"
by Josephine Peyton Young**

This chapter focuses on how CDA facilitated the study of the discourses of masculinity. Young adapted Gee's (1999, chap. 2, this volume) guidelines for CDA and used Fairclough's (1995, chap. 10, this volume) work as a lens for her interpretations. CDA made visible how Chavo's (a middle-class Hispanic 18-year-old male) constructions of masculinity shaped his participation in school literacy practices and, in turn, the way that school literacy practices and classroom contexts shaped his understandings of what it meant to be a boy in a literacy classroom. Using the four analytic tools (particularly cultural models) suggested by Gee (1999, chap. 2, this volume) for CDA as thinking devices, Young constructed four stories about Chavo's adolescent literacy experiences. As she constructed stories to represent the cultural models of Chavo, his mother, and his teacher, she conducted a micro-analysis on the form and function of the spoken language to inform her CDAs. This chapter demonstrated how an analysis based on the form and function of language worked in conjunction with a more macro-analysis of CDA to highlight the complexities inherent in discourses of masculinity and school literacy.

**"Chapter 8: Language, Power, and Participation:
Using Critical Discourse Analysis to Make Sense
of Public Policy"
by Haley Woodside-Jiron**

Different from the previous chapters in this book, this chapter looks at the use of CDA as a tool in the critical analysis of public policy. Drawing primarily from Fairclough's (1992, 1995; Chouliaraki & Faircough, 1999) frame, this work emphasizes the analysis of text, discourse practices, and social practices in policies related specifically to reading instruction in education. Through the close analysis of changes in reading policies in California between 1995 and 1997, and the more recent federal "No Child Left Behind" legislation, this research pushes beyond issues of form and function in language to deeper understandings of how specific texts, discourse practices, and social practices affect social arrangements, the naturalization of cultural models, and development of literate identities.

The chapter opens by situating CDA within the field of critical policy analysis. Kingdon's (1995) framework for policy analysis is compared with underlying tenants of critical theory to point toward overarching constructs that are important in the critical analysis of policy. The rest of the chapter is dedicated to the analysis of these constructs at a much more detailed analytic and interpretive level through CDA. Specifically, issues of authority, cohesion, intertextuality, and hegemony are examined. Through the analysis of intertextual consistency and consensus in the development of cohesion, we come to see how the naturalization of particular models and perceived consensus contribute to learning and social transformation. Here people are positioned in specific ways by policy professionals and related policies with respect to knowledge and what is thinkable/unthinkable (Bernstein, 1996). Such engineering of social change, Woodside-Jiron argues, reduces resistance and places specific, potentially hegemonic, restraints on our interactions.

**"Chapter 9: Locating the Role
of the Critical Discourse Analyst"
by Lisa Patel Stevens**

This chapter explores the concepts of reflexivity and the role of the public intellectual when using CDA in a field-based setting. The chapter draws on the metalanguage used by myself, as the critical discourse analyst, and a teacher who participated in a year-long study of her literacy practices and beliefs enacted in a middle-school science classroom. The data analyzed included conversations about my work in her classroom, observations, and the findings from CDA methods and frameworks. In turning the CDA framework back on my own work as a field-based researcher, Stevens poses questions about how CDA can be used with research participants, what its role might be as a communicative and transformative teaching and learning tool, and the responsibility of the discourse analyst to field-based participants.

The analysis within the chapter shows that the overt use of and meta-discussions about CDA provided openings and junctures for discussion between myself and the research participant. Further, applying Fairclough's orders of discourses to our conversations shed considerable light on the shifting positionalities, subjectivities, and school-based identities negotiated by and between the researcher and participants. Stevens concludes that using CDA within field-based settings demands a higher level of willingness for both parties to act as interlocuters than would normally occur through the analysis of public documents and texts. This shared sense of responsibility as interlocuters has the potential to draw on metalanguages to explore, unearth, and contest various plausibilities and claims based on the application of CDA.

"Chapter 10: Semiotic Aspects of Social Transformation and Learning" by Norman Fairclough

This chapter is framed by collaborative work between Fairclough and Bob Jessop and Andrew Sayer on theorizing discourse within a critical realist social ontology and epistemology (Fairclough, Jessop, & Sayer, forthcoming). The general question is: How do we interpret the effectiveness of discourse in the reproduction and transformation of social life? This entails addressing a number of other questions including: How do we see the relationship between discourse and nondiscursive (including material) aspects of social life? How do we see the constructive effects of the former on the latter? How do we see the relationship among concrete social events, social structures, and the agency of social actors, and how do we see particular texts, conversations, interviews, and so on as parts of social events? The particular focus in this chapter is on incorporating a theory of learning into this framework. What is the relationship between individual and collective learning and social reproduction and transformation? How does social science figure in processes of individual and collective learning in contemporary societies? How in particular can critical social scientists (including discourse analysts) envisage their contribution to individual and collective learning in ways that accord with the objectives of critical social science? How, finally, does discourse figure in individual and collective learning in its relation to social reproduction and transformation? How might critical discourse analysts envisage their particular contribution to projects of individual and collective learning and progressive social transformation?

"Chapter 11: Setting an Agenda for Critical Discourse Analysis in Education" by Rebecca Rogers

This final chapter looks closely at where CDA theories and methods overlap. The places where there are disjunctures can provide an intellectual road map for CDA in a broad range of educational contexts. I comment explicitly on each of the chapters within the themes of the book: form, function relationships, context and discourse, and CDA and learning.

ACKNOWLEDGMENTS

The 3-day working meeting took place at Washington University in St. Louis. I would like to thank the financial support provided through the Department of Education at Washington University. I would like to extend a special thanks to the chair of the Department of Education, James Wertsch, for his encouragement and support with this meeting during my first year as an assistant professor. I am also grateful that each of the study group members took the time to come to St. Louis to discuss, debate, and collaborate about CDA and education. Many thanks to Judith Solsken, who carefully reviewed an earlier version of this book. A special thanks to Melissa Kniepkamp and Elizabeth Malancharuvil-Berkes for their assistance in the preparation of this manuscript. Also, thank you to Naomi Silverman and Erica Kica at Lawrence Erlbaum Associates for all of their support.

—Rebecca Rogers
Washington University in St. Louis, MO

REFERENCES

Barton, D., & Hamilton, M. (1998). *Local literacies. Reading and writing in one community*. London: Routledge.

Barton, D., Hamilton, M., & Ivanič, R. (Eds.). (2000). *Situated literacies: Reading and writing in context*. London: Routledge.

Bernstein, B. (1996). *Pedagogy symbolic control and identity: Theory, research, critique*. Bristol, PA: Taylor & Francis.

Chouliaraki, L., & Fairclough, N. (1999). *Discourse in late modernity: Rethinking critical discourse analysis*. Edinburgh: Edinburgh University Press.

Cole, M. (1996). *Cultural psychology: A once and future discipline*. Cambridge, MA: Harvard University Press.

Cope, B., & Kalantzis, M. (Eds.). (2000). *Multiliteracies: Literacy learning and the design of social futures*. London: Routledge.

Davies, B., & Harré, R. (1990). Positioning: The discursive production of selves. *Journal for the Theory of Social Behavior, 20*(1), 43–63.

IDEA. *Inquiry into discourse and ethnographic analysis*. (June 9, 2001). Group meeting. Participants include: J. Gee, N. Fairclough, C. Lewis, R Rogers, S. Rowe, L. Sarroub, L. Stevens, and J.P. Young. St. Louis: Washington University.

Engestrom, Y. (1996). Learning by expanding. In H. Daniels (Ed.), *Introduction to Vygotsky* (pp. 123–142). New York: Routledge.

Fairclough, N. (1992). *Discourse and social change*. Cambridge: Polity Press.

Fairclough, N. (1995). *Critical discourse analysis: The critical study of language*. New York: Longman.

Fairclough, N. (2000). Multiliteracies and language. Orders of discourse and intertextuality. In B. Cope & M. Kalantzis (Eds.), *Multiliteracies: Literacy learning and the design of social futures* (pp. 162–181). London: Routledge.

Fairclough, N., Jessop, R., & Sayer, A. (forthcoming). Critical realism and semiosis. In J. Roberts (Ed.), *Critical realism, discourse, and deconstruction*. New York: Routledge.

Gee, J. (1992). *The social mind: Language, ideology, and social practice*. New York: Bergin & Garvey.

Gee, J. (1996). *Social linguistics and literacies: Ideology in discourses* (2nd ed.). London: Taylor & Francis.

Gee, J. (1999). *An introduction to discourse analysis: Theory and method*. New York: Routledge.

Goffman, E. (1959). *The presentation of the self in everyday life*. New York: Anchor.

Goffman, E. (1981). *Forms of talk*. Philadelphia: University of Pennsylvania Press.

Harré, R., & Van Langenhove, L. (1991). Varieties of positioning. *Journal for the Theory of Social Behaviour, 21*(4), 393–407.

Kamler, B. (1997). An interview with Terry Threadgold on critical discourse analysis. *Discourse, 18*(3), 437–452.

Kingdon, J. W. (1995). *Agendas, alternatives, and public policies* (2nd ed.). New York: Longman.

Kress, G. (1993). Against arbitrariness: The social production of the sign as a foundational issue in critical discourse analysis. *Discourse and Society, 4*(2), 169–191.

Lave, J., & Wenger, E. (1991). *Situated learning: Legitimate peripheral participation*. New York: Cambridge University Press.

Pecheux, M. (1975). *Language, semantics and ideology*. New York: St. Martin's Press.

Tomasello, M. (1999). *The cultural origins of human cognition*. Cambridge, MA: Harvard University Press.

Volosinov, V. (1973). *Marxism and the philosophy of language*. Berkeley: University of California Press.

Wenger, E. (1998). *Communities of practices*. Learning, meaning and identity. New York: Cambridge University Press.

Widdowson, H. G. (1998). The theory and practice of critical discourse analysis. *Applied Linguistics, 19*(1), 136–151.

Foreword

James Collins

I write this 1 week after the current U.S. president, a man distinguished by his fundamentalist religious certainty and his commitment to global military unilateralism, addressed a national TV audience, informing the U.S. Congress and the American people that the ongoing war/postwar in Iraq would cost much more and take much longer than confidently predicted a few months earlier. This instructive inability to carry through on high-tech military solutions for stabilizing a global order has its domestic concomitants. It comes from a president whose neoliberal economic policy of tax cuts and industrial deregulation has so far presented the country with the sobering prospect of massive federal deficits and ongoing job loss. It comes also from an administration notable for having early on pushed through legislation, called *Leave No Child Behind*, which greatly increases federal oversight of public education and, in particular, classroom literacy pedagogy. It provides a sharp reminder that we live in an era of globalized economic interconnectivity, increasing economic inequalities, coupled with fundamental cultural and political divisions, within and between nations—and a time in which debates about education have achieved an unparalleled public salience.

In addition to this particular conjuncture of political and economic volatility, during which questions of learning, identity, and power have become densely intertwined, the broader intellectual climate of our era—so-called late or postmodernity—is one of ongoing critique and uncertainty about the bases for knowledge and the grounds for effective action. One result has been a reconsideration of the relation between knowledge and action. As both social analysts and social actors feel the need to grapple with greater complexity under conditions of greater uncertainty, they do so with an increasing sense of ethical commitments. What can I/we do both to understand and change the world? How do I "apply" my research? These are insistent questions in education research as well as a range of traditional academic disciplines (Bauman, 1997). At a time of crises both public and private, when the general theories and "reliable" methodologies of decades past no longer seem adequate to understanding our globalized, diversified circumstances, when optimism about solutions to social problems is on the wane (Rorty, 1989), it is easy to understand the search for critical perspectives—that is, views, concepts, and ways of inquiring that offer some purchase on broad questions of power while also permitting study of particulars, the situated activities and events in which life occurs.

Concern with critique of social injustice, often focused on educational topics, if not educational sites per se, has a reasonable pedigree in sociolinguistics and linguistic anthropology. A founder of quantitative sociolinguistics, Labov (1972) wrote a scathing critique in the late 1960s of the then-prevalent notion that nonstandard speakers were somehow linguistically deficient (educationally "at risk" in the current jargon). Gumperz and Hymes, founding figures in the "ethnography of communication" paradigm, were writing from the 1970s onward about how language difference interacted with social inequalities in school and nonschool settings (Cazden, Hymes, & John, 1970; Gumperz, 1986; Gumperz & Hymes, 1986; Hymes, 1980).

However, what is now propitious about the current period, and shown in this collection, as well as some of the other work discussed later, is that groups of researchers are taking up a common set of goals. Most broadly they seek to combine systematic language analysis, ethnographic grounding, and social theory engagements to develop studies of education that are also inquiries into contemporary life: how we engage each other, learn in groups, develop identities, oppress, and resist oppression.

The chapters in this volume variously argue that critical perspectives require attention to discourse—language use and the social worlds it both presupposes and brings into being—analytical attention informed by debates within social theory. They do so by presenting arguments, concepts, and analyses from the Upper- and lowercase: CDA and critical discourse analysis. In capitalized form, Critical Discourse Analysis is a research program associated with the work of Fairclough and students and collaborators (Chouliaraki & Fairclough, 1999; Fairclough, 1995; Tusting, 2000). Fairclough's framework is grounded in readings of social theory and systemic functional linguistics, and features a three-part scheme of analysis: text (roughly, words and phrasal units), discourse practice (roughly, communicative events and their interpretation), and social practice (roughly, society-wide processes). Analyses have tended to focus on the critique of large-scale media and formal bureaucratic institutions. CDA has been credited with putting questions of power and social injustice squarely on the agenda of UK and European sociolinguistics (Slembrouck, 2001), but it has also been criticized for regularly neglecting to analyze context (Widdowson, 1998) and for its First World parochialism (Blommaert, 2003). Critical discourse analysis, in the lowercase, refers to a range of research efforts in Europe, the UK, and North America, which grapple with questions of language, ideology, and power.

A very influential strand in education-related critical discourse analysis is the work of James Gee (1996, 1999, chap. 2, this volume). His framework features an unusual synthesis of insights from formal and functional linguistics, cognitive sciences, postmodern literary theory, and more work-a-day historical and sociological research on society, schooling, and literacy. His work offers a range of creative, shrewd analyses of policy documents, stories, video games, and found texts (such as aspirin bottle labels). The play of capitals is also important in Gee's work: His distinction between lowercase discourse and uppercase Discourse has been widely discussed in education research, including several chapters in this volume.

Rebecca Rogers, the editor of this collection, is to be lauded for taking the lead in pulling together this timely exchange among young, critically minded education researchers and two major discourse theorists. Her editorial Introduction and Conclusion clearly present the relations between Fairclough's CDA and Gee's discourse/Discourse while also calling for more attention to questions of learning and more fully developed qualitative cases. Among the specific studies contained in this volume, those by Rogers, Young, and Woodside-Jiron provide the most extensive case material. They present suggestive analyses and methodological explorations pertaining to learning practices and participant alignment within influential discourses of being a "kind" of student and a "kind" of African American (Rogers); to learning and identity as regulated within models of masculinity (Young); and to recent state and national struggles over the definition of legitimate pedagogy and literacy (Woodside-Jiron). Other contributions, such as those by Rowe and Sarroub, pose issues of long-standing interest to practitioners of discourse analysis and ethnography: Rowe's chapter addresses the relation between discourse and action as part of an inquiry into situated learning, and Sarroub addresses the relation between analysis of discourse excerpts, reflexive awareness among researchers and participants, and wider ethnographic understanding as part of an inquiry into conflict and decision making among teachers who grapple with assessment procedures.

It is appropriate that a volume arguing that learning often results from conflictual, contradictory juxtapositions of differing discourses contains uneven responses from both Gee and Fairclough. Gee's discussion of discourse, context, and learning occurs early in the collection, treats each concept at length, and argues for a clear distinction between CDA and the wider currents of critical discourse analysis. Fairclough, near the end of the volume, addresses learning as part of "a theoretical reflection on semiotic aspects of social transformation. . . ." In short, he goes "meta"—that is, he translates the question of learning into the problem of emergence, which is part of a general discussion of structural determinants and social change. In reading Gee and Fairclough, in relation to the other contributors as well as each other, one is forced to acknowledge what is at times a fertile tension and at times a chasm between theoretical and descriptive accounts. Working within this tension, the contributors of cases and their primary theoretical interlocutors push forward a discussion of practice-based learning that is sensitive to situation while also cognizant that we live in a world of fast-track capitalism and brutal inequality.

The cases, analyses, and arguments in *An Introduction to Critical Discourse Analysis in Education* can be seen as part of a wider (potential) dialogue about the need for conceptual debate as well as ethnographic grounding in discourse analysis, whether in education research or elsewhere. In presenting a set of comparable case studies engaging concepts of C/critical D/discourse A/analysis, contributors in this volume also develop the "extended case method," which Burawoy (1991), drawing on anthropological, sociological, and Marxist traditions, argued is essential for the production of rational, humane, and emancipatory knowledge about society, history, and our place therein. Turning to more immediate collective interlocutors, these would include the (a) U.S.-based conversations about the "Linguistic anthropology of education," an initial stage of which has been a book of the same name (Wortham & Rymes, 2003), and (b) lively discussion and practice of "Linguistic ethnography in the UK," occurring on a listserve (Ling-ethnog@jiscmail.ac.uk) and at a regular "Linguistic Ethnography Forum" held as part of the annual meetings of the British Association of Applied Linguistics.

In a recent reflective piece for the Linguistic Ethnography Forum, Ben Rampton addressed how being a former teacher influences the ethnographer's insights and anxieties about both description and theory. In general he challenges his audience to grapple with the philosophical, personal, and political issues raised by ethnographic inquiry. In his conclusion, he recalls that

> Twenty five years ago, Hymes outlined the vision of a democratic society where there was one pole with people who'd been professionally trained in ethnography; at the other pole, there was the general population, respected for their intricate and subtle knowledge of the worlds they lived in; and in between, were people who could "combine some disciplined understanding of

ethnographic inquiry with the pursuit of their vocation" (Hymes, 1980, p. 99).
(Rampton, 2003, p. 7)

It seems to me that the contributors in this volume share the Hymesian impulse to widen the reach of ethnography and critical social awareness. It is shown in their concern with reflexive practice, the reports of open exchanges with their research participants, and their desire to make the concepts and practices of critique, discourse analysis, and ethnographic inquiry available to a readership of practicing teachers as well as teacher educators. In this also they are to be commended for their efforts and to the readers of this volume.

REFERENCES

Bauman, Z. (1997). *Postmodernity and its discontents.* New York: Routledge.
Blommaert, J. (2003). *Discourse analysis: A critical introduction.* Cambridge: Cambridge University Press.
Burawoy, M. (1991). The extended case method. In M. Burawoy, A. Burton, A. Ferguson, K. Fox, J. Gamson, N. Gartrell, L. Hurst, C. Kurzman, L. Salzinger, J. Schiffman, & S. Ui (Eds.), *Ethnography unbound: Power and resistance in the modern metropolis* (pp. 271–290). Berkeley: University of California Press.
Cazden, C., Hymes, D., & John, V. (Eds.). (1970). *Functions of language in the classroom.* New York: Teachers College Press.
Chouliaraki, L., & Fairclough, N. (1999). *Discourse in late modernity.* Edinburgh: University of Edinburgh Press.
Fairclough, N. (1995). *Critical discourse analysis.* London: Longman.
Gee, J. (1996). *Social linguistics and literacies* (2nd ed.). London: Taylor & Maxwell.
Gee, J. (1999). *An introduction to discourse analysis.* New York: Routledge.
Gumperz, J. (1986). Interactional sociolinguistics in the study of schooling. In J. Cook-Gumperz (Ed.), *The social construction of literacy* (pp. 45–68). New York: Cambridge University Press.
Gumperz, J., & Hymes, D. (Eds.). (1986). *Directions in sociolinguistics* (2nd ed.). Oxford: Blackwell.
Hymes, D. (1980). *Language in education: Ethnolinguistic essays.* Washington, DC: CAL.
Labov, W. (1972). *The logic of nonstandard English, Language in the inner city.* Philadelphia: University of Pennsylvania Press.
Rampton, B. (2003). *Coming to linguistic ethnography from a background in teaching.* Paper presented at the annual meeting of the British Association of Applied Linguistics.
Rorty, R. (1981). *Contingency, irony, and solidarity.* New York: Cambridge University Press.
Slembrouck, S. (2001). Explanation, interpretation and critique in the analysis of discourse. *Critique of Anthropology, 21,* 33–57.
Tusting, K. (2000). *Written intertextuality and the construction of Catholic identity in a parish community: An ethnographic study.* Unpublished doctoral dissertation, Lancaster University, Lancaster.
Widdowson, H. (1998). The theory and practice of critical discourse analysis. *Applied Linguistics, 19,* 136–151.
Wortham, S., & Rymes, B. (Eds.). (2003). *Linguistic anthropology of education.* Westport, CT: Praeger.

About the Authors

EDITOR

Rebecca Rogers

Rebecca Rogers is an Assistant Professor in the Department of Education at Washington University in St. Louis. She teaches courses in critical discourse analysis, sociolinguistics, critical literacy, and literacy methods for teachers. Her current research investigates how both adults who are labeled as "low literate" and elementary school children accelerate as readers and writers within a crticial literacy/social justice framework. Set in both elementary and adult learning sites, Rogers is developing a life-span perspective of critical literacy development. She is the author of *A Critical Discourse Analysis of Family Literacy Practices: Power in and out of Print* (Erlbaum, 2003).

AUTHORS

Norman Fairclough

Norman Fairclough is a Professor of Language in Social Life at Lancaster University. His books include *Language and Power, Critical Language Awareness, Discourse and Social Change,* and *Critical Discourse Analysis.*

James Gee

James Paul Gee is the Tashia Morgridge Professor of Reading at the University of Wisconsin–Madison. Among other books, he is the author of *Social Linguistics and Literacies, The Social Mind,* and *What Video Games Have to Teach Us About Learning and Literacy.*

Jean Ketter

Jean Ketter, who taught high school English and journalism for 12 years, is currently a Grinnell College associate professor of education. In addition to research interests in critical discourse analysis and the sociocultural aspects of multicultural literature instruction, she researches the political and pedagogical import of high-stakes reading and writing assessment. At Grinnell, she teaches classes in educational foundations, educational history, and the theories and methods of English and foreign language instruction.

Cynthia Lewis

Cynthia Lewis is Associate Professor at the University of Iowa where she coordinates the Language, Literacy, and Culture Program and teaches courses in critical discourse analysis, theoretical perspectives on literacy research, and children's literature. Her research focuses on literacy as a social and critical practice, with a particular interest in the discursive construction of power and identity in literacy teaching and learning. She is the author of *Literary Practices as Social Acts: Power, Status, and Cultural Norms in the Classroom* (Erlbaum, 2001), which received the Edward B. Fry Book Award and the Thomas N. Urban Research Award.

Shawn Rowe

Shawn Rowe holds a Ph.D. from Washington University in St. Louis, Department of Education. His research focuses on critical discourse analysis in informal learning sites such as science centers and museums. He teaches courses in sociolinguistics and research methods.

Loukia K. Sarroub

Loukia K. Sarroub is an Assistant Professor in the Department of Teaching, Learning and Teacher Education in the College of Education and Human Sciences at the University of Nebraska–Lincoln. Her research and teaching focus on literacy and discourse practices in and out of school, education and anthropology, youth cultures, immigrant communities, and ethnographic and qualitative research methods. She is the author of *All American Yemen Girls: Islam and Education in a Public School* (Forthcoming, University of Pennsylvania Press).

Lisa Patel Stevens

Lisa Patel Stevens is a lecturer in the Middle Years of Schooling program at the University of Queensland in Australia. Prior to taking up work as an academic, Lisa worked as a reading teacher, literacy specialist, and policy-maker. Her research interests include the intersections of language, literacy, and culture with young people, and the cultural construction of adolescence as a life stage.

Haley Woodside-Jiron

Haley Woodside-Jiron is an Assistant Professor in the Department of Education at the University of Vermont. Her teaching and research focus on educational policy, literacy methods, teacher change, and decision-making processes in education. Currently she is researching the federal Reading First initiative and how it is negotiated in different states, districts, and schools. She is also engaged in the discourse analysis of classroom talk and the effects of teacher prompts in student literacy development.

Josephine Peyton Young

Josephine Peyton Young is an Assistant Professor of Language and Literacy at Arizona State University. She teaches courses in content area literacy and adolescent literacy with a focus on gender. Her research focuses on issues related to adolescent literacy. Currently, she is studying the literate practices of adolescent males in relation to their beliefs about and constructions of masculinity.

An Introduction to Critical Discourse Analysis in Education

Rebecca Rogers
Washington University in St. Louis

Critical Discourse Analysis (CDA) holds much promise for educational research. Researchers using CDA can describe, interpret, and explain the relationships among language and important educational issues. One such issue is the current relationship among the economy, national policies, and educational practices. In what Gee and the New Literacy Scholars refer to as *fast capitalism*, the top–down model of business (and classroom) leadership has been abandoned for a "community of practice" model (e.g., Wenger, 1998; Wenger, McDermott, & Snyder, 2002) characterized by flattened hierarchies, the construction and distribution of knowledge, joint problem solving, and flexible and creative workers. Many new literacy classrooms fit this description. There is also a back-to-the-basics backlash at national and state levels—to return to an educational system reminiscent of factory models of education. Gee (2001) pointed out the contradictions embedded in such policies, especially when the world of work is moving in the opposite direction.

CDA is amply prepared to handle such contradictions as they emerge and demonstrate how they are enacted and transformed through linguistic practices in ways of interacting, representing, and being. Locating such relationships are at the heart of a CDA agenda, but are often difficult to pinpoint. To understand the power–knowledge relationships operating in a committee on special education meeting or in a second-grade classroom, analysts need to understand the relationship between language form and function, the history of the practices that construct present-day practices,

1

and how social roles are acquired and transformed. Each of these are threads that run through this book.

THE MULTIPLE MEANINGS OF CRITICAL DISCOURSE ANALYSIS

What is critical about CDA? Is all analysis of discourse, assuming that language is social and political, a CDA? Is there a specific sequence of methodological steps that qualifies an analysis as CDA? What aspects of language are important to analyze in conducting CDA? What is the difference between cda and CDA? How do we assess the validity and trustworthiness of such research?

CDA is both a theory and a method. Researchers who are interested in the relationship between language and society use CDA to help them describe, interpret, and explain such relationships. CDA is different from other discourse analysis methods because it includes not only a description and interpretation of discourse in context, but also offers an explanation of why and how discourses work. CDA is a domain of critical applied linguistics (e.g., Fowler, Hodge, Kress, & Trew, 1979; Kress & Hodge, 1979; Parker & the Bolton Discourse Group, 1999; Pecheux, 1975; Pennycook, 2001; Willig, 1999). There are many different approaches to CDA, including French discourse analysis (e.g., Foucault, 1972; Pecheux, 1975), social semiotics (Hodge & Kress, 1988), sociocognitive studies (van Dijk, 1993), and the discourse historical method (Wodak, 1996, 1999). Each of these perspectives on CDA can be applied to issues in education.

Fairclough and Wodak (1997) offered eight foundational principles of CDA. These principles are a useful starting point for researchers interested in conducting CDA. These are:

- CDA addresses social problems
- Power relations are discursive
- Discourse constitutes society and culture
- Discourse does ideological work
- Discourse is historical
- A sociocognitive approach is needed to understand how relations between texts and society are mediated
- Discourse analysis is interpretive and explanatory and uses a systematic methodology
- CDA is a socially committed scientific paradigm

Over the past two decades, much research has been conducted using these principles (see Rogers et al. [in progress] for a literature review). CDA is beginning to take hold in educational research in North America (see Siegel & Fernandez [2000] for an overview of critical approaches). Educational researchers are interested in how texts are put together (e.g., Bloome & Carter, 2001; Lemke, 1992; Peyton-Young, 2001), studies of policy (Collins, 2001; Corson, 2000; Woodside-Jiron, 2002, in press), and interactions in classrooms and schools (Bloome & Egan-Robertson, 1993; Kumaravadivelu, 1999; Moje, 1997; Rogers, 2003). All of these studies are linked in their inquiry into the relationship between language and social configurations of education. Although there is no formula for conducting CDA, researchers who use CDA are concerned with a critical theory of the social world, the relationship of language and discourse in the construction and representation of this social world, and a methodology that allows them to describe, interpret, and explain such relationships. As outlined in the next section, approaches to CDA may vary at the "critical," "discourse," or "analysis" sections of the method, but must include all three parts to be considered a CDA.

What Is the "Critical" Part of CDA?

The term *critical* in CDA is often associated with studying power relations. This concept of critical is rooted in the Frankfurt school of critical theory (Adorno, 1973; Adorno & Horkeimer, 1972; Habermas, 1976). Critical research and theory is a rejection of naturalism (that social practices, labels, and programs represent reality), rationality (the assumption that truth is a result of science and logic), neutrality (the assumption that truth does not reflect any particular interests), and individualism. Critical research rejects the overdeterministic view of social theory espoused by Marxists and instead argues for a dialectic between individual agency and structural determinism. As with all research, the intentions of critical discourse analysts are not neutral. Corson (2000) wrote that his aim is to, "explore hidden power relations between a piece of discourse and wider social and cultural formations" and have an interest in "uncovering inequality, power relationships, injustices, discrimination, bias, etc" (p. 95). Corson raised an important point concerning the nature of critical discourse work. The intentions of the analyst always guide the theory and method of CDA. Within this framework of "critical," the analyst's intention is to uncover power relationships and demonstrate inequities embedded in society. In this framework, the analyst may believe that the uncovering of power relationships in their analysis may lead to disrupting the power relations in the social contexts in which they study. They do not, however, include such political and social disruption in their analysis.

Another interpretation of the "critical" in CDA is an attempt to describe, interpret, and explain the relationship between the form and function of language. The form of language, as expanded on in a later section, consists of grammar, morphology, semantics, syntax, and pragmatics. The function of language includes how people use language in different situations to achieve an outcome. Critical discourse analysts believe there is a relationship between the form and function of language. Further, they start with the assumption that certain networks of form–function relationships are valued in society more than others. For example, the informal genre of storytelling combined with the anecdotal information a parent shares about their child as a reader at home carries less social value within the context of a Committee on Special Education (CSE) meeting than the formal genre of presenting test scores. A critical discourse analyst's goal is to study the relationships between language form and function and explain why and how certain patterns are privileged over others. In the sense that all systems of meaning are linked to socially defined practices that carry more or less privilege and value in society, such exploration is also an exploration into power and language. As Chouliaraki and Fairclough (1999) stated, "our view is that the links between particular discourses and social positions, and therefore the ideological effects of discourse, are established and negotiated in the process of articulation within a practice" (p. 150). The implication, in this perspective of "critical," is that although ideology inevitably exists, it is explicitly studied. In this perspective, the intention of the analyst is to explore the networks of discourse patterns that comprise social situations.

Another interpretation of "critical" is that CDA explicitly addresses social problems and seeks to solve social problems through the analysis and accompanying social and political action. The intention of the analyst in this view of "critical" is explicitly oriented toward locating social problems and analyzing how discourse operates to construct and is historically constructed by such issues. In this perspective, analysts believe that analyzing texts for power is not enough to disrupt such discursive powers. Instead the analyst must work from the analysis of texts to the social and political contexts in which the texts emerge. This is an explicitly action-oriented stance and is most often referred to as a form of critical language awareness.

What Is the "Discourse" Part of CDA?

Analysts of language have defined *discourse* in a broad number of ways. Stubbs (1983) defined it as, "language above the sentence or above the clause" (p. 1). Brown and Yule (1983) wrote, "the analysis of discourse is, necessarily, the analysis of language in use. As such, it cannot be restricted to the description of linguistic forms independent of the purposes or functions which these forms are designed to serve human affairs" (p. 1). Fairclough (1992a) wrote, "Discourse is, for me, more than just language use: it is language use, whether speech or writing, seen as a type of social practice" (p. 28).[1]

Discourse within a CDA framework traces its linguistic genealogy to critical linguistics and systemic functional linguistics (Fowler et al., 1979; Kress & Hodge, 1979). Within a functional approach to language (an area I address in depth later), linguists believe that language responds to the functions of language use and has different work (or functions) to perform. Within this discipline, discourse is a system of meanings or "systematically organized set of statements which give expression to the meanings and values of an institution" (Kress, 1985, p. 6).

Within a CDA framework, analysts of discourse start with the assumption that language use is always social and that analyses of language occur above the unit of a sentence or clause (e.g., Jaworski & Coupland, 1999). In this view, discourse both reflects and constructs the social world and is referred to as constitutive, dialectical, and dialogic. Discourse is never just a product, but a set of consumptive, productive, distributive, and reproductive processes that is in relation to the social world.

Gee (1996) made a distinction between little "d" and "D" discourse. Little "d" refers to language bits or the grammar of what is said. "D"iscourse refers to the ways of representing, believing, valuing, and participating with the language bits. Big Discourse includes language bits, but it also includes the identities and meanings that go along with such ways of speaking. This distinction helps us see that the form of language cannot exist independent of the function of language and the intention of speakers. Further, Gee (chap. 2, this volume) asserts that Discourse is not merely a pattern of social interactions, but is connected to identity and the distribution of social goods. Gee (1996) set forth a number of theoretical propositions about Discourses:

1. Discourses are inherently ideological. . . . They crucially involve a set of values and viewpoints about the relationships between people and the distribution of social goods, at the very least, about who is an insider and who is not, often who is "normal" and who is not, and often, too, many other things as well.

2. Discourses are resistant to internal criticism and self-scrutiny because uttering viewpoints that seriously undermine them defines one as being outside of them. The Discourse defines what counts as acceptable criticism.

---

[1]See K. Sawyer (2002) for an analysis of the concept of discourse within Foucault's writing.

3. Discourse-defined positions from which to speak and behave are not, however, just defined internally to a Discourse, but also as standpoints taken up by the Discourse in its relation to other, ultimately opposing, Discourses.

4. Any Discourse concerns itself with certain objects and puts forward certain concepts, viewpoints, and values at the expense of others. In doing so, it marginalizes viewpoints and values central to other Discourses. In fact, a Discourse can call for one to accept values in conflict with other Discourses of which one is also a member.

5. Discourses are intimately related to the distribution of social power and hierarchical structure in society, which is why they are always and everywhere ideological. Control over certain Discourses can lead to the acquisition of social goods (money, power, status) in a society. These Discourses empower those groups that have the least conflicts with their other Discourses when they use them. Let us call Discourses that lead to social goods in a society *dominant Discourses*, and let us refer to those groups that have the fewest conflicts when using them as *dominant groups*.

Critical discourse analysts treat language differently than linguists, sociolinguists, or conversation analysts. Discourse within a CDA framework is not a reflection of social contexts, but constructs and is constructed by contexts. Discourses are always socially, politically, racially, and economically loaded.

What Is the "Analysis" Part of CDA?

Although there are many principles about discourse that unite the research of CDA, there is also dissension within the community of CDA. Oftentimes this dissension revolves around analytic procedures.[2] The analytic procedures depend on what definitions of *critical* and *discourse* the analyst has taken up as well as his or her intentions for conducting the analysis. There are more and less textually oriented approaches to discourse analysis. Some methods are less linguistically focused and more focused on the context in which the discourse arises. Other methods are interested in the historical emergence of a set of concepts or policies. Other methods pay equal attention to language and social theory. Fairclough (1992a) referred to this method as a textually oriented approach to discourse analysis. The chapters in this book engage in textually oriented approaches to discourse analysis. Two of the most common sets of methodologies used by educational researchers are those of Gee (1999) and Fairclough (1992a, 1992b, 1995). As

---

[2]See also Titscher, Meyer, Wodak, and Vetter (2000) for an overview of CDA procedures and techniques.

I demonstrate in chapter 10, although there is a great deal of synergy among the frameworks, there are also places of conflict.

Fairclough's (1992, 1995) analytic procedures include a three-tiered model that includes description, interpretation, and explanation of discursive relations and social practices at the local, institutional, and societal domains of analysis. The local domain may include a particular text (e.g., a newspaper, political speech, or school board meeting). The institutional domain is the next level of abstraction and includes the social institutions that enable and constrain the local domain (e.g., political affiliation of the newspaper company, schools). The societal domain is the next level of abstraction and includes the policies and meta-narratives that shape and are shaped by the institutional and local domains. Each of these domains is in an ongoing dialogue with each other. Chouliaraki and Fairclough (1999) developed this analytic scheme even further by incorporating elements of systemic functional linguistics into the analytic framework. They referred to genre, discourse, and style as the three properties of language that are operating within and among the local, institutional, and societal domains. A critical discourse analyst using this set of procedures will continually move between a micro- and macroanalysis of texts. This recursive movement between linguistic and social analysis is what makes CDA a systematic method, rather than a haphazard analysis of discourse and power.

Gee's (1999) analytic procedures include a set of connection-building activities that includes describing, interpreting, and explaining the relationship between language bits (small "d") and cultural models, situated identities, and situated meanings (big "D"). The connection-building activities includes six that allow the analyst to construct meaning from a network of discourse patterns. The tasks include: semiotic building, world building, activity building, socioculturally situated identity building, political building, and connection building. Gee provided a useful list of questions to ask of each task. The questions consist of various aspects of grammar. For example, within "semiotic building," Gee asked the question: What sign systems are relevant (and irrelevant) in the situation? In world building, Gee posed the question: What are the situated meanings of some of the words and phrases that seem important in the situation? (see chap. 11 for a full discussion of Gee's methodology in relation to Fairclough's).

The CDA, then, is an analysis of not only what is said, but what is left out—not only what is present in the text, but what is absent. In this sense, CDA does not read political and social ideologies onto texts. Rather, the task of the analyst is to figure out all of the possible configurations between texts, ways of representing, and ways of being, and to look for and discover the relationships between texts and ways of being and why certain people take up certain positions vis-à-vis situated uses of language.

There are no formulas for conducting CDA. Deciding which set of analytic procedures to use depends on the practical research situation you are in, the texts you are studying, and your research questions. Each of the authors in this volume has chosen a different entry point for his or her analysis. What is necessary is attention to critical social theories and linguistic analysis of texts. What is important is that all three components of CDA (critical, discourse, and analysis) are embedded within a methodology. In this book, each of the authors attends to these components of CDA. We have also targeted three issues that we believe are important for CDA in educational research. The first is attention to the relationship between language form and language function. The second is attention to the relationship between discourse and contexts. The third is attention to what insights CDA provides us about learning. The following introduces some of the important concepts that appear in each of the chapters.

THE MAKING OF MEANING: FORM AND FUNCTION

Systemic functional linguistics is the linguistic backbone of CDA (Halliday, 1994; Halliday & Hasan, 1989). Systemic-functional linguistics (SFL) is a theory of language that focuses on the function of language. Although SFL accounts for the syntactic structure of language, it places the function of language as central (what language does, and how it does it), in preference to more structural approaches, which place the elements of language and their combinations as central. SFL starts at social context and looks at how language both acts on and is constrained by this social context.

Put simply, there are hard and soft structures to language. Hard structures include aspects of the linguistic system such as adjectives, nouns, and verbs. Soft structures include the function of language. They are referred to as *soft structures* because of the level of abstraction. The goal of an empirically based CDA is to describe, interpret, and explain the relationship between the hard and soft structures of language.[3] Halliday (1975) wrote,

> The viewpoint we are taking [with regard to language] is a functional one. We shall relate the meaning, in turn, to linguistic function, to the functions that language is made to serve in the life of the growing child . . . this gives us some insight into why the adult language has evolved in the way it has . . . we can see the adult linguistic study is structured in a way which reflects very closely its functional origins. (p. 8)

One of the underlying assumptions of SFL is that the object of language study should be a whole text, not a decontextualized sentence or utterance. SFL is committed to a view of language that focuses on meaning and the choices people make when making meaning. Unlike structural aspects of

---

[3]See Lynn and Cleary (1993) and Goatly (2000) for an introduction to linguistic concepts.

language systems (e.g., generative models of grammar), there are no sharp distinctions between the system (form) and the use of language (function). This means that the analyst can look to speech (discourse) as an artifact of the relationship between language and structure.

The assumption that language and literacy practices are socially situated *and* have underlying systems of meaning underlies an SFL approach to language. According to Halliday (1978), there is a deep organizing principle in the grammars of human language that distinguishes between the functions available in language. Halliday stated, "there is a systematic correspondence between the semiotic structure of the situation type (field, mode, tenor) and the functional organization of the semantic system" (p. 32). Within SFL, language is encoded in particular genres (e.g., poetry, sermon, informal talk among friends, political speech). This is referred to as the *mode* of language and is a primarily textual function. Every utterance also enacts certain social relationships. This is the *tenor* of the utterance, and the function is primarily interpersonal. Last, every utterance operates within a larger framework of what is possible given cultural constraints. This is referred to as the *field* of language, and the primary function is ideational. In other words, every utterance is made up of three different functions—textual, interpersonal, and ideational. There are parallels among SFL mode, tenor, and field and genre, discourse, and style within CDA (this relationship appears in chaps. 3, 6, and 11, this volume).

Another distinguishing feature of SFL is the conscious or unconscious choice of meaning. A set of options such as singular/plural, past/present/future tense, and positive/negative polarity is available to every speaker and is called a *system*—thus the name *systemic linguistics*. When language is described this way, every choice made also signifies choices *not* made. It would be naïve to think that all people have equal access to options when speaking. Indeed Fairclough (chap. 10, this volume) argues that social practices control the selection of certain structural possibilities and the exclusion of others.

Despite the centrality of SFL in discourse studies in general and CDA in particular, educational researchers in the American context have been reluctant to take up the work of SFL (Christie, 2002; Cope & Kalantzis, 2000; Goatly, 2000; Schleppegrell, 2001). Gee (chap. 2, this volume) points out that American linguists have a historical link to a Chomskian model of linguistics. This is a problem because autonomous models of syntax associated with Chomskian models of linguistics privilege language study as autonomous and disassociated parts—antithetical to the theoretical assumptions about discourse to which many analysts prescribe (see also Gee, chap. 2, this volume). In this volume, we argue that analysts should explicitly attend to theories of language and the relationship between form and function.

CONTEXT AND DISCOURSE

CDA starts with the assumption that language use is always inevitably constructing and constructed by social, cultural, political, and economic contexts. Fairclough (1995) outlined three contexts that are important for CDA: local, institutional, and societal. These contexts are especially relevant to educational researchers studying the interactions between teachers and students, curriculum documents, institutional meetings, state think tanks charged to address current educational issues, and so on.

We may also think about the CDA making up a context. For example, in an analysis of a conversation between a teacher and student, we may analyze the way in which the teacher and student are interacting (genre, mode), the relationship between them (tenor), and the way they call on larger discourses of achievement (field). This analysis of the way in which discourses are linked together is a context. What is important to remember is that every context has a history of discourse links and practices that are chained together in particular ways.

The relationship between context and discourse has a long and tumultuous history in linguistic analysis (for a current discussion, see Blommaert, 2001; Heller, 2001; Slembrouck, 2001). For conversation analysis, *context* is defined in terms of the immediate "here and now" of co-participants in a dialogue. Accordingly, the most important context for participants as well as analysts is the linguistic one (i.e., what has been said immediately prior to an utterance). In conversation analysis, the immediate physical context is of equal importance to the reconstruction of the meaning of a given utterance. Yet Linell (1998) argued that, for methodological reasons articulated most clearly in Schegeloff (1991), larger sociocultural contexts have generally been ignored in conversation analysis (CA). As a result, CA does not pay close attention to the social and political contexts in which the everyday interactions it chooses for analysis take place. Ethnographies of speaking (Briggs, 1996), interactional sociolinguistics (Gumperz, 1982), forms of discourse analysis (Linell, 1998; Rommetviet & Blakar, 1979; Scollon, 2001), as well as CDA (Fairclough, 1995; Gee, 1999) have used CA methods. Indeed to carry out CDA, the analyst must attend to traditional conversation analysis. These analyses have extended the account of what constitutes meaningful contextual resources (Linell, 1998) to include some of the culturally, historically, and institutionally situated affordances and constraints on ways of speaking that shape speakers' meaning-making activity (see Jaworski & Coupland [1999] for an overview of approaches). CDA, in contrast, although making social and political analyses and claims, has often been critiqued for decontextualizing the discourse analyses, erring by either attending to social theory or detailed linguistic analyses (Widdowson, 1998). Blommaert (2001) stated,

One of the most important methodological problems in discourse analysis in general is the framing of discourse in particular selections of contexts, the relevance of which is established by the researcher but is not made into an object of investigation . . . this problem is especially pressing in the case of CDA, where the social situatedness of discourse data is crucial and where context is often taken to include broad systematic and institutional observations. (p. 5)

CDA insists on an analysis of context to understand language in use. As Gee (chap. 2, this volume) states, an issue for the analyst is determining which context to include—or what he refers to as the *frame* problem. Obviously a CDA cannot attend to all contexts at the same time. What is important to remember is that there is attention paid to the ways in which the local, institutional, and societal domains construct and are constructed by discourses and how these contexts change over time. Such contexts must be linked to the questions that are asked and the assertions that can be made from the analysis.

CRITICAL DISCOURSE ANALYSIS IN EDUCATIONAL SETTINGS

The current state of educational affairs is a result of interlocking social, cultural, economic, and epistemological factors. As Young (1990) wrote,

the modern educational crisis is a product of the one-sided development of our capacity for rational management of human affairs and rational problem solving. The institution of mass schooling can be either a source of the problem or a possible vehicle for the changes in learn level we require. (p. 23)

The crisis is an educational one because powerful groups seek to use educational means to bring about what they see as resolutions to current problems. For schooling to continue to be educational, it must solve the modern educational problem.

The contributors to this volume define *education* as including informal and formal learning opportunities for preservice and inservice teachers for elementary and adult students. Learning opportunities occur in the local community, within the school building (e.g., in classrooms as well as meeting rooms), and are shaped by the national policies. One of the central concerns in education is the discrepancy in achievement between mainstream and working class and minority children. The No Child Left Behind Act rhetorically argues for the importance of reading polices and practices that are scientific, reliable, and replicable so that every child has the opportunity to learn how to read. As researchers interested in discourse, we understand that *opportunity* is a cultural model that can take on different meanings depending on the speaker's intention. When we talk about matters of achievement, within the national rhetoric of achievement, we often measure achievement as an in-the-head phenomenon rather than a set of practices that are socially and culturally situated. Further, achievement is often measured in terms of a set of outcomes (e.g., proficiency in math problems, an increase in reading levels).

The methodologies that are espoused as valuable are increasingly positivistic, reliable, and replicable. Only methodologies that are rational and replicable are given credence. Such a narrow methodology can only examine learning (and other educational issues) from one point of view.

In educational settings, language is the primary mediational tool through which learning occurs. Sociocultural learning theorists have not attended to matters of inequity and privilege, nor have critical discourse theorists attended to matters of learning. In this volume, we argue that CDA contributes to an understanding of learning in two primary ways. First, analyzing discourse from a critical perspective allows one to understand the processes of learning in more complex ways. Indeed the close analysis of the networking of language allows the analyst insight into aspects of learning that other theories and methods might have missed. Second, in the process of conducting CDA, researchers' and participants' learning is shaped (also an aspect of reflexivity addressed in chap. 11).

Discourse theories have not historically attended—or been applied—to matters of learning. Gee (1992, 1994, 1996, 1997, 1998, 2000) is an exception. Gee (2000) wrote, "knowing is a matter of being able to participate centrally in practice and learning is a matter of changing patterns of participation (with concomitant changes in identity)" (p. 181). After Tomasello (1999), Gee defined his approach to learning as pattern recognition.[4] As Gee points out, one can only generate paradoxes or problems about learning with regard to specific perspectives on what learning is, and the problems and paradoxes shift with different perspectives.

This is where Gee's (1996) theory of learning and acquisition adds to a discussion of shifting identities across contexts. Gee distinguished between learning and acquisition. He defined *learning* as:

A process that involves conscious knowledge gained through teaching (though not necessarily from someone officially designated as a teacher) or

---

[4]Michael Tomasello is a cognitive psychologist who asserts that learning is a form of pattern recognition. He suggests that linguistic competence and performance is one example of learning how to negotiate pattern recognition. From a cognitive psychology perspective, Tomasello argues for the cultural and social origins of language acquisition. His work is important for critical discourse theory and learning because it provides a starting point for theorizing about the way in which negative or self-defeating "cultural models" are acquired as individuals interact with the social world.

through certain life experiences that trigger conscious reflection. This teaching or reflection involves explanation and analysis, that is, breaking down the thing to be learned into its analytic parts. It inherently involves attaining, along with the matter being taught, some degree of meta-knowledge about the matter. (p. 138)

He defined *acquisition* as:

A process of acquiring something (usually subconsciously) by exposure to models, a process of trial and error, and practice within social groups, without formal teaching. It happens in natural settings which are meaningful and functional in the sense that acquirers know that they need to acquire the thing they are exposed to in order to function and they in fact want to so function. This is how people come to control their first language. (p. 138)

According to Gee, learning occurs within secondary institutions (e.g., schools and businesses). Acquisition occurs within primary discourses (e.g., home, community, church in some communities). Other research (Rogers, 2002) has pointed out that the boundaries between learning and acquisition are not so clearly defined. Indeed negative ideologies are acquired on a routine basis in schools. Learning involves changes in participation and the subsequent shifts in identity. Such changes construct and are constructed by social change or social transformation. Wenger, McDermott, and Snyder (2002) wrote, "the knowledge of experts is an accumulation of experience—a kind of 'residue' of their actions, thinking, and conversations—that remains a dynamic part of their ongoing experience" (p. 9). Lave (1996) argued that learning may be traced through changing participation and the related changes in identity in social practices. In this view, learning is related to social transformation.

Learning as social transformation is important to realizing a vision of democratic education. Systems of education—including school systems and higher education—are not the only vehicles for which such learning can be realized. However, schools are highly organized institutions through which critique of society can be coupled with hope and possibility of constructing more social just spaces. CDA holds much promise for educational research—as we see in each of the chapters in this volume—because it starts with the contradictions or what Fairclough (1995) referred to as *cruces*.

CRITIQUES OF CDA

CDA could not be considered a critical methodology if it did not attend to critiques of theory and method. A number of position papers and reviews (Bloome, 1997; Fairclough & Wodak, 1997; Janks, 1997; Wodak, 1999), theoretical papers (Blommaert, 2001; Hammersely, 1997; Kress, 1993), and critiques and responses to critiques (Flowerdew, 1999; Pennycook, 2001; Price, 1998; Toolan, 1997; Tyrwhitt-Drake, 1999; Verschueren, 2001; Widdowson, 1998) have been written concerning the theoretical and methodological basis of CDA. CDA is often critiqued around the following dimensions (e.g., Tyrwhitt-Drake, 1999; Widdowson, 1998). First, political and social ideologies are projected onto the data rather than being revealed through the data. This means that analysts begin their analysis knowing what they are going to "find" before they begin, and their analysis simply confirms what they suspected. A second critique is that there is an unequal balance between social theory and linguistic method. Depending on the background and training of the analyst (e.g., either as a Chomskian linguist or an ethnographer), the analysis may more strongly attend to descriptions of language or the context in which the language use unfolds. A third critique is that many discourse analyses are extracted from social contexts. This is the case in many discourse analyses conducted on political speeches, government documents, and newspaper reports (e.g., written documents). A fourth critique is that the methodology is not systematic or rigorous. In this volume, the authors add two additional critiques of CDA. One is that CDA has not been applied to or attended to matters of learning—an issue addressed in the previous section. The second critique is that there has been little attention paid to the nonlinguistic aspects of discourse such as activity and emotion. This absence is ironic given that emotions are the stronghold of ideology.

Although there are conflicting opinions on the extent to which the linguistic analysis should and can be "systematic" (Bucholtz, 2001; Flowerdew, 1999; Pennycook, 2001; Price, 1998; Widdowson, 1998), what researchers engaging with CDA want to avoid is what Widdowson (1998) referred to as an analysis that is, "a record of whatever partial interpretation suits your own agenda" (p. 149). Fowler (1996) agreed that critical linguistics might represent theoretical positions rather than empirical insights. He wrote,

> the original linguistic model, for all its loose ends, at least possessed a certain theoretical and methodological compactness, and I think it is important now to consolidate and develop this (essentially Hallidayian) model. If this is not done, the danger is that "critical linguistics" in the hands of practitioners of diverse intellectual persuasions will come to mean loosely any politically well-intentioned analytic work on language and ideology, regardless of method, technical grasp of linguistic theory or historical validity of interpretations. (p. 6)

When *critical* is interpreted as the disruption of power relations rather than as the systematic investigation of the relationships among genres, discourse, and style, and how some meanings are privileged over others, such critiques may be warranted. Indeed Widdowson (1998) pointed out, "if all discourse is ideological then ideological significance can never be discovered, for it is always a function of a particular ideological partiality" (p. 149). What Widdowson left out is that it is the task of the analyst to study how discourse practices construct (and are constructed by) social practices. Ideology is not a static set of relations.

In this book, the authors argue that this is not an inherent flaw in the method and theory, but the way in which the research has been taken up. Indeed *critical* can also mean a set of choices within a linguistic system that has vast meaning-making potential. The sense that some choices are seen as more valuable or privileged leads to an analysis of power and language. In this book, we take this charge seriously and set out to explore the relationship between discourse practices, rather than assume power is embedded in language. While not denying the exposure of inequity as an important goal, it should not be seen as the social scientific goal of critical discourse analysis. Pennycook (2001) wrote,

if we take power as already sociologically defined and we see our task as using linguistic analysis of texts to show how that power is used, our task is never one of exploration, only of revelation. If, on the other hand, we are prepared to see power as that which is to be explained, then our analyses of discourse aim to explore *how* power may operate, rather than to demonstrate its existence. (p. 93; italics added)

To be a critical social scientific method, CDA needs to reflexively demonstrate the changing relationship between social theory and linguistic structures and how this fits into evolving social and linguistic theories and methodologies.

REFERENCES

Adorno, T. (1973). *Negative dialectics.* New York: Seabury.
Adorno, T., & Horkheimer, M. (1972). *Dialectic of enlightenment.* New York: Herder & Herder.
Blommaert, J. (2001). Context is/as critique. *Critique of Anthropology, 21*(1), 13–32.
Bloome, D. (1997). Book review of critical discourse analysis. *Reading Research Quarterly.*
Bloome, D., & Egan-Robertson, A. (1993). The social construction of intertextuality and classroom reading and writing. *Reading Research Quarterly, 28*, 303–333.
Bloome, D., & Power-Carter, S. (2001). Lists in reading education reform. *Theory Into Practice, 40*(3), 150–157.
Briggs, C. (Ed.). (1996). *Disorderly discourse: Narrative, conflict, and inequality.* New York: Oxford University Press.
Brown, G., & Yule, G. (1983). *Discourse analysis.* Cambridge: Cambridge University Press.
Bucholtz, M. (2001). Reflexivity and critique in discourse analysis. *Critique of Anthropology, 21*(1), 165–183.
Chouliaraki, L., & Fairclough, N. (1999). *Discourse in late modernity: Rethinking critical discourse analysis.* Edinburgh, Scotland: Edinburgh University Press.

Christie, F. (2002). *Classroom discourse analysis: A functional perspective.* New York: Continuum Press.

Collins, J. (2001). Selling the market: Educational standards, discourse and social inequality. *Critique of Anthropology, 21,* 143–163.

Cope, B., & Kalantzis, M. (Eds.). (2000). *Multiliteracies: Literacy learning and the design of social futures.* London: Routledge.

Corson, D. (2000). Emancipatory leadership. *International Journal of Leadership in Education, 3*(2), 93–120.

Fairclough, N. (1992a). *Discourse and social change.* Cambridge, England: Polity Press.

Fairclough, N. (1992b). Intertexuality in critical discourse analysis. *Linguistics and Education, 4,* 269–293.

Fairclough, N. (1995). *Critical discourse analysis. The critical study of language.* New York: Longman.

Fairclough, N., & Wodak, R. (1997). Critical discourse analysis. In T. van Dijk (Ed.), *Discourse as social interaction* (pp. 258–284). London: Sage.

Flowerdew, J. (1999). Description and interpretation in critical discourse analysis. *Journal of Pragmatics, 31,* 1089–1099.

Foucault, M. (1972). *The archeology of knowledge and the discourse on language.* New York: Pantheon Books. Originally published as *L'Archeologie du Savoir* (Paris: Editions Gallimard, 1969).

Fowler, R. (1996). On critical linguistics. In Caldas-Coulthard & Coulthard (Eds.), *Texts and practices: Readings in critical discourse analysis* (pp. 1–15). London: Routledge & Kegan Paul.

Fowler, R., Hodge, R., Kress, G., & Trew, T. (1979). *Language and control.* London: Routledge & Kegan Paul.

Gee, J. P. (1992). *The social mind: Language, ideology, and social practice.* New York: Bergin & Garvey.

Gee, J. P. (1994). First language acquisition as a guide for theories of learning and pedagogy. *Linguistics and Education, 6,* 331–354.

Gee, J. P. (1996). *Social linguistics and literacies: Ideology in discourses* (2nd ed.). London: Taylor & Francis.

Gee, J. P. (1997). Thinking, learning, and reading: The situated sociocultural mind. In D. Kirshner & J. A. Whitson (Eds.), *Situated cognition: Social, semiotic, and psychological perspectives* (pp. 37–55). Mahwah, NJ: Lawrence Erlbaum Associates.

Gee, J. P. (1999). *An introduction to discourse analysis.* London: Routledge.

Gee, J. P. (2000). New people in new worlds: Networks, the new capitalism, and schools. In B. Cope & M. Kalantiz (Eds.), *Multiliteracies: Literacy learning and the design of social futures* (pp. 43–68). London: Routledge.

Gee, J., & Green, J. (1998). Discourse analysis, learning, and social practice: A methodological study. *Review of Research in Education, 23,* 118–169.

Goatly, A. (2000). *Critical reading and writing: An introductory coursebook.* New York: Routledge.

Gumperz, J. (1982). *Discourse strategies.* New York: Cambridge University Press.

Habermas, J. (1976). *Legitimation crisis.* London: Heinemann Educational Books.

Halliday, M. (1978). *Language as social semiotic: The social interpretation of language and meaning.* London: Edward Arnold.

Halliday, M. (1985). *An introduction to functional grammar.* London: Edward Arnold.

Halliday, M. (1994). *An introduction to functional grammar* (2nd ed.). London: Edward Arnold.

Halliday, M., & Hasan, R. (1989). *Language, context and text: Aspects of language as a social-semiotic perspective.* Oxford, England: Oxford University Press.

Hammersley, M. (1997). On the foundations of critical discourse analysis. *Language and Communication, 17*(3), 237–248.

Heller, M. (2001). Critique and sociolinguistic analysis of discourse. *Critique of Anthropology, 21*(1), 117–141.

Janks, H. (1997). Critical discourse analysis as a research tool. *Discourse: Studies in the Politics of Education, 18*(3), 329–342.

Jaworski, A., & Coupland, N. (1999). *The discourse reader.* London: Routledge.

Kress, G. (1985). *Linguistic processes in sociocultural practice.* Victoria, Australia: Deakin University.

Kress, G. (1993). Against arbitrariness: The social production of the sign as a foundational issue in critical discourse analysis. *Discourse and Society, 4*(2), 169–191.

Kress, G., & Hodge, R. (1979). *Language as ideology.* London: Routledge & Kegan Paul.

Kumaravadivelu, B. (1999). Critical classroom discourse analysis. *TESOL Quarterly, 33*(3), 453–484.

Lave, J. (1996). The practice of learning. In J. Lave & S. Chaiklin (Eds.), *Understanding practice: Perspectives on activity and context* (pp. 3–32). Cambridge: Cambridge University Press.

Lave, J., & Wenger, E. (1991). *Situated learning: Legitimate peripheral participation.* New York: Cambridge University Press.

Lemke, J. (1992). Intertextuality and educational research. *Linguistics and Education, 4,* 257–267.

Linnell, P. (1998). *Approaching dialogue. Talk, interaction, and contexts in dialogical perspectives.* Amsterdam: John Benjamins Publishing Company.

Lynn, M., & Cleary, L. (1993). *Linguistics for teachers.* New York: McGraw-Hill.

Moje, E. (1997). Exploring discourse, subjectivity, and knowledge in chemistry class. *Journal of Classroom Interaction, 32*(2), 35–44.

Parker, I., & the Bolton Discourse Group. (1999). *Critical textwork. An introduction to varieties of discourse analysis.* Buckingham: Open University Press.

Pecheux, M. (1975). *Language, semantics and ideology.* New York: St. Martin's Press.

Pennycook, A. (2001). *Critical applied linguistics. A critical introduction.* Mahwah, NJ: Lawrence Erlbaum Associates.

Peyton-Young, J. (2001). Displaying practices of masculinity: Critical literacy and social contexts. *Journal of Adolescent and Adult Literacy, 45*(1), 4–14.

Price, S. (1998). Critical discourse analysis: Discourse acquisition and discourse practices. *TESOL Quarterly, 33*(3), 581–595.

Rogers, R. (2002). Between contexts: A critical analysis of family literacy, discursive practices, and literate subjectivities. *Reading Research Quarterly, 37*(3), 248–277.

Rogers, R. (2003). *A critical discourse analysis of family literacy practices: Power in and out of print.* Mahwah, NJ: Lawrence Erlbaum Associates.

Rommetveit, R., & Blakar, R. (Eds.). (1979). *Studies of language, thought and verbal communication.* London: Academic Press.

Sawyer, K. (2002). A discourse on discourse: An archeological history of an intellectual concept. *Cultural Studies, 16*(3), 433–456.

Schegloff, E. (1991). Reflections on talk and social structure. In D. Boden & D. Zimmerman (Eds.), *Talk and social structure: Studies in ethnomethodology and conversation analysis* (pp. 44–70). Cambridge: Polity.

Schleppegrell, M. (2001). Linguistic features of the language of schooling. *Linguistics and Education, 12*(4), 431–459.

Scollon, R. (2001). *Mediated discourse analysis: The nexus of practice.* London: Routledge.

Siegel, M., & Fernandez, S. (2000). Critical approaches. In M. Kamil, P. Mosenthal, P. D. Pearson, & R. Barr (Eds.), *Methods of literacy research. The methodology chapters from the handbook of reading research* (Vol. III, pp. 65–75). Mahwah, NJ: Lawrence Erlbaum Associates.

Slembrouck, S. (2001). Explanation, interpretation, and critique in the analysis of discourse. *Critique of Anthropology, 21*(1), 33–57.

Stubbs, M. (1983). *Discourse analysis: The sociolinguistic analysis of natural language.* Oxford: Basil Blackwell.

Titscher, S., Meyer, M., Wodak, R., & Vetter, E. (2000). *Methods of text and discourse analysis.* London: Sage.

Tomasello, M. (1999). *The cultural origins of human cognition.* Cambridge, MA: Harvard University Press.

Toolan, M. (1997). What is critical discourse analysis and why are people saying such terrible things about it? *Language and Literature, 6*(2), 83–103.

Tyrwhitt-Drake, H. (1999). Resisting the discourse of critical discourse analysis: Reopening a Hong Kong case study. *Journal of Pragmatics, 31,* 1081–1088.

van Dijk, T. (1993). Principles of critical discourse analysis. *Discourse and Society, 4*(2), 249–283.

Verschueren, J. (2001) Predicaments of criticism. *Critique of Anthropology, 21*(1), 59–81.

Wenger, E. (1998). *Communities of practices. Learning, meaning and identity.* New York: Cambridge University Press.

Wenger, E., McDermott, R., & Snyder, W. (2002). *Cultivating communities of practice: A guide to managing knowledge.* Cambridge, MA: Harvard Business Press.

Widdowson, H. G. (1998). The theory and practice of critical discourse analysis. *Applied Linguistics, 19*(1), 136–151.

Willig, C. (Ed.). (1999). *Applied discourse analysis: Social and psychological interventions.* Buckingham: Open University Press.

Wodak, R. (1996). *Disorders of discourse.* London: Longman.

Wodak, R. (1999). Critical discourse analysis at the end of the 20th century. *Research in Language and Social Interaction, 32*(1 & 2), 185–193.

Woodside-Jiron, H. (2002). *The language of politics and the politics of language: A critical discourse analysis of California reading policy.* Unpublished doctoral dissertation, State University of New York Press, Albany.

Woodside-Jiron, H. (in press). Critical policy analysis: Researching the roles of cultural models, power, and expertise in reading policy. *Reading Research Quarterly, 38*(4).

Young, R. (1990). *A critical theory of education. Habermas and our children's future.* New York: Teachers College Press.

Chapter 2

Discourse Analysis:
What Makes It Critical?

James Paul Gee
University of Wisconsin–Madison

CENTRAL CONCEPTS

All discourse analysis that intends to make empirical claims is rooted in specific viewpoints about the relationship between *form and function* in language, although these are rarely spelled out in discourse analytic work in education. Further, empirically motivated work in discourse is based, in part, on *specific analytic techniques* for relating form and function in oral and/or written texts. Critical discourse analysis (CDA) involves, beyond relating form and function in language, specific empirical analyses of how such form–function correlations *themselves* correlate with specific *social practices* that help constitute the very nature of such practices. Because social practices inherently involve social relationships where issues of solidarity, status, and power are at stake, the flow is bottom–up from work in CDA and are themselves empirical claims. *Learning* is a type of social interaction in which knowledge is distributed across people and their tools and technologies, dispersed at various sites, and stored in links among people, their minds and bodies, and specific affinity groups. Such a view of learning allows an integration of work in CDA, situated cognition, and sociocultural approaches to language and literacy.

INTRODUCTION

What makes a piece of research discourse analysis? What makes it critical discourse analysis? I offer one opinion about these questions in this chapter. My considerations are basic because I want to illuminate what I take to be fundamental issues—ones often obscured in work in education where

19

discourse analysis sometimes means no more than anecdotal reflections on written or oral texts. As to critical discourse analysis, sometimes this seems to amount to proselytizing for one's own politics in the absence of any close study of oral or written language.

A note before I start: I personally associate the term (letters) *CDA* with Fairclough's (1992, 1995) approach to discourse analysis and the term (spelled out) *critical discourse analysis* with a wider array of approaches, including Fairclough's, my own, and others. When I get to the question, "What makes something *critical* discourse analysis?" (as opposed to plain old discourse analysis), I mean this question generally, and not just about Fairclough's work.

Although both Fairclough and I have been influenced by poststructuralist thought (e.g., Foucault, Bourdieu, and Bakhtin) and neo-Marxist critical theory (e.g., Althusser, 1971; Gramsci, 1971), the linguistic side of Fairclough's work is based on (his own version of) a Hallidayian model of grammatical and textual analysis (Halliday, 1994)—a model more pervasive in England and Australia than in the United States. The linguistic side of my own work is based on (my own version of) American non-Hallidayian models of grammatical and textual analysis (e.g., Chafe, 1979; Givon, 1979) and sociolinguistics (Gumperz, 1982; Hymes, 1974, 1981; Labov, 1972a, 1972b), combined with influences from literary criticism (e.g., Chatman, 1978). The two models are not incompatible, and the differences reflect differences in training and background and not (for the most part) principled disagreements.

Approaches to discourse analysis that avoid combining a model of grammatical and textual analysis (of whatever sort) with sociopolitical and critical theories of society and its institutions are not forms of critical discourse analysis. At the same time, there are many, especially in education, who combine aspects of sociopolitical and critical theory with rather general (usually thematic) analyses of language not rooted in any particular linguistic background or theory. Such work is a form of critical discourse analysis, although it may not always be referred to as such.

Much work in discourse analysis, especially in the field of linguistics, has no particular interest in education or issues germane to education. This is true of work in critical discourse analysis as well. My own work in both areas (Gee, 1992, 1996, 1999) has often centered on education, although not always on schools. In this chapter, from time to time, I discuss the relevance of discourse analysis and critical discourse analysis to controversial issues in education.

SOME CRUCIAL DISTINCTIONS

At the outset, I want to make a couple of distinctions that are important from a linguistic point of view, although often ignored in discourse-related work in education. The first distinction, one with a long and controversial history in linguistics and the philosophy of language, is between *utterance-type meaning* and *utterance-token meaning* (Levinson, 2000).

When we interpret any piece of language, we have *general expectations* about how our language is normally used. Another way to put this is to say that any word or structure in language has a certain "meaning potential"— that is, a range of possible meanings that the word or structure can take on in different contexts of use. Thus, for example, the word *cat* has to do broadly with felines; the (syntactic) structure "subject of a sentence" has to do, broadly, with naming a "topic" in the sense of "what is being talked about." This is utterance-type meaning. Utterance-type meanings are general meanings, not situation-specific meanings (although we could say that they are, in reality, connected to the prototypical situations in which a word or structure is usually used).

In actual situations of use, words and structures take on much more specific meanings within the range of (or at least related to the range of) their meaning potentials. This is utterance-token meaning, or what I call *situated meaning* (Gee, 1996, 1999). Thus, in a situation where we are discussing species of animals and say something like, "The world's big cats are all endangered," *cat* means things like lions and tigers; in a situation where we are discussing mythology and say something like, "The cat was a sacred symbol to the ancient Egyptians," *cat* means real and pictured cats as symbols; and in a situation where we are discussing breakable decorative objects on our mantel and say something like, "The cat broke," *cat* means a statue of a cat.

Turning to structures, rather than words: Although the subjects of sentences are always topiclike (this is their utterance-type meaning) in different situations of use, subjects take on a range of more specific meanings. In a debate, if I say, "The constitution only protects the rich," the subject of the sentence ("the constitution") is an entity about which a claim is being made; if a friend of yours has just arrived and I usher her in saying, "Mary's here," the subject of the sentence ("Mary") is a center of interest or attention; and in a situation where I am commiserating with a friend and say something like, "You really got cheated by that guy," the subject of the sentence ("you") is a center of empathy (signaled also by the fact that the normal subject of the active version of the sentence—"That guy really cheated you"—has been "demoted" from subject position through use of the "get-passive").

The second distinction is between vernacular styles of language and nonvernacular styles (Labov, 1972a, 1972b). Save in the case of massive social disruption, every human being acquires a native language in his or her early years. Most linguists, at least in the United States, believe that this process of native language acquisition is partly under biological control (Chomsky, 1986, 1995; Pinker, 1994). That is, for human beings, language is akin to an instinct (like the instinctual knowledge some bird species have of how to build their species-specific nest or sing their species-specific song). Faced with input from a specific human language (e.g., English or Russian), the child builds a language out of those resources that, although superficially different from other languages, is, at a level of basic design features, fundamentally the same as all other languages. No teaching is required. This argument means that people's native languages, or native dialects within a larger language like English or Russian, are all "equal," in the sense of being equally rule-governed, complex, and fully communicative (Chomsky, 2002). (Perhaps I should point out here as well that, although Chomsky's work is of a major importance, not least because it clearly demonstrates that at a grammatical level all languages and dialects are equally good, his work offers little help in analyzing language in use at the discourse level. His work is focused on sentence-level grammar [for the most part] and deals with the most basic aspects of grammatical structure, not the full set of communicative resources people put to use in specific instances of verbal interaction.)

People use their native language initially and throughout their lives to speak in the vernacular style of language—that is, the style of language they use when they are speaking as "everyday" people and not as specialists of various sorts (e.g., biologists, street-gang members, lawyers, videogame adepts, postmodern feminists, etc.). Thus, another way to put the claim in the last paragraph would be to say that everyone's vernacular style is as good as anyone else's. Of course a given society can designate one variety as *standard* and others as *nonstandard*, but this distinction is social and political (Milroy & Milroy, 1991). From a linguistic point of view, it is meaningless because each native speaker speaks a dialect of his or her language that is, again, from a linguistic point of view equally as good (complex, communicative, rule governed) as anyone else's.

Of course this claim—commonplace among linguists—bears importantly on issues in education. From a linguistic point of view, no child comes to school with a worse or better language than any other child's (barring massive social disruption—simply being poor does not count or at least need not count as massive social disruption, which is meant to cover cases like putting children in closets or otherwise depriving children of access to linguistic data and social interaction). A child's language is not lesser because that child speaks a so-called *nonstandard* dialect. These claims are not politically contentious in modern linguistics, they are simply empirical. At the same time, a good deal of educational research is devoted to showing the social and political advantages middle-class children gain from bringing a dialect close to the standard to school, thanks to the fact that schools value these dialects more positively and build on them more adeptly.

Nearly everyone comes to acquire nonvernacular styles of languages later in life, styles used for special purposes such as religion, work (e.g., a craft), government, or academic specialties. Let us call all these *social languages* (Gee, 1996, 1999) and say that, although everyone acquires a vernacular social language (a different dialect for different groups of people) connected to his or her native language (e.g., English), people usually also go on to acquire different nonvernacular social languages connected to different social groups (e.g., one person may become adept at the language of Christian fundamentalist theology and someone else at the language of modern mathematics).

Although the process of acquiring a vernacular form of one's language is biologically specified and every later social language does indeed build on the resources of one's vernacular, acquiring various nonvernacular social languages is not a process that is biologically specified (Gee, 2001). Evolution surely aided humans in acquiring the capacity for language in the sense of one's native vernacular (or we humans, like the other primates, would have no language at all), but it did not aid us in acquiring the social language of physics, for instance, because physics and its style of language have been around way too short a time to have been given any evolutionary aid beyond the basic language resources that the language of physics, like all other later social languages, draws from vernacular forms of language.

Thus, consider the following two sentences:

1. Hornworms sure vary a lot in how well they grow.
2. Hornworm growth displays a significant amount of variation.

The first sentence is a vernacular style of language. Everyone who is a native speaker of English, regardless of their dialect, can utter some equally good variant of this sort of sentence (if they know what hornworms are—green caterpillar-like creatures with yellow horns). The second sentence is in an academic social language. Although every native speaker's grammar contains all the grammatical structures that this sentence contains (e.g., nominalizations), not every speaker knows that *combining them in just this way* is called for by certain social practices of certain academic (and school-based) domains ("Discourses"). *This has to be learned, and this knowledge is not acquired on the basis of any biological capacity for language.* It is manifestly the case that many children in school struggle to acquire forms of language like that in Sentence 2, although none (if they are native speakers) struggles with the forms of language like that in Sentence 1.

Again every native speaker of English has a grammar that contains all of the grammatical structures used in Sentence 2. All of them are used at times in vernacular forms of language. However, to produce a sentence like 2, you must know more than this. You must know that, in this style of language, verbs naming dynamic processes (e.g., *grow* and *vary*) are turned into nouns naming abstract things (e.g., *growth* and *variation*). You have to know that in this form of language emotive markers like *sure* are not used. You have to know that in this form of language a vague phrase like *a lot* must be replaced by a more explicit one like *significant variation* (where *significant* has a fairly precise definition in areas like biology). You have to know that subjects of sentences in this form of language will often not be simple nouns (like *hornworms*), but nominalizations (like *hornworm growth*) expressing a whole clause worth of information (i.e., hornworms grow) as an abstract concept. Most important, you have to know all these things together and that these linguistic features, in fact, tend to go together—to pattern together—in this form of language.

By *patterning* I mean only that certain grammatical devices go or hang together in a certain way—for example, nominalizations, a lack of emotive markers, technical terms, copulative or presentational verbs, and complex subjects in the case of sentences like the one in 2. Just as a person wearing a sun hat, tank top, swim suit, and open sandals tells us that that person is ready for the beach or some other outdoor activity in the sun (because these items of clothing go together or pattern together for that sort of purpose), so too these grammatical devices go together to tell us that this sort of sentence belongs to an academic form of language used for certain sorts of characteristic activities.

This discussion bears importantly on a current educational debate. Many pro-phonics advocates have made the following sort of argument (see Gee [2001] for further discussion). The acquisition of one's native oral language is biologically specified (aided by our human biological capacity for language) and, thus, requires no overt teaching or learning. Yet written language has been on the historical scene too short a time to have this sort of biological support. Thus, it is not acquired in the same way that one's native oral language is—that is, through immersion in practice (exposure to data), but requires overt teaching and learning through which the child is overtly told the nature of the code (the mapping between phonemes and graphemes).

This argument does not work despite that some linguists have made it. Social languages like the one represented in Sentence 2 often have both oral and written forms (not necessarily the same). Their oral versions, as we have seen, are not supported by biology—indeed children manifestly struggle to acquire them in school, and different children acquire them better and worse than others (which is not true of people's native vernacular dialects). Nonetheless, there is no evidence that social languages are primarily learned through overt instruction. Although teachers calling students' attention to some of their features and developing a common meta-language within which to talk about those features with their students is probably efficacious (Gee, 2002; Martin, 1990), no one knows how to describe—and, thus, to overtly tell—all the features and combinations of features that make up such academic social languages. It is unlikely that any physicist, for instance, believes he or she learned the social language of physics through grammar drills or overt instruction on its features and combinations of features. It seems that immersion in practice and participation with those who speak (and write) such social languages is still crucial. Furthermore, the contrast between oral and written language development, in the case of nonvernacular social languages, is not as sharp as some linguists and pro-phonics advocates have claimed (Gee, 2001, 2002).

None of this says phonics is right or wrong. What is says is that, from a sociolinguistic point of view, people learn new styles of oral and written language (new social languages) in school and later in life—styles that are not biologically specified, but rather the results of history and culture. Immersion and participation surely play a strong role in this process, as does active intervention and help from teachers, although we know little about what are the most effective overt teacher interventions. It may be better to give people overt information in the midst of practice, when they need it, rather than outside practice—but much remains to be studied here despite simplifications common among the advocates of things like scripted instruction.

TWO TASKS: THE UTTERANCE-TYPE MEANING TASK

Discourse analysis of any type (Jaworski & Coupland, 1999; van Dijk, 1997a, 1997b), whether critical or not, can undertake one or both of two related tasks. One task is what we call the *utterance-type meaning task*. This task involves the study of correlations between form and function in language at the level of utterance-type meanings. *Form* here means things like morphemes, words, phrases, or other syntactic structures (e.g., the subject position of a sentence). *Function* means meaning or the communicative purpose a form carries out.

The other task is what we call the *utterance-token meaning* (or situated meaning) *task*. This task involves the study of correlations between form and function in language at the level of utterance-token meanings. Essentially, this task involves discovering the situation-specific or situated meanings of forms used in specific contexts of use.

Failing to distinguish between these two tasks can be dangerous because different issues of validity come up with each of these tasks as we see later. Let me start with an example of the utterance-type meaning task. Specific forms in a language are prototypically used as tools to carry out certain communicative functions (i.e., to express certain meanings). For example, consider the following sentence labeled (1) (adapted from Gagnon, 1987):

1. Though they were both narrowly confined to the privileged classes, the Whig and Tory parties represented different factions.

This sentence is made up of two clauses: an independent (or main) clause ("the Whig and Tory parties represented different factions") and a dependent clause ("Though they were both narrowly confined to the privileged classes"—the conjunction *though* here marks this clause as subordinated to, dependent on, the following independent clause). These are statements about form. An independent clause has as one of its functions (at the utterance-type level) that it expresses an assertion—that is, it expresses a claim that the speaker/writer is making. A dependent clause has as one of its functions that it expresses information that is not asserted, but rather assumed or taken for granted. These are statements about function (meaning).

Normally (i.e., technically speaking, in the unmarked case) in English dependent clauses follow independent clauses—thus, Sentence (1) might more normally appear as: "The Whig and Tory parties represented different factions, though they were both narrowly confined to the privileged classes." In Sentence (1), the dependent clause has been fronted (placed in front of the whole sentence). This is a statement about form. Such fronting has as one of its functions that the information in the clause is thematized (Halliday, 1994)—that is, the information is treated as a launching-off point or thematically important context from which to consider the claim in the following dependent clause. This is a statement about function.

In summary, in respect to form–functioning mapping at the utterance-type level, we can say that Sentence (1) renders its dependent clause ("Though they were both narrowly confined to the privileged classes") a taken-for-granted, assumed, unargued for (i.e., unasserted), although important (thematized), context from which to consider and, perhaps, argue over the main claim in the independent clause ("The Whig and Tory parties represented different factions"). The dependent clause is, we might say, a concession. Other historians might prefer to make this concession the main asserted point and, thus, would use a different grammar, perhaps saying something like: "The Whig and Tory parties were narrowly confined to the privileged classes, though they represented different factions of those classes."

All approaches to discourse analysis, in their consideration of form, go beyond grammatical structures as traditionally construed (which are restricted to relationships within sentences) to consider structures or patterns across sentences. For example, consider the following two sentences (adapted from Gagnon, 1987):

2. The age of popular democracy lay far ahead. But the principle of representative government was already secure, as was the rule of law, which promised to protect all citizens from arbitrary authority of any kind.

The first sentence has the subject "the age of popular democracy," and the second has the subject "the principle of representative government." The subject position (a form) in a declarative sentence is a grammatical structure that expresses the "topic" (a function) of the sentence in the sense of naming the entity or topic about which a claim is being made and in terms of which the claim should be disputed. The conjunction *but*, beginning the second sentence, is a form that sets up a contrast in meaning (a function) between these two topics (i.e., "the age of popular democracy" and "the principle of representative government"), making it clear that for the author a government could be representative without representing all the people in a country (i.e., being popular democracy). Here we see how patterns of form across sentences, not just within sentences, relate to functions (meanings).

At a fundamental level, all types of discourse analysis involve, however tacitly they may be acknowledged, claims about form–function matching at the utterance-type level. This is so because if one is making claims about a piece of language, perhaps at a much more situated and contextualized level than we are now talking about, but these claims violate what we know about how form and function are related to each other in language at the utterance-type level, then these claims are quite suspect unless there is evidence that the speaker or writer is trying to violate these sorts of basic grammatical relationships in the language (e.g., in poetry).

Of course different approaches to discourse analysis have different viewpoints on how to talk about form and function. For instance, some approaches have an expanded notion of form in which not only grammatical and cross-sentence patterns are considered, but also things like pausing, repetitions, repairs, eye gaze, speech rate, and timing of turn taking (Ochs, Schegloff, & Thompson, 1997). Each of these latter are, in turn, related to various utterance-type functions they serve in interaction (as well, of course, to more specific situated or contextualized meanings of the utterance-token type).

Furthermore, different approaches to discourse analysis have different views about how to explicate what it means to say that form *correlates* with function at the utterance-type level. One perspective with which I am sympathetic would explicate this idea as follows: A particular form, thanks to a history of repeated and partially routine interaction among a group or groups of people, comes to function so as to have a particular sort of prototypical meaning or expected range of meanings when considered apart from any specific context of use.

As already indicated, the meanings with which forms are correlated at the utterance-type level are rather general (meanings like "assertion," "taken-for-granted information," "contrast," etc.). In reality, they represent only the meaning potential or range of a form or structure, as we have said.

The more specific or situated meanings that a form carries in a given context of use must be figured out by an engagement with our next task—the utterance-token (situated) meaning task discussed in the next section.

When one asks what makes a piece of discourse analysis valid at the utterance-type level, the matter is settled by appeal to theories of grammar in the sense of theories about how form and function correlate in language, both at the level of language universals (e.g., dependent clauses are never assertions) and in the case of specific languages. Of course one can argue over who has the best theory of grammar in this sense. Yet once one accepts a given theory and accepts that the data have been described adequately (e.g., that the researcher has correctly identified main and dependent clauses), the issue of validity is settled.

There is a problem, however. Thanks to the prevalence of varieties of Chomskian theories of grammar, theories that have little or nothing to do with form–function mappings in language, there has been, especially in the United States, much less work—and much less agreement—on functional theories of grammar of the sort we have been discussing. The best-known functional theory (although in reality it is but one of several) is Halliday's (1994) work. See also Martin, Matthiessen, and Painter's (1997) theory of systematic functional grammar, a theory much less used in the United States than in England and Australia (Halliday might say that the utterance-type and utterance-token meaning distinction I have made is a matter of the "delicacy" of one's analysis).

TWO TASKS: THE UTTERANCE-TOKEN (SITUATED) MEANING TASK

A second task that any form of discourse analysis, critical or otherwise, can undertake is what I called the utterance-token (situated) meaning task. For simplicity's sake, I now call this the *situated meaning task*. As I pointed out earlier, language forms have both utterance-type and utterance-token meanings. At the utterance-type level, we are concerned that there are certain *types* of forms in a language like English (words, morphemes, phrases, and other structures) and they are associated with certain *types* of functions—what I called *meaning potentials* previously. However, when we actually utter or write a sentence, it also has what I called an *utterance-token meaning* or what I call here a *situated meaning* (Gee, 1996, 1999). Situated meanings arise because particular language forms take on specific or situated meanings in specific contexts of use.

Context refers to an ever-widening set of factors that accompany language in use (and thus is often used in the plural, *contexts*). These include the material setting, the people present (and what they know and believe), the language that comes before and after a given utterance, the social relationships of the people involved, and their ethnic, gendered, and sexual identities, as well as cultural, historical, and institutional factors. Most contemporary approaches to discourse analysis assume a reflexive view of the relationship between language and context. *Reflexive* here means that, at one and the same time, an utterance influences what we take the context to be, and context influences what we take the utterance to mean. For example, if I say "How are ya?" versus "Whatnthehell is wrong with you?" as I pass you in the corridor, these utterances lead you to construe the context in a certain way (friendly vs. hostile), although everything else going on may make you interpret each utterance in quite specific ways—for example, you may hear the latter utterance as just kidding.

Consider the word *coffee* as a simple example of how situated meaning differs from utterance-type meaning. *Coffee* is an arbitrary form (other languages use different sounding words for coffee) that correlates with meanings having to do with the substance coffee (this is its meaning potential). At a more specific level, however, we have to use context to determine what the word means in any situated way. In one context, *coffee* may mean a brown liquid; in another one, it may mean grains of a certain sort; in another, it may mean berries of a certain sort; and it will mean other things in other contexts (e.g., a certain flavor or skin color).

To see a further example of situated meanings at work, consider Sentence (1) again ("Though they were both narrowly confined to the privileged classes, the Whig and Tory parties represented different factions"). We said earlier that an independent clause represents an assertion (a claim that something is true). Yet this general form–function correlation can mean different specific things in actual contexts of use and can indeed even be mitigated or undercut altogether.

For example, in one context, say between two like-minded historians, the claim that the Whig and Tory parties represented different factions may be taken as a reminder of a fact they both agree on. However, between two quite diverse historians, the same claim may be taken as a challenge (despite *your* claim that shared class interests mean no real difference in political parties, the Whig and Tory parties in 17th-century England were really different). Of course on stage as part of a drama, the claim about the Whig and Tory parties is not even a real assertion, but a pretend one.

Furthermore, the words *privileged, contending,* and *factions* take on different specific meanings in different contexts. For example, in one context, *privileged* might mean "rich," whereas in another context, it might mean "educated," "cultured," "politically connected," "born into a family with high status," or some combination of these or something else altogether.

To analyze Gagnon's sentence, his whole text, or any part of it at the level of situated meanings—that is, to carry out the situated meaning task—

would require a close study of some of the relevant contexts within which that text is placed and that it, in turn, helps to create. This might mean inspecting the parts of Gagnon's text that precede or follow a part of the text we want to analyze. It might mean inspecting other texts related to Gagnon's. It might mean studying debates among different types of historians and debates about educational standards and policy (because Gagnon's text was meant to argue for a view about what history should be taught in schools). It might mean studying these debates historically across time and in terms of the actual situations Gagnon and his text were caught up in (e.g., debates about new school history standards in Massachusetts—a state where Gagnon once helped write a version of the standards). It might mean many other things as well. Obviously there is no space in a chapter of this scope to develop such an analysis.

The issue of validity for analyses of situated meaning is quite different than the issue of validity for analyses of utterance-type meanings. We saw before that the issue of validity for analyses of utterance-type meanings basically comes down to choosing and defending a particular grammatical theory of how form and function relate in language at the level of utterance-type meanings, as well as of course offering correct grammatical and semantic descriptions of one's data. However, the issue of validity for analyses of situated meaning is much harder. In fact it involves a deep problem known as the *frame problem.*

The frame problem is this: Any aspect of context can affect the meaning of an (oral or written) utterance. Context, however, is indefinitely large, ranging from local matters like the positioning of bodies and eye gaze, through people's beliefs, to historical, institutional, and cultural settings. No matter how much of the context we have considered in offering an interpretation of an utterance, there is always the possibility of considering other and additional aspects of the context, and these new considerations may change how we interpret the utterance. Where do we cut off consideration of context? How can we be sure any interpretation is right if considering further aspects of the context might well change that interpretation?

Let me give an example of a case where changing how much of the context of an utterance we consider changes significantly the interpretation we give to that utterance. Biologist Roger Lewontin (1991) pointed out in his book *Biology as Ideology* that it is a truism in medical science that the cause of tuberculosis is the *tubercle bacillus.* Lewontin went on to point out that tuberculosis was a common disease in the sweatshops and factories of the 19th century, whereas it was much less common among rural people and in the upper classes. So why don't we conclude that the cause of tuberculosis is not the *tubercle bacillus,* but unregulated industrial capitalism? In fact in light of the history of health and disease in modern Europe, that explanation makes good sense. An examination of the causes of death, first systematically recorded in the 1830s in Britain and a bit later in North America, shows that most people did indeed die of infectious diseases. As the 19th century progressed, however, the death rate from all these diseases continuously decreased:

> Smallpox was dealt with by a medical advance, but one that could hardly be claimed by modern medicine, since smallpox vaccine was discovered in the eighteenth century and already was quite widely used by the early part of the nineteenth. The death rates of the major killers like bronchitis, pneumonia, and tuberculosis fell regularly during the nineteenth century, with no obvious cause. There was no observable effect on the death rate after the germ theory of disease was announced in 1876 by Robert Koch. The death rate from these infectious diseases simply continued to decline as if Koch had never lived. By the time chemical therapy was introduced for tuberculosis in the earlier part of this century, more than 90 percent of the decrease in the death rate from that disease had already occurred. (Lewontin, 1991, pp. 43–44)

It was not modern sanitation or less crowding in cities that led to the progressive reductions in the death rate because the major killers in the 19th century were respiratory and not waterborne, and parts of our cities are as crowded today as they were in the 1850s. More likely, Lewontin argued, the reduction in death from infectious diseases is due to general improvement in nutrition related to an increase in the real wage in developed countries: "In countries like Brazil today, infant mortality rises and falls with decreases and increases in the minimum wage" (Lewontin, 1991, p. 44).

Lewontin showed that the meaning—in this case, even the truth value that one attaches to a statement like "the cause of tuberculosis is the tubercle bacillus"—changes as one widens the context within which the meaning of this statement is considered. In this case, he widened the context from medicine as an academic research area to include social and industrial concerns.

What this example shows is that the frame problem is something of a double-edged sword for discourse analysis. Discourse analysts can change the contextual frame of utterances to bring out new meanings—ones that may change how we think about certain issues. At the same time, critics can always ask of any discourse analysis whether the situated meanings attributed to pieces of language in the analysis would not change, perhaps even significantly, if the analyst had considered other aspects of the context (wider aspects or just additional features at the same level of detail). We should point out that everyday people in interpreting any language directed to them face the frame problem just as do discourse analysts when they seek to analyze discourse. Everyday people must, however unconsciously, apply (in part culturally relative) standards of what constitutes relevant and irrelevant aspects of context in interpreting utterances. That is, they must cut off the consideration of context *someplace* if they are to get about the business of communicating and leading their lives. Indeed an important topic of some research in linguistic semantics and the philosophy of language is the specifics of such standards of relevance (e.g., Sperber & Wilson, 1986).

All discourse analysts can do to deal with the frame problem is offer arguments that the aspects of context they have considered, in a particular piece of research, are the important and relevant ones for the people whose language is being studied and for the analytic purpose of the researcher. Further, the researcher or other researchers can seek out additional aspects of context and see if this changes, in significant ways, the original analysis offered. Of course they can never exhaust all potentially significant aspects of context—that is indeed what the frame problem is all about. In that sense, discourse analysis, at the level of situated meanings, is always open to further revision as we learn more about the context of the data analyzed. This is indeed typical of all interpretive methods of research.

Reflection and Action

Deciding which social, cultural, political, economic, and geographic contexts to include in CDA is part of what Gee referred to as the *frame problem*. The lens researchers bring to their analysis is another part of the frame problem. Consider the various aspects of the frame problem in your work as a critical discourse analyst.

CRITICAL DISCOURSE ANALYSIS

Some forms of discourse analysis add a third task to the two (the utterance-type meaning task and the situated meaning task) discussed so far. They also study the ways in which either or both language–form correlations at the utterance-type level (Task 1) and situated meanings (Task 2) are associated with social practices (Task 3).

It is here where critical approaches to discourse analysis diverge from noncritical approaches. Noncritical approaches (e.g., Pomerantz & Fehr, 1997) tend to treat social practices solely in terms of patterns of social interaction (e.g., how people use language to *pull off* a job interview). Thus, consider again the sentence from Gagnon we discussed above:

1. Though they were both narrowly confined to the privileged classes, the Whig and Tory parties represented different factions.

A noncritical form of discourse analysis could point out that using "though they were both narrowly confined to the privileged classes" as a de-

pendent (and, thus, assumed and unasserted) clause sets up a social relationship with the reader in terms of which the reader should accept as given
and assumed. That is, that distinctions of wealth in a society are less central
to the development of democracy than political differences within elites in
the society (which the main asserted clause is about). Readers who do not
want to make this assumption without argument, which the use of the dependent clause encourages them to do, are going to find this relationship
uncomfortable. Of course people with a political bent are liable to find this
sort of claim full of potential important for issues of power, inside and outside academic history, but the noncritical discourse analyst need not pursue
the matter further, beyond explicating what sort of position the reader is
placed in by the text (or encouraged to take up).

Critical approaches (e.g., Chouliaraki & Fairclough, 1999; Fairclough,
1992, 1995; Gee, 1999; Luke, 1995; van Dijk, 1993; Wodak, 1996), however,
go further and treat social practices not just in terms of social relationships.
They also treat social practices in terms of their implications for things like
status, solidarity, distribution of social goods, and power (e.g., how language in a job interview functions as a gate-keeping device allowing some
sorts of people access and denying it to others). In fact critical discourse
analysis argues that language in use is always part and parcel of, and partially constitutive of, specific social practices, and that social practices always
have implications for inherently political things like status, solidarity, distribution of social goods, and power.

Social practices are (partially) routine activities through which people
carry out (partially) shared goals based on (partially) shared (conscious
or unconscious) knowledge of the various roles or positions people can
fill within these activities. Practices are embedded within practices. Thus,
one session of a graduate seminar is a social practice, as is the whole seminar course. Some practices are more routinized than others that may be
more open ended and fluid. The world is full of social practices: a medical
exam; eating in a fancy restaurant; exercising in a health club; engaging in
a gang drive-by shooting; a police interrogation; a direct instruction reading lesson in a first-grade classroom; an election; giving a political speech;
applying for a prestigious college; trading Pokemon cards; advocating for
what history should be taught in schools (as Gagnon is); and so forth
through an endless array.

One way in which we can define *politics* is to say that it *involves any social relationships in which things like status, solidarity, or other social goods are potentially
at stake.* In this sense of politics, social practices are inherently and inextricably political because by their very nature they involve social roles or positions that have implications for potential social goods, such as who is an insider and who is not to the practice (and its associated social groups).
Because critical discourse analysis argues that language in use is always part

and parcel of, and partially constitutive of, one or more specific social practices, language in use is inherently and inextricably political.

So the issue becomes this: Is it enough to leave the analysis of the social at the level of how talk and texts function in social interactions or do we need to go further and consider, as well, how talk and text function *politically* in social interactions (using politics in the sense developed earlier)? Does the latter task render discourse analysis—and, thus, perforce critical discourse analysis—unscientific or unacademic a mere matter of advocacy?

My view is that there are solid linguistic, even grammatical, grounds on which to argue that all language in interaction is inherently political and, thus, that all discourse analysis, if it is to be true to its subject matter (i.e., language in use) and in that sense scientific, must be critical discourse analysis. Sociolinguists have known for years that all social languages, vernacular or otherwise, regardless of the larger language from which they are drawn (e.g., English, Russian, etc.), display variability (Labov, 1972a, 1972b; Milroy, 1987a, 1987b; Milroy & Milroy, 1991). One sort of variability that any social language displays is variation on a continuum that runs between informal and formal forms. Another related sort of variability that any social language displays is variation on a continuum that runs between marking solidarity (lack of deference) with others and marking status or deference between or among people. All languages and social languages have grammatical ways to mark these distinctions—that is, degrees of informality and formality and degrees of solidarity and deference—and can in fact do so in complicated ways.

For example, consider first the following two excerpts (Gee, 1996). In sentence (3), a young woman tells her parents about how she ranked, on a scale of morality, some characters in a story she had heard in a class she was taking at a university. She tells her boyfriend the *same thing* in sentence (4):

3. Well, when I thought about it, I don't know, it seemed to me that Gregory should be the most offensive. He showed no understanding for Abigail, when she told him what she was forced to do. He was callous. He was hypocritical, in the sense that he professed to love her, then acted like that.

4. What an ass that guy was, you know, her boy friend. I should hope, if I ever did that to see you, you would shoot the guy. He uses her and he says he loves her. Roger never lies, you know what I mean?

These two texts are both in versions of the vernacular—that is, in neither case is the young woman trying to speak like a specialist in some specialized social language (but see later text about the connections between the form of language in (3) and school). However, the first text (3) is more formal and creates a certain sense of deference in talking to her parents, whereas the second text (4) is more informal and creates a certain sense of solidarity with her boyfriend.

Some of the grammatical markers that create these distinctions in these two texts are: To her parents, the young woman carefully hedges her claims ("I don't know," "it seemed to me"); to her boyfriend, she makes her claims straight out. To her parents, she uses formal terms like *offensive, understanding, callous, hypocritical,* and *professed*; to her boyfriend, she uses informal terms like *ass* and *guy*. She also uses more formal sentence structure to her parents ("it seemed to me that . . . ," "He showed no understanding for Abigail, when . . . ," "He was hypocritical in the sense that . . .") than she does to her boyfriend (". . . that guy, you know, her boy friend," "Roger never lies, you know what I mean?").

The young woman repeatedly addresses her boyfriend as "you," thereby noting his social involvement as a listener, but does not directly address her parents in this way. In talking to her boyfriend, she leaves several points to be inferred—points that she spells out more explicitly to her parents (e.g., her boyfriend must infer that Gregory is being accused of being a hypocrite from the information that, although Roger is bad, at least he does not lie, which Gregory did in claiming to love Abigail).

Although different dialects would mark such distinctions in formality and deference differently, all people have vernacular forms of language in which they can and do do such things. However, an important and much studied educational issue arises here. Formal forms of the vernacular in the style of (3)—roughly (very roughly), more formal forms of standard English—are often well utilized and privileged in school as a bridge to academic social languages. Formal forms of the vernacular in other dialects are usually poorly utilized and unprivileged, if not even demonized. (By the way, it does not matter whether we call [3] and [4] two styles of a vernacular social language or two different vernacular social languages.)

It is not just the vernacular that marks out these sorts of distinctions around formality/informality and deference/solidarity. Specialist social languages do so as well. Indeed any use of language must mark where it is in terms of these sorts of distinctions; it is part of the grammar of languages to do so. Thus, consider the two excerpts from the following written texts, both written by the same biologist (Myers, 1990). The first appeared in a professional biological journal, the second in a popular science magazine:

5. Experiments show that *Heliconius* butterflies are less likely to oviposit on host plants that possess eggs or egg-like structures. These egg-mimics are an unambiguous example of a plant trait evolved in response to a host-restricted group of insect herbivores.

6. *Heliconius* butterflies lay their eggs on *Passiflora* vines. In defense the vines seem to have evolved fake eggs that make it look to the butterflies as if eggs have already been laid on them.

It does not matter whether we say that these two excerpts are from different, but related, social languages (professional biology and popular biology) or are stylistic variants of the same social language (a certain type of biology), although my preference is the first choice. The fact remains that the first excerpt (5) is more technical and formal in a way that creates solidarity with other professional biologists, but separation from nonprofessionals. Note that *more* formality here, unlike in the case of the vernacular, creates *more* solidarity, in part, because it creates separation of specialists from nonspecialists. The second excerpt, although still formal when compared with the vernacular variant in (4), is less formal than the excerpt in (5). It creates much less of a separation from the nonprofessional audience, although it is still not anywhere near as "bonding" as the vernacular form in (4).

Again these differences—that is, those between (5) and (6)—are marked grammatically. The first extract, from the professional scientific journal, is about the conceptual structure of a specific theory within the scientific discipline of biology. The subject of the initial sentence is *experiments*—a methodological tool in natural science. The subject of the next sentence is *these egg mimics*: Note how plant parts are named not in terms of the plant itself, but in terms of the role they play in a particular theory of natural selection and evolution—namely, coevolution of predator and prey (i.e., the theory that predator and prey evolve together by shaping each other). Note also, in this regard, the earlier host plants in the preceding sentence, rather than the vines of the popular passage.

In the second sentence, the butterflies are referred to as "a host-restricted group of insect herbivores," which points simultaneously to an aspect of scientific methodology (like experiments did) and the logic of a theory (like egg mimics did). Any scientist arguing for the theory of coevolution faces the difficulty of demonstrating a causal connection between a particular plant characteristic and a particular predator when most plants have so many different sorts of animals attacking them. A central methodological technique to overcome this problem is to study plant groups (like *Passiflora* vines) that are preyed on by only one or a few predators (in this case, *Heliconius* butterflies). "Host-restricted group of insect herbivores," then, refers to both the relationship between plant and insect that is at the heart of the theory of coevolution and to the methodological technique of picking plants and insects that are restricted to each other so as to control for other sorts of interactions.

The first passage, then, is concerned with scientific methodology and a particular theoretical perspective on evolution. The second extract, from a popular science magazine, is not about methodology and theory, but about animals in nature. The butterflies are the subject of the first sentence, and the vine is the subject of the second. Further, the butterflies and the vine are labeled as such, not in terms of their role in a particular theory.

The second passage is a story about the struggles of insects and plants that are transparently open to the trained gaze of the scientist. Further, the plant and insect become intentional actors in the drama: The plants act in their own defense and things look a certain way to the insects; they are deceived by appearances as humans sometimes are.

These two examples replicate in the present a historical difference. In the history of biology, the scientist's relationship with nature gradually changed from telling stories about direct observations of nature (in a form closer to the vernacular, although still different from it) to carrying out complex experiments to test complex theories (Shapin & Schaffer, 1985) using a form of language far removed from the vernacular. In fact, Myers (1990) argued that professional science is now concerned with the expert "management of uncertainty and complexity" and popular science with the general assurance that the world is knowable by and directly accessible to experts. This change in science also coincided with the growth of the sharp separation between amateurs and professionals doing science—a separation that previously was not that strong.

If all this is right—that is, that all social languages, whether vernacular forms or not, must mark out, grammatically, distinctions having to do with things like status, deference, solidarity, separation, and bonding—then all social languages are inherently political because these things (i.e., status, deference, solidarity, separation, and bonding) have clear implications for the distribution of obvious social goods in society. They have to do with who is or can be an insider or outsider vis-à-vis the social groups and social practices in a society. If this is part and parcel of the workings of all language— indeed part of the form–function mapping and situated meanings of all language—then any form of discourse analysis, if it is to be complete, must be critical and political. This amounts, then, not (just) to a political claim, but to an empirical one.

In terms of our earlier remarks about patterning, I should point out here that, once again, what is at stake is how various grammatical features "hang together," not any one feature in and of itself. For example, hedges, Latinate terms (like *offensive*), more complex syntax (e.g., "it seemed to me that . . ."), a degree of vagueness, address as "you," and other features all go together to make (3) less formal and more bonding than (4).

Reflection and Action

Gee (1999, chap. 5) presents six building tasks (e.g., semiotic building, world building, activity building, relationship building, political building, and connection building) and the grammatical devices that accompany each of these building tasks. In light of Gee's prior discussion about patterning, what connections can you make between the tasks to correlate the form and function of utterances with particular social practices?

LEARNING

If one is going to engage in discourse analysis applied to educational issues, the notion of *learning* becomes crucial. Because discourse analysis is about the inextricably political marriage between form and function within social practices, some perspectives on learning fit better with discourse-analytic research than do others. For example, a view of learning that focuses only on changing representations inside people's heads fails to engage with form and function out in the world of social practices. Discourse analysis is as much (or more) about what is happening among people out in the world (sociology) than it is about what is happening in their minds (psychology).

The approach to learning that is most compatible, in my opinion, with discourse analysis is one that defines *learning* as *changing patterns of participation in specific social practices* (Lave, 1988, 1996; Lave & Wenger, 1991; Rogoff, 1990; Rogoff & Lave, 1984; Wertsch, 1985, 1991). Because social practices set up roles or positions within which people become insiders, outsiders, or marginal with respect to the social groups whose practices these are, it follows that social practices create what we can call *socially situated identities* (e.g., tough-guy cop, rookie, by-the-books cop; devout Catholic, lapsed Catholic, Catholic in name only; veteran street-gang member, core younger member, hanger-on; etc. through a great many distinctions for which the labels do not matter, only the ways in which people, often unconsciously, recognize and react to each other within various and specific social practices). It follows, then, that changes in one's patterns of participation with specific social practices constitute changes in these socially situated identities. Thus, in these terms, learning is change in a socially situated identity.

This view of learning requires us to see that people's activities are often part of larger communities of practice—that is, groups of people ongoingly engaged in (partially) shared tasks or work of a certain sort, whether these be people in an elementary school classroom, members of a street gang or an academic discipline, affiliates of a cause (e.g., *greens*), or participants in a specific business organization. Such communities of practice produce and reproduce themselves through the creation of a variety of characteristic social practices, and within these they *apprentice* new members.

Communities of practice, then, in this respect, are related to institutions. Indeed institutions are often composed of a variety of communities of practice, although communities of practice can be more or less institutionalized (they are always institutionalized to a some extent). When we define *learning* as changing patterns of participation in specific social practices within communities of practice, it becomes apparent that we can equally talk about individuals' learning or communities of practice (or organizations or institutions) themselves, in whole or in part, learning (Senge, 1991). A discourse analytic analysis of learning, then, needs to show how a distinctive community of practice is constituted out of specific social practices (across time and space) and how patterns of participation systematically change across time, both for individuals and the community of practice as a whole (or distinctive parts of it).

Some have criticized the notion of a *community of practice* because groups of people engaging in repeatable sorts of social practices need not be a *community* in any romantic sense of this term. There is, of course, "honor among thieves," as they say, and communities of practice in a modern business may share little, besides their practices, beyond the desire for profit (e.g., Bauman, 1995).

A related term that has sometimes been used for a notion closely related to communities of practice is *Discourses* (used with a capital "D" to clarify that it means more than just using language to discourse about something; Gee, 1996, 1999). Discourses are distinctive ways people talk, read, write, think, believe, value, act, and interact with things and other people to get recognized (and recognize themselves) as a distinctive group or distinctive kinds of people (Hacking, 1986). They do so by engaging in distinctive and repeatable social practices, whether these be members of an L.A. street gang, lawyers or biologists of a certain sort, mental patients of a certain type, or members of a first-grade classroom.

Forms of discourse analysis that marry the study of form and function with the study of social practices, on the one hand, and the study of changing patterns of participation within communities of practice or Discourses, on the other, tend to place the study of socially situated identities at the heart of the enterprise. It is here, too, that a good deal of the educational implications of such work follows. Schools recruit culturally and historically distinctive social languages, social practices (within which specific situated meanings are formed), and Discourses to form and reform, reward and punish, distinctive kinds of people (i.e., distinctive socially situated identities) with sociopolitical implications that shape our lives and societies. Because discourse analysis, construed in the sorts of ways I have here construed it, can speak to such matters, it is a potentially powerful tool for research in education.

CULTURAL MODELS

When people participate in a community of practice or enact and recognize a Discourse (socially situated identity), they learn cultural models. Cultural models (Strauss & Quinn, 1997) are everyday theories (i.e., storylines, images, schemas, metaphors, and models) about the world that tell people what is typical or normal, not universally, but from the perspective of a particular Discourse.

For example, certain types of middle-class people in the United States (Harkness, Super, & Keefer, 1992) hold a cultural model of child development in terms of which a child is born dependent on her parents and grows up by going through (often disruptive) stages toward greater and greater independence (and independence is a high value for this group of people). In contrast, certain sorts of working-class families (Philipsen, 1975) hold a cultural model of child development in terms of which a child is born unsocialized and with tendencies to be selfish. The child needs discipline from the home to learn to be a cooperative social member of the family (a high value of this group of people).

These different cultural models are not true or false. Rather, they focus on different aspects of childhood and development. Cultural models are partially in people's minds (by no means always consciously) and partially in the objects, texts, and social practices that surround them. For example, many guidebooks supplement and instantiate the above middle-class cultural model of childhood and stages. In contrast, many religious materials supplement and instantiate the above working-class model of childhood.

Sometimes people get confused over the distinctions among situated meanings, cultural models, social languages, and Discourses. A situated meaning is the meaning a word or phrase is given in an actual context of use (e.g., "Get the mop, the coffee spilled" vs. "Get the broom, the coffee spilled"). A cultural model is an often tacit theory or story about how things work in the world (e.g., children throw tantrums because they are undergoing stages toward greater independence). A social language is a pattern of grammatical devices associated with a given social practice, activity, or socially situated identity (e.g., "Experiments show that *Heliconius* butterflies are less likely to oviposit on host plants that possess eggs or egg-like structures"). A Discourse is a whole package: a way of using not just words, but words, deeds, objects, tools, and so forth to enact a certain sort of socially situated identity (e.g., a Latino street-gang member in L.A.).

Discourses recruit specific social languages (ways with words) and cultural models (taken-for-granted stories), which in turn encourage people to construct certain sorts of situated meanings—that is, encourage them to read context in given ways. For example, many academic Discourses (e.g., professional biology) use social languages (like the one in "Hornworm growth displays a significant amount of variation" as opposed to "Hornworms sure vary a lot in how well they grow") that disallow markers of affect or emotion (or, more generally, involvement). This is related to a cultural model that is something like this: Emotion clouds reason and leads to a lack of objectivity; dispassionate people reason better and are objective. In turn, this may lead people in these sorts of Discourses to interpret words and phrases in their social languages, in actual contexts of use, in certain ways. For example, a word like *significant* in "Hornworm growth displays a significant amount of variation" may, in context, take on a meaning of not just statistically significant, but more real and truthful than claims made on non-quantifiable bases.

Reflection and Action

Think about the multiple situated identities you embody in your work as a teacher educator, teacher, researcher, or educational advocate. What discourse practices are associated with each identity? How does your identity fluctuate across the contexts in which you work? What cultural models comprise each situated identity?

ONE STYLE OF CDA

My own work (Gee, 1996, 1999) represents but one approach to critical discourse analysis. It primarily appeals to four analytic tools: social languages, situated meanings, cultural models, and Discourses (with a capital "D"). In the following, I elaborate on each of these a bit more. Because there is no space here for anything like a full discourse analysis, I merely want to show the sorts of questions and issues to which these tools can give rise with regard to specific pieces of data.

Social Languages

My approach to social languages (what are sometimes called *registers*) is to define them as follows: A social language is a way of using language so as to enact a particular socially situated identity (i.e., to be a specific socially meaningful "kind of person"). For example, there are ways of speaking like a (specific type of) doctor, street-gang member, postmodern literary critic, football fanatic, neoliberal economist, working-class male, adaptationist bi-ologist, and so on through an endless array of identities. Of course often we can recognize a particular socially situated "kind of person" through his or her use of a given social language without actually being able to enact that kind of person.

In no way do I wish to imply that enacting and recognizing *kinds of people* (Hacking, 1986; Hicks, 2000) is a matter of people falling into rigid kinds. Enacting and recognizing kinds of people is all about negotiating, guessing, and revising guesses about kinds of people; it is all about contesting and re-sisting being positioned as a certain kind of person. Thus, there are often no strict boundaries to social languages.

In examples 1 to 4, we saw different social languages (i.e., two styles of a vernacular social language or two different vernacular social languages de-pending on how one wants to put the matter, and two styles of a biological social language or two different biological social languages, again depend-ing on how one wants to put the matter).

Consider the following two short passages from an interview with a mid-dle-school teacher (7) from an impoverished postindustrial urban city and a college professor (8) from the same city. Both women were being inter-viewed about their views on racism and poverty in their city (see Gee [1999] for the transcription conventions used next).

7. *Interviewer:* ... *would you ever tie that into like present power relations or just individual experiences of racism in their* [her student's] *lives or something like that.*
   Uh I talk about housing,
   We talk about the [????] we talk about a lot of the low-income things,
   I said "Hey wait a minute,"
   I said, "Do you think the city's gonna take care of an area that you don't take care of yourself?" [I: uh-huh]
   I said, "How [many of] you [have] been up [NAME] Street?"
   They raise their hands,
   I say "How about [NAME] Ave.,"
   That's where those gigantic houses are,
   . . .
   I said, "How many pieces of furniture are sitting in the front yard?" [I: mm-hm] "Well, none."
   I said "How much trash is lying around?" None."
   I said, "How many houses are spray painted?
   How many of them have kicked in, you know have broken down cars

8. *Interviewer:* . . . *How, do you see racism happening, in society, let's put it that way.*

Um, well, I could answer on, on a variety of different levels. [I: uh-huh]

Um, at the most macrolevel, um, I think that there's um, um,

I don't want to say this in a way that sounds like a conspiracy, [I: mm-hm]

But I think um, that um, basically that the lives of people of color are are, are irrelevant to the society anymore. [I: mm-hm]

Um, they're not needed for the economy because we have the third world to run away into for cheap labor, [I: uh-huh]

Um, and I think that, that the leadership, this country really doesn't care if they shoot each other off in in the ghettos,

Um, and, and so they let drugs into the ghettos,

And they, um, they, let people shoot themselves, shoot each other,

And they don't have, a police force that is really gonna, um, work,

And they cut the programs that might alleviate some of the problems, and, um.

So I think there's, that it's manifested at, at the most, structural level as, um, you know, a real hatred, of, of, of uh people of color.

In these passages, these two women are using different social languages. The middle-school teacher uses a style of language in which often when she is asked about her classroom or her students, she mimics a dialogue she might have with her students, using a fairly informal vernacular style of language. We found this style not only with this teacher, but with a number of other teachers in this city. The college professor—a professor of anthropology—uses a social language that mixes a somewhat more formal vernacular style with some features from a style of language from the social sciences ("different levels," "macrolevel," "the third world," "structural level," etc.).

The middle-school teacher's style is certainly a distinctive style of language, recruiting its own special grammatical resources. Identifying it as a grammatical pattern is only one step in the analysis, however. We have to go on to form hypotheses about what communicative function or functions it serves (at the utterance-type and/or utterance-token level) and how it helps, with a great many other things to constitute particular socially situated identity for this teacher and other teachers in her city (not all of course). The grammatical pattern, then, leads us to look in a particular way for particular things, and that is of course one of the reasons for using discourse analysis as a research tool. The same could be said of the college professor.

There are a good many other differences between the two forms of language shown earlier. For example, the college professor uses lots of words and phrases for things that are social, but general and abstract (e.g., *people of color, the society, the economy, third world, cheap labor, the leadership, this country, our leadership*). The middle-school teacher uses more colloquial and concrete terms (e.g., *a little bit, playing the game, teaching the kids, the low-income things, wait a minute, gigantic houses, lying around*). There are syntactic and discourse-level differences as well.

It is also important to note that these two women co-construct the social language they use with the interviewer. In these interviews, the interviewer nearly always asks the middle-school teacher her views as they are related to or affect her role as a teacher in her classroom. Of course this encourages answers that are local to her classroom, although it does not necessitate constructing mini-dialogues. However, the interviewer never asks the college teacher about her views on racism and poverty in relation to her teaching or even her city, but in a more global way, encouraging the college professor to answer in a more theoretical and nationally focused way.

Situated Meanings

As we saw earlier, within social languages, words do not have just utterance-type meanings. They also have meanings that are specific and situated in the actual contexts of their use. Words, phrases, and utterances in use act as clues or cues that guide active construction of meaning in context.

The most interesting issue of situated meaning in the college professor's text involves trying to understand what her words for the social but abstract agents she so emphasizes might mean: words like *society* (which can find certain sorts of people irrelevant), *the leadership* or *this country* (which cannot care and can view certain sorts of people as expendable), or *people in power* (which can have a point of view). The situated meaning of these terms seems to be something like a "deep, hidden, and all-powerful structural agent, operating at a national or global level, that operates behind the scenes to cause effects on local circumstances whose real significance is not readily apparent."

In the middle-school teacher's text, we might consider what situated meanings can be attributed to words and phrases like *job, white middle-class brought up person,* and *low-income things.* Given the rest of her interview not printed here, it is clear that *job* here means something like "low, entry-level service job." *White middle-class brought up person* does not seem to mean only White people, but people who, in situations where power and status are at stake, "play the game." Coupled with *job* as *service job* here, it seems to mean also "people who behave subserviently even in lowly positions in something like a Horatio Alger way." *Low-income things* seems to mean, in the context of this text, "the sorts of nonmiddle-class behaviors and neighborhood settings that lead one to be rejected by middle-class people as untrustworthy and undeserving."

Cultural Models

The situated meanings of words and phrases within specific social languages trigger specific cultural models in terms of which speakers (writers) and listeners (readers) give meaning to texts. Cultural models are not static (they change and are adapted to different contexts; Gee, 1992), and they are not purely mental (but distributed across and embedded in socioculturally defined groups of people and their texts and practices).

People sometimes pick up cultural models overtly by being told or having read them. More often they pick them up as *found* items in the midst of practice in a particular domain (often inside particular institutions), whether this be romance, doing literacy in school, raising children, playing computer games, going to a doctor, engaging in Alcoholics Anonymous (AA) sessions, and so on (see Holland, Lachicotte, Skinner, & Cain, 1998). People more adept at the domain pass on cultural models through shared stories, practices, and procedures that get newcomers to pay attention to salient features of prototypical cases in the domain—the ones that best reflect the cultural models in a domain. In turn cultural models get reinforced and relatively ritualized as they are used in repeated practice. The models and allegiance to the models also become an important bonding cement within the social groups associated with a given domain of practice.

Cultural models are a good analytic device with which to deal, in part, with the frame problem mentioned earlier. Cultural models help people determine, often unconsciously, what counts as relevant and irrelevant in given situations. The college professor applies a widespread academic cultural model in terms of which actual behavior or events (the appearances) follow from larger, deeper, more general, underlying, and hidden causes. This model, in fact, is at the foundation of many of the sciences. Appearances are deceiving, and a deeper, truer reality lies behind the appearances. This deeper reality (the real reality) is discoverable only by people with special knowledge, tools, or insight, not by common (everyday, colloquial language-speaking) people. Plato's myth of the shadows in the cave is one early instantiation of this cultural model in Western culture.

The middle-school teacher applies a widespread cultural model in terms of which people's problems flow from their own behaviors as individuals, and it is through correct behavior and proper appearances that one achieves success. In terms of this model, victims are responsible for their own problems, which they bring on themselves by their own refusal to behave properly (i.e., like a middle-class person). This cultural model has long roots in Anglo history, where the model citizen is someone who owns enough to be motivated to behave in such a way as to uphold the social and political structures that protect his or her property (John Locke is a key figure here).

Ironically, the college professor's cultural model is almost the inverse of the middle-school teacher's. In terms of the college professor's model, people's actual behavior and interactions are really the effect of deeper and hidden causes over which they have little control. In terms of the middle-school teacher's model, people's poverty and powerlessness are not due to the workings of power and the forces of politics, but rather to their own attitudes and behaviors. These two models clash in the public sphere of our political life.

Discourses

A person cannot enact a particular kind of person all by themselves and by using only language. A *Discourse* (with a capital "D"—I use "discourse" with a little "d" just to mean language in use) is a distinctive way to use language *integrated* with "other stuff" so as to enact a particular type of (however negotiable and contestable) socially situated identity (type of person).

What is this "other stuff"? It is distinctive ways of thinking, being, acting, interacting, believing, knowing, feeling, valuing, dressing, and using one's body. It is also distinctive ways of using various symbols, images, objects, artifacts, tools, technologies, times, places, and spaces. Think of what it takes to be/do a tough-guy detective (in the Philip Marlowe mode, say), a traditional Catholic nun, or a Gen-X e-entrepreneur in the new economy (magazines like *Fortune* regularly discuss—or did so before the collapse of e-stocks—the details of this latter Discourse).

Discourses are always defined in relationship to other Discourses. For example, the Discourse of Los Angeles African-American teenage gang members exists and has changed through history in reciprocal relations with the Discourse of Los Angeles policemen, as well as a good many other related civic-, community-, and church-related Discourses. So, too, the Discourse of neo-Darwinian biologists exists and has changed through history in reciprocal relations with various religious Discourses, including, especially since the 1950s, the Discourse of American creationists.

We have no space here to do justice to all the elements involved in the professor's and teacher's respective Discourses. Hence, let me consider just one example here of how language relates to or aligns with nonlanguage stuff. The middle-school teacher's text aligns her with her *local* area and her specific classroom. The college professor's text aligns her with the *national–global* world. As pointed out earlier, the interviewer co-constructs this alignment, always forming her questions and responses to the teacher and professor so as to assume and invite these orientations—orientations that neither interviewee ever rejects or attempts to break out of.

Both the middle-school teacher and college professor are of course speaking out of professional Discourses. However, the middle-school teacher enacts her expertise in terms of a more colloquial (everyday) social language and in terms of the actual dialogues and procedures of her day-to-day work. Thus, her expertise is aligned not only with the local, but with the everyday and with her specific actions as a teacher. The professor enacts her expertise in a specialist, noncolloquial language and in terms of distanced viewpoints, not in terms of the actual dialogues and procedures of her day-to-day work.

We can note, too, that the teacher's Discourse is aligned with the local and colloquial, in part, because of the ways it is currently and has been historically positioned in terms of status and power in relation to the professor's Discourse and in relation to other Discourses, such as those of professors in Schools of Education (which mediate between noneducational specialist Discourses and the multiple Discourses of teachers and schools). This is not to say, by any means, that one or other of these Discourses is always and everywhere the more (or less) politically powerful one.

To see that power can run in both directions, one need only look at the current stance of many neoliberal politicians (e.g., George W. Bush). On the one hand, such politicians tend to privilege certain specialist Discourses (e.g., in testing and reading instruction) over teacher Discourses in determining curricula, pedagogy, and accountability. On the other hand, the tend to consider academic Discourses like that of our college professor as elitist viewpoints in relation to the everyday and populist wisdom of the teacher's colloquial language and cultural models (models that hold that anyone can *make it* if they just behave correctly).

In the end, I would argue that critical literacy involves using discourse analysis in such a way that we see that language is always fully situated in social and political contexts. It is always caught up with the ways individuals must, in using language, give voice to Discourses in interaction, now and throughout history, with each other. These interactions are the sites where power operates. They are also the sites at which humans can make and transform history.

This chapter has given a few hints at how the analyses of social languages, situated meanings, cultural models, and Discourses can lead to certain sorts of hypotheses and the consideration of certain sorts of issues. These hypotheses and issues, in turn, can often lead to fruitful collaborations between discourse analysis and other methods of research in areas like sociology, political theory, anthropology, and so forth.

Many of the chapters in this volume take off from the sorts of basic considerations about discourse analysis discussed here and move more broadly into other areas, often utilizing other forms of research as well—forms that they fruitfully combine with discourse analysis of language proper. In my view, however, the basic premise of the whole enterprise of discourse analysis is this (see also Scollon & Scollon, 1981): *How* people say (or write) things (i.e., form) helps constitute *what* they are doing (i.e., function). In turn, *what* they are saying (or writing) helps constitute *who* they are being at a given time and place within a given set of social practices (i.e., their socially situated identities). Finally, *who* they are being at a given time and place within a given set of social practices produces and reproduces, moment by moment, our social, political, cultural, and institutional worlds.

RECOMMENDED READINGS

Gee, J. P. (1994). First language acquisition as a guide for theories of learning and pedagogy. *Linguistics and Education, 6,* 331–354.

Gee, J. P. (2000). Communities of practice in the new capitalism. *The Journal of the Learning Sciences, 9,* 515–523.

Gee, J. P. (2002). Learning in semiotic domains: A social and situated account. In D. Schalert, C. Fairbanks, J. Worthy, B. Maloch, & J. Hoffman (Eds.), *The 51st yearbook of the National Reading Conference* (pp. 23–32). Oak Creek, WI: NRC.

Kress, G. (2000). Design and transformation: New theories of meaning. In B. Cope & M. Kalatzis (Eds.), *Multiliteracies: Literacy learning and the design of social futures* (pp. 153–161). London: Routledge.

Tomasello, M. (1999). *The cultural origins of human cognition.* Cambridge, MA: Harvard University Press.

REFERENCES

Althusser, L. (1971). Ideology and ideological state apparatuses. In L. Althusser (Ed.), *Lenin and philosophy and other essays.* London: New Left Books.

Chafe, W. L. (1979). The flow of thought and the flow of language. In T. Givon (Ed.), *Syntax and semantics 12: Discourse and syntax.* New York: Academic Press.

Chatman, S. (1978). *Story and discourse: Narrative structure in fiction and film.* Ithaca, NY: Cornell University Press.

Chomsky, N. (1986). *Knowledge of language.* New York: Praeger.

Chomsky, N. (1995). *The minimalist program.* Cambridge, MA: MIT Press.

Chomsky, N. (2002). *On nature and language.* Cambridge: Cambridge University Press.

Chouliaraki, L., & Fairclough, N. (1999). *Discourse in late modernity.* Edinburgh: Edinburgh University Press.

Fairclough, N. (1992). *Discourse and social change.* Cambridge: Polity.

Fairclough, N. (1995). *Critical discourse analysis.* London: Longman.

Gagnon, P. (1987). *Democracy's untold story: What world history textbooks neglect.* Washington, DC: American Federation of Teachers.

Gee, J. P. (1992). *The social mind: Language, ideology, and social practice.* New York: Bergin & Garvey.

Gee, J. P. (1996). *Social linguistics and literacies: Ideology in discourses* (2nd ed.). London: Taylor & Francis.

Gee, J. P. (1999). *An introduction to discourse analysis: Theory and method.* London: Routledge.

Gee, J. P. (2001). Progressivism, critique, and socially situated minds. In C. Dudley-Marling & C. Edelsky (Eds.), *The fate of progressive language policies and practices* (pp. 31–58). Urbana, IL: NCTE.

Gee, J. P. (2002). Literacies, identities, and discourses. In M. Schleppegrel & M. C. Colombi (Eds.), *Developing advanced literacy in first and second languages: Meaning with power* (pp. 159–175). Mahwah, NJ: Lawrence Erlbaum Associates.

Givon, T. (1979). *On understanding grammar.* New York: Academic Press.

Gramsci, A. (1971). *Selections from the prison notebooks.* London: Lawrence & Wishart.

Gumperz, J. J. (1982). *Discourse strategies.* Cambridge: Cambridge University Press.

Hacking, I. (1986). Making up people. In T. C. Heller, M. Sosna, & D. E. Wellbery (Eds.), *Reconstructing individualism: Autonomy, individuality, and the self in Western thought* (pp. 222–236). Stanford, CA: Stanford University Press.

Halliday, M. A. K. (1994). *An introduction to functional grammar* (2nd ed.). London: Edward Arnold.

Harkness, S., Super, C. M., & Keefer, C. H. (1992). Learning how to be an American parent: How cultural models gain directive force. In R. D'Andrade & C. Strauss (Eds.), *Human motives and cultural models* (pp. 163–178). Cambridge: Cambridge University Press.

Hicks, D. (2000). Self and other in Bakhtin's early philosophical essays: Prelude to a theory of prose consciousness. *Mind, Culture, and Activity, 7,* 227–242.

Holland, D., Lachicotte, W., Skinner, D., & Cain, C. (1998). *Identity and agency in cultural worlds.* Cambridge, MA: Harvard University Press.

Hymes, D. (1974). *Foundations of sociolinguistics.* Philadelphia: University of Pennsylvania Press.

Hymes, D. (1981). *"In vain I tried to tell you": Essays in Native American ethnopoetics.* Philadelphia, PA: University of Pennsylvania Press.

Jaworski, A., & Coupland, N. (Eds.). (1999). *The discourse reader.* London: Routledge.

Labov, W. (1972a). *Language in the inner city: Studies in Black English vernacular.* Philadelphia: University of Pennsylvania Press.

Labov, W. (1972b). *Sociolinguistic patterns.* Philadelphia, PA: University of Pennsylvania Press.

Lave, J. (1988). *Cognition in practice.* Cambridge: Cambridge University Press.

Lave, J. (1996). Teaching, as learning, in practice. *Mind, Culture, and Activity, 3,* 149–164.

Lave, J., & Wenger, E. (1991). *Situated learning: Legitimate peripheral participation.* Cambridge: Cambridge University Press.

Levinson, S. C. (2000). *Presumptive meanings: The theory of generalized conversational implicature.* Cambridge, MA: MIT Press.

Lewontin, R. C. (1991). *Biology as ideology: The doctrine of DNA.* New York: Harper.

Luke, A. (1995). Text and discourse in education: An introduction to critical discourse analysis. In M. W. Apple (Ed.), *Review of research in education 21* (pp. 3–48). Washington, DC: AERA.

Martin, J. R. (1990). Literacy in science: Learning to handle text as technology. In F. Christe (Ed.), *Literacy for a changing world* (pp. 79–117). Melbourne: Australian Council for Educational Research.

Martin, J. R., Matthiessen, C., & Painter, C. (1997). *Working with functional grammar.* London: Arnold.

McWorter, J. (2002). *The power of Babel: A natural history of language.* New York: W. H. Freeman.

Milroy, L. (1987a). *Language and social networks* (2nd ed.). Oxford: Blackwell.

Milroy, L. (1987b). *Observing and analysing natural language.* Oxford: Blackwell.

Milroy, J., & Milroy, L. (1991). *Authority in language: Investigating language prescription and standardisation* (2nd ed.). London: Routledge.

Myers, G. (1990). *Writing biology: Texts in the social construction of scientific knowledge.* Madison: University of Wisconsin Press.

Ochs, E., Schegloff, E. A., & Thompson, S. A. (Eds.). (1997). *Interaction and grammar.* Cambridge: Cambridge University Press.

Philipsen, G. (1975). Speaking "like a man" in Teamsterville: Culture patterns of role enactment in an urban neighborhood. *Quarterly Journal of Speech, 61,* 26–39.

Pinker, S. (1994). *The language instinct: How the mind creates language.* New York: William Morrow.

Pomerantz, A., & Fehr, B. J. (1997). Conversation analysis: An approach to the study of social action as sense making practices. In T. A. van Dijk (Ed.), *Discourse as social interaction: Discourse studies 2: A multidisciplinary introduction* (pp. 64–91). London: Sage.

Rogoff, B. (1990). *Apprenticeship in thinking: Cognitive development in social context.* New York: Oxford University Press.

Rogoff, B., & Lave, J. (Eds.). (1984). *Everyday cognition: Its development in social context.* Cambridge, MA: Harvard University Press.

Scollon, R., & Scollon, S. W. (1981). *Narrative, literacy, and face in interethnic communication.* Norwood, NJ: Ablex.

Senge, P. M. (1991). *The fifth discipline: The art & practice of the learning organization.* New York: Doubleday.

Shapin, S., & Schaffer, S. (1985). *Leviathan and the air-pump.* Princeton, NJ: Princeton University Press.

Sperber, D., & Wilson, D. (1986). *Relevance: Communication and cognition.* Cambridge: Cambridge University Press.

Strauss, C., & Quinn, N. (1997). *A cognitive theory of cultural meaning.* Cambridge: Cambridge University Press.

van Dijk, T. A. (1993). Principles of critical discourse analysis. *Discourse and Society, 4*(2), 249–283.

van Dijk, T. A. (Ed.). (1997a). *Discourse as structure and process: Discourses studies 1: A multidisciplinary introduction.* London: Sage.

van Dijk, T. A. (Ed.). (1997b). *Discourse as social interaction: Discourse studies 2: A multidisciplinary introduction.* London: Sage.

Wertsch, J. V. (1985). *Vygotsky and the social formation of mind.* Cambridge, MA: Harvard University Press.

Wertsch, J. V. (1991). *Voices of the mind: A sociocultural approach to mediated action.* Cambridge, MA: Harvard University Press.

Wodak, R. (1996). *Disorders of discourse.* London: Longman.

A Critical Discourse Analysis of Literate Identities Across Contexts: Alignment and Conflict

Rebecca Rogers
Washington University in St. Louis[1]

CENTRAL CONCEPTS

Orders of discourse—Orders of discourse is a heuristic that illustrates the relationship among texts, social practices, and identities. Orders of discourse include genre, discourse, and style and have equivalents in Systemic Functional Linguistics of mode, tenor, and field.

Genre—Genres include the organizational properties of interactions. They include "ways of interacting" that reference the mode of communication (e.g., sermon, lecture, rap song).

Discourse—Discourses are systematic clusters of themes that include contradictions. Discourses may be thought of as "ways of representing." Use Gee's distinction between d/Discourse (see chap. 11).

Style—Style is the domain closest to identity or "ways of being" and includes aspects of grammar that signify how people are drawn into and compose social structures.

Learning—Learning involves shifts in ways of interacting, representing, and being across time and over contexts.

Alignment—Alignment is the consistency between ways of interacting, representing, and being either within or across contexts.

Conflict—Conflict is a disjuncture between ways of interacting, representing, and being either within or across contexts.

---

[1]This research was supported by the Sociological Initiatives Foundation.

Identity—I use Gee's definition of *situated identities* that include the use of language and other semiotic tools to participate in meaningful ways within a particular Discourse. This participation includes cultural models—or storylines—that people carry with them about their various social roles. The construct of situated identities assumes that any one individual has more than one identity in various contexts. Further, an individual may have more than one identity that is in conflict or alignment with another part of their identity—this tension between situated identities may be referred to as *subjectivities*.

INTRODUCTION

Adults and children participate in many Discourses and communities of practice (Cole, 1996; Lave & Wenger, 1991) including work, home, and peer groups. For the 20 million adults in the United States who are considered to be living below the "literacy line" (Costa, 1988), the focus participants in this research, the communities of practice often include continuing education. These adults, the most marginalized in our society—the poor, often minority, and undereducated—participate in multiple, sometimes competing, and sometimes completely aligned communities of practice.[2] As adults cross the multiple Discourses of their daily lives, Discourses that often involves participating in formal educational contexts with their children, they construct and reconstruct what Gee (1996) referred to as *situated identities*. Situated identities are the toolkits that include the use of language and other social semiotic tools to participate in meaningful ways within a particular Discourse. Indeed situated identities are the nexus for Discourses and practices as people construct and are constructed by their social world (Antaki & Widdicombe, 1998; Bucholtz, Liang, & Sutton, 1999; Sawin, 1999).

What is deeply problematic is that, despite proficiency and competency in a great number of contexts, adults (and children) often do not see themselves as competent and carry a negative sense of self, shaped by their history of participation[3] with schools, into learning environments, shaping their own and their children's education. What is needed, I argue, are a set of theories, methods, and instructional interventions that allow edu-

---

[2]In this chapter, I refer to *alignment* as a consistency among learning objectives, strategies, or ways of interacting, representing, and being that are associated with a community of practice or discourse.

[3]Rogers (2003) defined *history of participation* as "a set of values, beliefs, and networks of practices that people bring with them from their experiences in a range of discursive contexts. People have histories of participation that are networks of practices that may either conflict or be in alignment with the network of practices that constitute various contexts" (p. 128).

cators to describe and explain how people can see themselves as proficient in one context and deficient in another. I propose CDA can do this. In this chapter, I make an argument for the study of socially situated identities (specifically in three contexts—history with school, involvement with children's education, and outside of school literacy) through the empirical and theoretical tools of CDA (Chouilaraki & Fairclough, 1999; Fairclough, 1995; Gee, 1999). I also demonstrate that this description offers insight into particular networking of practices that offers insight into learning in and out of schools. I do this through one case study. Specifically, the research question that guided this inquiry was: What is the relationship between linguistic resources within and across contexts for an adult who has been labeled as low literate?

METHODOLOGY

Context: Race and Education

St. Louis, the city where this study takes place, has been cited as the fourth most segregated city, the highest rate of adult illiteracy in the country (Racial and Ethnic Residential Segregation in the United States: 1980– 2000), and has the highest percentage of adult illiteracy in the country (Reder, 2002). The history of race and public education in St. Louis is interwoven with the history of segregation (Stuart-Wells & Crain, 1997). Missouri established free public schools in 1839—years before many states. These schools were designed to provide education to all White citizens according to their ability. African-American students were systematically denied access to free public schools, and in 1846, Missouri passed a law explicitly prohibiting the education of "Negroes" (Stuart-Wells, 1997, p. 75). Despite institutional segregation, African Americans have a history of struggling for educational opportunities. Freedom Schools were established to provide free education to African-American children. The schools were held on steamboats on the Mississippi River. In the late 1800s, as a response to the inadequate and substandard schools that African-American children were sent to, African-American parents in St. Louis built a school at their own expense and donated it to the Board of Education. As Anderson (1988) pointed out, the efforts by African-American leaders and parents to force the all-White St. Louis school board to provide greater educational opportunities for African-American children were representative of the value that African-American families in St. Louis placed on education. Stuart-Wells and Crain (1997) pointed out that before Missouri passed a compulsory school attendance law in 1905, there were more African-American children in St. Louis enrolled in schools than there were of White children with similar economic status. In the years following the Brown decision, a group of 15 parents formed the "Concerned Parents of North St. Louis" to protest the continued segregation of their schools. This initiative became known as the first phase of desegregation in St. Louis. Recently, the Black Leadership Roundtable declared a state of emergency based on achievement differences between African-American and White students (Bower, 2001; Jackson & Denson, 2001).[4]

African-American parents in St. Louis have always struggled and fought for the best educational opportunities for themselves and their children. They fought to attend city schools. They fought to attend integrated schools. The struggle continues. Many of the parents have not had the educational opportunities that their children may have. Many of the parents in this study were students in the St. Louis school system and dropped out of the system. These institutional and societal contexts form the backdrop of the participants' lives and struggle for educational equity.

Research Design[5]

Data Collection.   I interviewed 20 adults who were enrolled in adult literacy programs. My selection criteria was that the adults attended the classroom regularly, they had children enrolled in the St. Louis Public School system, and they were willing to talk with me about their experiences and their families' experiences with the educational system. Each of the interviews was semistructured. I followed the interview protocol, but let the participants decide which domain they wanted to discuss first. Each interview ranged from 2 to 6 hours long, and many of them stretched across a period of 2 or 3 days. This allowed both the participants and me a chance to reflect on the questions and raise new questions and insights. All of the interviews were conducted at the adult literacy centers. When possible, I observed in the adult literacy classroom prior to conducting the interviews. The pur-

---

[4]The racial segregation that exists between the city and county of St. Louis, the history of inequitable funding between schools, the disproportionate amount of African-American students in special education services within the city schools, and yet the continued belief in schools as an institution for upward social mobility characterizes the local, institutional, and societal domains of CDA. In this chapter, I draw on interview data from adults who have grown up and have had children within these social contexts. I primarily rely on the interview data and network of linguistic practices within three contexts in the interview. I do, however, recognize the way in which the individual interviews are connected to, constructed by, and construct the larger local, institutional, and societal contexts of which they are a part.

[5]The larger research project inquires into the relationship between literate resources and identities for adults and children in St. Louis. This is a three-phase project where I work with parents of children enrolled in elementary schools who also participate in GED programs, teachers as a part of a literacy action group, and teachers in their classrooms developing curriculum and studying literacy achievement. This chapter reports on one section of Phase I of the research.

pose of these observations was to start the interviews with a shared set of experiences. I took notes during the interviews.

I built three contexts into the interview protocol to evoke different discursive contexts to study the relationship between linguistic resources and social languages (Rogers, 2002). The three contexts included: history and present-day experiences with education, experiences with children's education, and out-of-school literacy experiences (see Appendix A for interview protocol). Cultural models serve to define people's beliefs, values, and choices based on achieving objects related to work, school, and relationships (Gee, 1999; Holland & Quinn, 1987). These objects are linked to particular story lines or cultural models. Significant cultural models prompted for in the interviews were the cultural model of reading/literacy and the cultural model of schooling. Indeed I wanted to know how the adults thought about reading, literacy, and education within different domains of experience. I also built into the methodology the flexibility to bring contradictions, or what Fairclough (1992) referred to as "cruces,"[6] which emerged from their interviews back to the participants and to ask them to make sense of the contradictions.

Analysis. All of the interviews were audiotaped and transcribed with the adult's permission.[7] My intention was to systematically study the relationship between discourses and contexts. I took Fairclough's (2000a) advice, "we cannot take the role of discourse in social practices for granted, it has to be established through analysis. Any discourse may be more or less important and salient in one practice of set of practices than in another and may change in importance over time" (p. 1).

Analysis of the data took a number of recursive stages. I read and reread the transcripts and had discussions about the general themes, patterns, and observations from each of the interviews. I coded each transcript for the three domains of "history and present day experiences with school," "in-

---

[6]Fairclough (1992a) suggested selecting cruces or moments of crisis in the data as an entry point into the analysis. These are moments in the discourse when it is evident something is going wrong. Fairclough wrote, "such moments of crisis make visible aspects of practices which might normally be naturalized, and therefore difficult to notice; but they also show change in process, the actual ways in which people deal with the problematization of practices" (p. 230).

[7]Transcription conventions:

[ ] - overlapping utterances
( ) - inaudible speech
(n.0) - length of silence or pause in seconds
- - haltering or stammering
Italics - tonal emphasis
= - continuous but nonoverlapping speech
Lines are divided by idea units.
Adapted from Jefferson's transcription notation.

volvement with children's education," and "literacy at home and in the community." I defined each of the domains by the definition provided under each of the themes in the interview protocol. I cross-checked the domains after coding with a research assistant. From here I went through a series of discourse and ethnographically oriented analytic steps. I defined each of the domains and clustered all of the examples of these domains under each of the domains, recognizing that there was overlap. I allowed the categories and themes from the participants' interviews and my observations of them in their classroom and in their child's classroom focus the sections of the interview we chose to focus our in-depth CDA.

I define CDA as the systematic study of ways of interacting (genre), ways of representing (discourse), and ways of being (style). I conducted the CDA in several stages. I conducted a paper-and-pencil analysis of the domains as well as a N-Vivo analysis. I chose sections of the transcript to focus on that provided the greatest conceptual leverage (i.e., where there was an obvious mixing of domains and/or the places where I could clearly see each of the domains so that I could code each of the excerpts from each of the domains with orders of discourse to begin to look for patterns within and across the domains).

Working from Chouliaraki and Fairclough's (1999) definition of *genre*, *Discourse*, and *style*, I coded each of the selected excerpts from the domains (history with education, involvement with children's education, out-of-school literacy activities) for genre, Discourse, and style (see CDA chart, Appendix B).[8] *Genre* is defined as "ways of interacting" or a description of the organizational properties of interactions. Aspects of genre include: thematic structure of the text, cohesion devices (parallel structure, repetition), wording, metaphors, politeness conventions, turn-taking structures, and interactional patterns. Interactional markers of African-American language such as narrative sequencing, call and response, and metaphorical language were coded under this domain (Morgan, 2002). *Discourses* are ways of representing and include what Luke (2000) referred to as "systematic clusters of themes, statements, ideas and ideologies." Discourses also include the chain of production, consumption, and distribution of texts and talk. Discourses necessarily embody tensions. For example, within the Discourse of literacy, there is a code for *literacy as purposeful* as well as *literacy as memorized skills*. Culturally relevant Discourses for the African-American participants emerged from the analysis (e.g., discourse of church, discourse of ministering). *Styles* are ways of being and include active/passive voice, modality (e.g., tense and affinity), transitivity (e.g., action, affective, state, abil-

---

[8]CDA is grounded in systemic functional linguistics (SFL; Halliday, 1978). SFL emphasizes the relationship between the form and function in language. Each utterance is believed to have a social function that is textual, interpersonal, or ideational. Related, each utterance can be analyzed for its mode (method of presentation), tenor (interpersonal relations), and field (connection to social world). Genre, discourse, and style are roughly equivalent to mode, tenor, and field.

ity, cognitive statements), and pronoun use. This domain also includes linguistic variations at the morphological level (e.g., suffix variation, third-person singular -s, past-tense markers), phonological features (e.g., consonant cluster simplification, deletion or reduction in medial syllable), and at the syntactic level (e.g., copula deletion, *they* possessive, future tense *be*, multiple negation; Fairclough, 1992, chap. 10, this volume).

After coding each of the excerpts for genre, Discourse, and style with different colored highlighters, I entered the data into N-Vivo. Because of the limitations of N-Vivo working with the complexity of CDA, I used the software for looking at the general patterns that emerged within and across the domains (e.g., clusters of discourses) and then returned to the paper-and-pencil method to include the complexity of the boundary crossings with the ethnographic data I collected.

I coded each of the transcripts at the level of the clause or what Gee (1999) called *idealized lines.* Within any one line there may be overlapping nodes of genre, discourse, and style or multiple occurrences of any of the orders of discourse. After constructing the codebook and coding the data, I ran a set of descriptive analysis in N-Vivo to see the patterns that emerged across the domains. I ran each analysis within each domain ($n = 3$) for each participant. I then printed out the reports and analyzed the patterns within and across the domains. I then looked at the configuration of Discourse practices across people. After each stage in the analysis, I returned to the whole interview, the themes I had generated, and the fieldnotes for each participant.

Case Selection. I chose to represent Natasha for this chapter because she illustrates various complexities of orders of discourse within and across the three domains. Because I discuss only relatively small parts of long oral history interviews, and do so in a discontinuous manner that cannot present the material in a chronological manner, I first summarize parts of her life story. I present a general description of the configuration of practices (genre, Discourse, style) in each of the domains and then across each of the domains. I have included analytic notes in the chapter to illustrate to the reader the configuration of Discourses. I also provide parenthetical analytic commentary to guide the reader as I trace Discourse practices within and across domains. I present a summary of the Discourse practices within and across domains for Natasha in Appendix C.

NATASHA

Natasha is an African-American woman in her early 20s. Natasha was placed in a special education class in fifth grade and was taken out of it at the end of her 10th-grade year. She dropped out of school in 11th grade and returned to adult education because she wanted to "be somebody." She has two children who she wants to show the value of education. She has to contend with the mutual demands of mothering and schooling. She attends family literacy classes at the elementary school as part of her GED classes.

"There's Something in Me That Slows Me Down": History With Schooling

Natasha was placed in special education when she was in the 5th grade and stayed there until she was in the 10th grade. She reported that her mother did not like to talk about her placement in special education, and she did not agree with the school's recommendation to place her in special education, but wanted her to get the extra support. She stated, "only the teachers know the students and their learning ability. My mother wouldn't know that." In this comment, Natasha reinforced the split between the home and school (Lareau, 1989). When I asked Natasha to describe what special education was like for her, she responded:

HISTORY WITH SCHOOLING	ORDERS OF DISCOURSE
1. It feel comfortable.	Positive Affective statement (S^9); Special
2. You don't have to worry	Education (D)
3. about asking the question.	
4. You know,	Connection building (G)
5. the other kids	
6. would laugh	Special education (D), Negative ability
7. because you're asking	(S), Deficit (S)
8. the question, right?	
9. When you was in that class,	African-American language (G/S^{10})
10. you could ask a question.	
11. If it was wrong or if it was right,	Schooling (D)
12. the teacher would just answer the	

[9]G represents genre, D represents discourse, and S represents style. Each of the codes in the right hand of the column represents the coding of the line-by-line transcript represented in the left of the chart.

[10]I coded aspects of African-American Language (AAL; Morgan, 2002; Smitherman, 2000) at the syntactic level as both genre (ways of interacting) and as style (ways of being). Natasha spoke in African-American language—including the syntactic, phonological, and morphological structures—when she spoke with peers in her classroom. I noticed aspects of African-American language in all domains of the interviews. I did notice code switching in the adults' interviews. I did not, however, notice that there was more code switching in any one of the domains. Myers-Scotton (1993) defined code switching as, "involving the use of two or more languages in the same conversation, usually within the same turn, or even within the same sentence of that turn" (p. 1). Myers-Scotton is a sociolinguist who collected linguistic data in Kenya for 20 years and focuses on the sociopsychological functions of code switching in African languages and their emergence in the United States.

12a.	question for you.	
13.	The high school kids,	
14.	"oh she didn't even get that word right."	Revoicing (S)
15.	So I'm reading out loud,	Rdg as individual (D)/Negative affective (S)
16.	and then you get that response	Passive construction (S)
17.	and you feel	Negative affective statement (S)/Reading (D)
18.	uncomfortable.	
19.	Then once you in a class like this	Special Education (D), Positive affective
20.	you feel	statements (S)
21.	like three or four students	
22.	they can't laugh at you,	Special Education (D), Negative Ability
23.	because they are in the same position	(S), Identity (S)
24.	that I'm in.	

Natasha's talk about her past learning was laced with deficit statements. She viewed school as irrelevant to her life and saw reading as figuring out words and concentrating. Natasha admitted her contradictory belief in special education as a place that "marked her," but also a place where she was not laughed at and was able to ask questions of the teacher. The Discourse of reading in this domain was represented as reading to get the words right (Lines 14–15). Natasha revoiced her high school peers who made fun of her as she was reading out loud (Line 14). The Discourse of reading for accuracy was coupled with negative affective statements "you feel uncomfortable" (Lines 17–18). The Discourse of learning in this domain was defined by a transmission model of education, where the teacher holds all of the knowledge, and learning was defined by memorization rather than constructing knowledge (Line 12). There was a shift in sense of self in this domain as Natasha described movement into a special education class where all of the students "are in the same position that I'm in" (Lines 23–24). The Discourse of reading and learning stayed the same, but the style shifted from negative affective statements to positive affective statements. Natasha felt more comfortable when she was in a special education classroom. Many of the beliefs she had about herself in high school stayed with her as she discussed her present-day school experiences at the adult learning center.

Natasha, like other adult education students, often discussed returning to school as a desire to "be somebody." However, as Luttrell (1997) pointed out, there is often a contradiction between schooling and mothering, where women see schooling as a desire rather than a fundamental right. To further compound this, when the adults talked about dropping out of and returning to school, they usually did so by positioning themselves as agents in the decision. Natasha expressed the tension between schooling and mothering: "I was having kids early. That is taking away from education.

You figure that I can't—I won't be able to continue my education, because I have this big responsibility—is to take care of life, that you work here, and so it is your responsibility you have for your education right then ... I mean, the education is because of the responsibility to take care of the child." Natasha discussed returning to school "for my education, and to become somebody. I don't want to be sitting around with no education and have to clean or something. I do that at home. I want to come and get an education so I can get to be somebody for my kids." When I asked Natasha to tell me about her experiences in adult education, she expressed that the adult education teacher took time with her, unlike her high school teacher. However, she noticed that she was not making progress in some areas like she thought she would. She stated,

PRESENT-DAY EXPERIENCES WITH SCHOOL	ORDERS OF DISCOURSE
1. I just feel it is me.	School (D), Negative ability (S)
2. Because if I really focus on something,	Reading as focusing; Individual (D)
3. Even though it is so boring for me to learn,	Learning as work (D)
4. If I really focus on it,	Individual (D)
5. I will get it right.	Positive cognitive statement (S)
6. But if I'm not interested in it,	Learning as not relevant (D)
7. I will just write anything,	Transitivity (S)
8. Just to get it over with.	Learning as not relevant (D)

In this excerpt, Natasha continued to set forth the Discourse of reading as an individual endeavor—one that requires "focus" (Line 2). This Discourse is coupled with negative ability statements ("I just feel it is me"; Line 1). Similar to her past experiences with school, she continued to define the Discourse of learning as defined by work and a set of tasks she generally was not interested in, rather than as a constructive process (Lines 4–5).

Natasha's statements of returning to school were based on decisions she made for her children, and she actively made these decisions. Her narrative of returning to school demonstrated her continued belief in education and also her shift in how she saw herself as an active part of her education—perhaps for the first time in her educational career.

Family and Community Literacy Practices

Reading the Bible and interacting with texts at church were two of the themes in Natasha's family and community literate life.[11] She shared these

[11]Moss (2001) described in detail the literate events of African-American churches. Some of the literacy practices include reciting memorized scriptures, reading from passages, highlighting and discussing passages of the Bible, making connections between the text and their lives, making intertextual connections between written and spoken genres, call and response with

literacy experiences with her daughter Amanda. Unlike her history with the
school domain, Natasha took an active stance when she discussed the education of her daughter and her involvement with her daughter's education.
However, her agentic stance was based on her own history of participation
with school and thus led her to make many of the same decisions that did
not work well for her. A frequent network of patterns in this domain was
"reading as purposeful" (Discourse) and "active construction of self" (style).

FAMILY AND COMMUNITY LITERACY PRACTICES	ORDERS OF DISCOURSE
1. I been reading the Bible	Active construction (S), AAL
2. to her a lot.	(G/S) Involvement (D)
3. I just go through	Active construction (S)
4. the index	Parallel with schooled literacy
5. and say, for instance,	(D)
6. some type of feeling I have,	Affective (S)
7. you know,	Connection (G)
8. and reading the scripture I read.	Reading, Purpose (D), Active (S)
9. If I'm feeling happy or angry	Affective (S)
10. yeah	Affective (S)
11. Or feeling to myself for,	Affective (S)
12. like or just feeling against the world	Active construction (S)
13. I just go	Active (S)
14. and try to find some part	Reading as purposeful (D)
15. Of the Bible that deals with it particularly	Active (S), Reading as purposeful (D)
16. I go to it and read.	

Natasha integrated her value of the church in their life into her involvement with her daughter's education, typical of many of the adults in the African-American community. In the prior excerpt, Natasha referred to reading the Bible for the purpose of dealing with emotional aspects of her life:
"I just go and find some part of the Bible that deals with it particularly I go
and read it" (Lines 13–16) (Discourse of reading). This comment reflected
that she saw reading, within the domain of the church, as meaningful and
purposeful—something that shifted when she discussed schooled literacy.
Connected to the Discourse of reading as purposeful/involvement in her
children's education, Natasha positioned herself as an agent through active
construction of herself. For example, in Lines 1 and 2, she stated, "I been
reading the Bible to her a lot." Another Discourse embedded in this excerpt was that of learning as observation, guided practice, and independent

---

the minister, and singing. Some of these literacy events include practices that would seem to
facilitate the boundary crossing between church and academic literacy (e.g., reading passages,
highlighting and discussing passages). Other aspects of the literacy events such as the merging
of oral and written texts as well as the participatory style of the interactions between the rever-
end and the congregation might separate the church discourse from academic discourse.

practice. Her daughter was learning about the forms and functions of texts as Natasha read the Bible to her.

Reflection and Action

Identify students in your research or teaching who have been assigned a label. Talk to them about their uses of reading, writing, and language in different areas of their life. What do you notice about how they use literacy and language in different domains? What interactional patterns do you notice? What discourses or cultural models are evident in their talk? How do they position themselves in relation to literacy in each domain (e.g., active? passive?)? (See e.g., Rogers, Light, & Curtis [in press] for an interview protocol used with 5th-grade students.)

Involvement with Children's Education

Remember that Natasha's mother did not think special education was a good placement for Natasha, and yet she agreed to put her into it so she could get additional resources. It is important to note that this is the only place in the interview where Natasha discussed a disagreement with the values and decisions of the school. Despite the disagreement, or conflict between the school and home, there was a strong enough alignment in the value of education that silenced Natasha's mother, and she conceded to the placement of Natasha in special education. The same cycle was repeated with Natasha and her own child. Despite recognizing that her daughter's teachers went too fast during instruction and her daughter was bright both in and out of school, Natasha still believed her daughter should be placed in special education. In the intercontextual connections (between the domain of history with school and involvement with children's education), we can begin to see the discursive and material reproduction of subject positions. In the domains of her own and her daughter's education, Natasha expressed a value in education and reinforced the cultural model of reading as subskill processes and an individual endeavor rather than a social phenomenon. I asked Natasha to tell me about her daughter as a reader.

INVOLVEMENT WITH CHILDREN'S EDUCATION	ORDERS OF DISCOURSE
1. As a reader, she can see a word	Reading as "seeing words" (D)
2. and she'll just say it backwards	Reading "saying words" (D)
3. or something.	
4. She just twists it a little bit.	Reading (D)/Deficit construction (S)
5. When I read to her	Involvement (D)/Active construction (S)
6. and she reads it back	Learning as observation, guided practice (D)

7. it won't always be the way I said it.	Reading as saying words (D)
8. I think she tries hard in her classroom	Cognitive statement (S), Reading as Work (D)
9. to impress her teacher	Value in education (D)
10. She try hard.	Value in education (D), Reading as Work (D),
11. She just has something	
12. that slows her down	Deficit as individual (D/S)
13. but I don't know what it is.	Deficit (D/S)
	Negative cognitive statement (S)

Natasha was very involved with her daughter's education, both at home and at school. She spoke of teaching her daughter how to read. She stated, "I really get down and help her." When she helped her daughter with reading, she helped her sound out words and pronounce the words right. The Discourse of reading was the same as her past experiences with education. Her sense of self shifted, however, from negative to positive ability and from passive to active construction. Not only did Natasha see herself as knowledgeable, she took the role of her daughter's teacher.

In the prior excerpt, Natasha's assertion that there was something that "slows [her daughter] down" echoed how she discussed her own history with school. She stated, "I don't know what it is, it's just something that's based in me" (Discourse, style). This is evidence of the alignment of negative ways of thinking about self (style) in relation to a particular type of literacy (Discourse) that was consistent across the domains of "history with schooling" and "involvement with children's education." As we hear Natasha discuss her daughter as a reader, we hear discursive artifacts of how she understood reading as a cultural model.

Natasha defined the Discourse of reading as "seeing words" (Line 1) and "saying" words (Line 2). This reinforced the schools' vision of reading as a subskill process (Discourse, alignment with the school). While she displayed her involvement with her daughter, she also showed her value and belief in the educational system. As she talked about her daughter as a learner in the classroom, she evoked the Discourse of learning as hard work, "she tries hard" (Lines 8, 10). She went on to demonstrate her belief that there are individual deficits (Discourse/style) with her daughter. "She just has something that slows her down but I don't know what it is." Her expression of a negative cognitive statement, "I don't know what it is," demonstrated the likelihood of Natasha turning to the experts of the school to provide her with a diagnosis of her daughter's difficulties (Discourse, style, alignment with the school). Despite telling me that her daughter was competent in many areas outside of school, including learning the songs at church and learning and teaching other children hopscotch songs, Natasha decided that she wanted to recommend her daughter for special education so she could receive additional resources. She stated:

INVOLVEMENT WITH CHILDREN'S EDUCATION	ORDERS OF DISCOURSE
1. I will recommend it for her.	Mothering (D)/Active stance (S)
2. I mean cause I know how hard	Cognitive statement (S)
3. it is for a teacher	Value in education (D)
4. to have a whole bunch of students	
5. and all the kids	
6. are not on the same level.	Discourse of ability (S/D)
7. So it will be good	Positive statement (S)
8. for the kids	
9. that she takes out	
10. they are a little slower	Special education (D)/Negative Ability (S)
11. than the other ones	
12. pull those kids out	
13. two or three hours of the school hours	Special Education, Time (D)
14. and go with them	
15. one on one	Reading as one-to-one (D)
16. and you see,	
17. you do that every day	Mothering/Schooling (D)/Learning as
18. through the school year	transmission (D)
19. that child would learn more.	Learning as work (D)

In the involvement with children domain, the primary configuration of Discourse patterns revealed that Natasha constructed herself as active with regard to literacy (style). She reinforced the school's vision of reading as a subskill process that is done individually and is measured through tests (Discourse). For example, in Line 15, she referred to "one-on-one support" and taking the slower children out of the classroom (Line 9). She also reiterated the importance of education and her value in it (Discourse). This value was apparent despite that, through the logic of school, she represented her daughter as not able and not competent (Discourse, style).

Within this domain, Natasha fluctuated between seeing reading as purposeful and as a subskill process (Discourse of reading). Across all of the examples, Natasha reported a value and commitment to education (Discourse) for both herself and her children. She actively constructed herself as an agent within this domain (style) and discussed how she was involved with her children's education (e.g., active construction of the pronoun, positive cognitive statements, and implicit references to herself as a teacher). However, she did construct her daughter with negative deficit and ability statements (style) as she showed an alignment with the discourse of the school and reading characterized by subskill processes and one-on-one instruction—an individual rather than a social phenomenon.

Reflection and Action

What are possible theories to explain why Natasha would recommend her daughter for special education when it did not work for herself as a learner and she already said (within the interview) that she did not want to refer her daughter? What are the local, institutional, and societal contexts that influence Natasha's decision making? What are possible ways to interrupt this cycle?

An Interdiscursive Perspective on Learning

To this point, I have argued that cultural models of literacy and learning are attached to ways of being/identities that shifts across various contexts. This is similar to the way Lave discussed learning in terms of changing participation in changing practices that include changes in identity rather than a change in the mind. Lave (1996) stated,

> There are ways of becoming a participant, ways of participating, and ways in which participants and practices change. In any event, the learning of specific ways of participating differs in particular situated practices. The term "learning mechanisms" diminishes in importance, in fact it may fall out altogether, as "mechanisms" disappear into practice. Mainly, people are becoming kinds of persons. (p. 157)

I continue with this line of reasoning and argue the need to look at such shifts in discourse patterns as *learning*. Shifts in the Discourse patterns can occur within a domain (intertextual) or across domains (intercontextual). Similarly, the configuration of Discourse practices can shift in one area across or within the context and not in others (e.g., ways of thinking about self can shift, but the cultural model of literacy as individual endeavor can stay the same).

I focus on the shifts between domains—or the intercontextual shifts. In both Natasha's history with education and her involvement with children's education, she expressed a Discourse of reading as a set of subskill processes that involved reading words and memorizing. The Discourse of reading shifted in the family and community literacy practices domain as Natasha discussed reading as a purposeful endeavor. Although the Discourse of reading stayed the same in both her history with school and her involvement with her daughter's education, the style connected to the Discourse shifted from negative ability and passive construction to positive ability and active construction of self. This shift in sense of self, even if it is accompanied by the same Discourse of reading, demonstrates learning.

Context 1   **Context 2**   **Context 3**

Family and Community   **Involvement with Children's**   **Past and Present**
Literacy Practices   **Education**   **Experiences with**
                                                               School

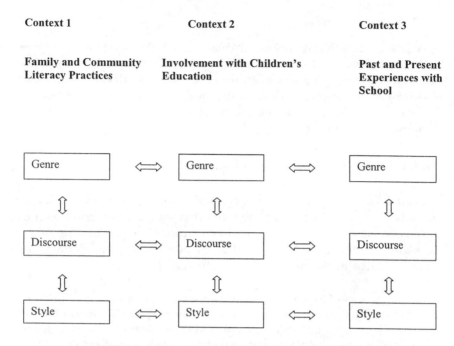

FIG. 3.1.   CDA and social transformation heuristic.

In this perspective, learning is a network of social practices, which changes over time and varies from place to place. Figure 3.1 is a simplified heuristic that represents potential shifts representing social transformation and learning in genre, Discourse, and style within and across three discursive contexts.

Analyzing the configuration of social practices and the shifts across time and context can help educators describe, interpret, and explain the ways of interacting, representing, and being that accompanies learning. Such configurations of practice often rub up against one another and are not mutually exclusive. Gee (1996) discussed this patterning in terms of boundary crossing and Fairclough (1995) in terms of manifest and constitutive intertextuality. What is important to draw out of both frameworks is that the boundary crossings and existence of discourses that cross at the domain of genre, Discourse, and/or style may be in *conflict* or *alignment* with the dominant Discourse. Often we think about clashes between groups in power and groups without power in terms of *conflict* among discourses, ways of interacting, representing, and being. However, we need to be just as concerned about the places where there is Discourse *alignment* as when there is Discourses conflict. The prime example in the data I have displayed is that each of the adults values education and upholds a view of themselves and of reading that is in alignment with the views of the school. It is this *alignment* that causes them to more readily believe when the school tells them that they or their children are deficient, or disabled, because they so readily believe in and value the institution of the school.

I argue that this view of learning—one that takes into account the configuration of practices and a theory for what such configurations can possibly mean—is especially important for marginalized learners. It allows the complexity of shifting identity—and the attendant discourses—to emerge. This is necessary to uncover and interrupt the acquisition of problematic identities as in Natasha's case. The question then is: How do we halt the (re) production of problematic ideologies in relation to literacy development? As noted in the research design, I conducted the interviews over 2 or 3 days so that both the participants and myself had time to reflect on the interview. During this time, I would pull out instances where there was inconsistency between the domains and ask the adults to make sense of this with me. For example, if the adults noted that they were ministers and constructing sermons, but then stated that they could not read, I would ask them why they thought this. The following conversation is an example of this member checking that occurred between Natasha and myself:

RR: You know, you sound like you don't have a memory problem. It's not a comprehension problem, because you told me stories about your life that had made sense to you.

N: Right. Yeah. It's not in comprehending, but I don't know what it is. It's—it's just—it's something, it's based on me. I don't know what it is, but I don't think I'm a slow learner, 'cause I learn fast on my job and everywhere I go. And, uh, they really think she's not—she don't have a bad attitude. And that's the first thing, I come to them with a positive attitude, no matter what. And they get a sense of me towards that, carries from them [inaudible] positive attitude, so I think that is one way that people really need to see, that be negative all the time, it's not worth it.

In this excerpt, there was a shift in Natasha's "ways of being" that demonstrates she was on the edge of thinking that her learning difficulty was not an internal deficit, but rather something that came from the instructional contexts of which she was a part. Her shift in thinking was represented by an increase in negative cognitive statements, showing that she was rethinking ideas that she believed in (i.e., she is deficient). The crucial line, "I don't know what it is, but I don't think I'm a slow learner, cause I learn fast on my job and everywhere I go," indicated that Natasha started to see herself not solely in terms of how the school saw her, but as a person with multiple identities across contexts. Jonassen (2000) wrote, "what causes change in activity systems are contradictions that emerge from them" (p. 107). Although Natasha realized that there was a distinction between her out-of-school and school representation of self, there were also traces of the same "language bits" she used when she spoke about her daughter as a learner. For some of the other adults in this study, shifts in Discourse patterns occurred within domains (e.g., there were shifts in style within the domain of schooling or involvement with children's education).

In these excerpts, we start to see shifts in Discourse patterns both within and across domains, which is evidence of learning. Without a systematic study of the relationships among genre, Discourse, and style, such shifts may have gone unnoticed. I argue that these shifts in ways of interacting, ways of representing, and ways of being that constitute the repositioning of self (and others) within various contexts that counts as learning and, consequently, transformation of self. As Sfard (1998) wrote,

> Being in action means being in a constant state of flux. The awareness of the change that never stops means refraining from a permanent labeling. Actions can be clever or unsuccessful, but these adjectives do not apply to the actors. For the learner, all options are always open, even if he or she carries a history of failure. Thus, quite unlike the [acquisition metaphor] the participation metaphor seems to bring a message of an everlasting hope: Today you act one way; tomorrow you may act differently. (p. 8)

This constant state of flux is certainly apparent in Natasha's literate life.

Conclusions and Discussion

This chapter has set forth two related sets of propositions. First, I argued and demonstrated that for CDA to be a trustworthy methodological tool in the social sciences it must be conducted in a standardized manner (i.e., researchers should avoid starting their data analysis assuming power is embedded in the data). In this study, I was not interested in studying power per se (e.g., Pennycook, 2001). Rather, I set out to study the relationship between discourse configurations and socially situated identities as it can be understood through an investigation of genre, Discourse, and style within three domains of practice and across domains of practice. In the sense that the analysis demonstrates a particular configuration of genre, Discourse, and style across the domains and such configurations are never value free, I concede this has been a study of language and power.

An implication for adult literacy research and instruction is that across almost all of the interviews, the analysis demonstrated that there was a shift for the adults in terms of how they viewed themselves in schools in their past and present classrooms (style). They did, however, continue to believe in and reinforce the cultural model of reading in the same way. This suggests that the adult literacy classrooms, at least the ones that were a part of this study, are doing a good job of setting up what Cambourne (1995) referred to as the "conditions for learning," where the adults see themselves as successful learners as a result of being engaged in their learning and seeing it as relevant to their lives. However, it also suggests that the reading instruction that is part of their adult education classrooms is similar to the type of reading instruction that they were a part of in their elementary and high school careers—reading instruction that did not work well for them the first time around.

All of the adults' talk consisted of hybrid discourse structures, either within or across domains, or both. The more hybrid the discourse, the more room for transformation and social change. Fairclough (2000b) wrote, "texts that are hybrid, or mixed in the discursive practices they draw upon, texts that are linguistically heterogeneous, are not exceptional and abnormal. Rather, they are quite normal, especially in a period of intensive change like the present" (p. 173). Educators and researchers should look for instances of hybridity, and indeed encourage them, as moments for potential reconfiguration of practices.

The second objective accomplished in this chapter is demonstrating that shifts in Discourse are equivalent to social transformation and learning. Each of the cases demonstrates evidence of intertextual (within domain) and intercontextual hybridity. Such shifts in Discourse represent places of learning. If literacy learning involves, as the new literacy scholars argue, shifts in knowing, participation, and identity, then teachers and researchers need to become proficient in looking for and documenting shifts in interacting, representing, and ways of being within multiple, and sometimes competing, Discourses.

This chapter demonstrated *how* discursive positions are held together, which has everything to do with learning. As people position themselves and are positioned in particular ways within Discourses, we can see how a person can embody a Discourse at one point in time and resist it at another point in time. This makes a compelling argument for the integration of diverse ways of interacting, representing, and being into classrooms and other learning environments because we want to build on the places that are the least conscious, and consequently where people—both adults and children—are most likely to be successful.

Learning is indeed a set of practices that involves activities and talk with concomitant shifts and changes across domains of interacting, representing, and being with such practices. Comprised of as a set of practices and interactions, educational sites hold the potential for analysis and subsequent transformation through a structural analysis of orders of discourse and intertextual, interactional analysis (between and within orders of discourse). Further, education is located at local, institutional, and societal modes of practice, and thus offers the potential for a multilayered approach to analysis. In the sense that literacy learning includes shifts in ways of interacting with texts, ways of representing and ways of being, the combined theories and methods of Gee and Fairclough make sense.

One of the major findings of this research that is of immediate concern to literacy researchers and practitioners is the distinction between *conflict* and *alignment* of Discourses. I demonstrated in Natasha's case that she valued education across all three domains of practice. The puzzling matter is that she continued to think about themselves as literate differently in each of the domains. This is problematic because she demonstrated a high degree of alignment with the schools (indeed she has come back to school to pursue her GED), and yet she does not see herself as competent and proficient within that institution. Further, she tended to reiterate the dominant values that were attached to the institution of school through reading. She saw reading as memorizing words, concentrating, work, and an individual endeavor. Thus, there was a high degree of alignment among her understandings of what literacy was, who and what it was for, and if she was capable of being literate in this domain. Traditionally, we do not speak of alignment between individuals and institutions, especially for those who are trying to gain access to mainstream codes of power as problematic. It is conflict that is cited in the literature as problematic. The adults do not see their literacy as mattering, especially the literacies that are the closest to their primary identities (e.g., church, home, community literacies). This makes the alignment between schooled literacy easier for the adults because it is the only literacy that matters. This allows for the school's "mark," as Natasha put it, to be believable by the adults for themselves and, as we saw from the adults oral histories, for their children as well. The adults do not see the contradictions embedded across the domains. A practical implication of this research is pointing out the places where what the adults say and how they think about themselves as literate do not match across domains. This is where the work of the new literacy studies is important to bring out-of-school literacies into school to increase the recognition work of marginalized literacies.

Methodological Implications

This chapter attended to learning, critical discourse, and identities across and within various contexts. In doing so, as in the other chapters in this volume, I kept the common critiques of CDA in the back of my mind. Two of the most common critiques of CDA are: (a) reading power and ideology onto the data instead of letting ideological relationships emerge from the data, and (b) an imbalance between linguistic analysis and context. In this collection, we have added a third critique—that is, the lack of attention to learning by CDA (see chap. 11).

CDA is often critiqued for being too heavy handed in its approach to language and to decontextualizing examples of language. In this study, I have used the combined frameworks of Gee and Fairclough to present a systematic study of the relationship among ways of interacting, ways of representing, and ways of being. As all of the chapters in this book do, I have attended to the structure of language. I have followed Fairclough's conceptualization of orders of discourse.

Balancing ethnographic and discourse analytic contexts is a struggle with which each of the authors in this book have dealt. In this chapter, I moved back and forth between the context of the three domains in the interview and the contexts of my ethnographic observations in the adult literacy classrooms to validate (or not) the patterns I was seeing in my CDA. Viewing *context* as a balance among local, institutional, and societal domains and genre, Discourse, and style may be a useful framework for literacy researchers. This study has focused on the context of genre, discourse, and style within the local context of the interview. However, as noted earlier, the stories that each of the participants told are structured by and structure the institutional and societal contexts in which they emerge. Future ethnographic studies should be conducted to investigate the relationships documented in this research.

Presently, SFL, the basis of CDA, is used as a resource rather than as a system of meaning making for analysis, especially in American contexts (see chap. 1, this volume, for a discussion of SFL). I argue the need for continued attention to social theory, an articulation of flexible system, and the relationship within and across systems is essential for the study of literacy. Such a framework has methodological implications that are of importance to the study of literacy.

There are limitations in this research. First, I have provided the case of Natasha not as representative of all of the adults I have interviewed, but for the purpose of theory and methodology building. The domains I evoked in the interviews may be read as artificially contrived domains. I realize the limitations in evoking discursive contexts to study the relationships between linguistic resources and identities. The primary limitation is that I am relying on the adults explicitly telling me what they are proficient with and in which context. Part of being proficient, Gee would argue, is that the strategies and skills associated with the proficiency are largely subconscious, and people are not readily aware of them. Despite the limitations embedded in using interviews as a methodology, important linguistic distinctions between contexts did emerge. Future research should follow these interviews with more across domain observations and follow-up interviews (Rogers, under review). In the meantime, the theoretical and methodological resources demonstrated in this chapter might provide a resource for other educational researchers interested in semiotic tools, CDA, and social transformation.

RECOMMENDED READINGS

Morgan, M. (2002). *Language, discourse, and power in African American culture.* Cambridge, MA: Cambridge University Press.
Pennycook, A. (2001). *Critical applied linguistics. A critical introduction.* Mahwah, NJ: Lawrence Erlbaum Associates.
Rogers, R. (2003). *A Critical Discourse Analysis of family literacy practices: Power in and out of print.* Mahwah, NJ: Lawrence Erlbaum Associates.

REFERENCES

Anderson, J. (1988). *The education of blacks in the south, 1860–1935.* Chapel Hill: University of North Carolina Press.
Antaki, C., & Widdicombe, S. (Eds.). (1998). *Identities in talk.* London: Sage.
Bower, C. (2001, June 27). Black leaders decry gap in academic achievement. *St. Louis Post Dispatch*, p. C1.
Bucholtz, M., Liang, A. C., & Sutton, L. (Eds.). (1999). *Reinventing identities. The gendered self in discourse.* New York: Oxford University Press.
Cambourne, B. (1995). Toward an educationally relevant theory of literacy learning. Twenty years of inquiry. *The Reading Teacher, 49*(3), 182–190.
Chouliaraki, L., & Fairclough, N. (1999). *Discourse in late modernity: Rethinking critical discourse analysis.* Edinburgh, Scotland: Edinburgh University Press.
Cole, M. (1996). *Cultural psychology: A once and future discipline.* Cambridge, MA: Harvard University Press.
Costa, M. (1988). *Adult literacy/illiteracy in the United States.* Santa Barbara, CA: ABC-CLIO.
Fairclough, N. (1992). *Discourse and social change.* Cambridge, England: Polity.
Fairclough, N. (1995). *Critical discourse analysis. The critical study of language.* New York: Longman.
Fairclough, N. (2000a). Discourse, social theory and social research. *Journal of Sociolinguistics, 4*(2), 163–195.
Fairclough, N. (2000b). Multiliteracies and language. Orders of discourse and intertextuality. In B. Cope & M. Kalantzis (Eds.), *Multiliteracies: Literacy learning and the design of social futures* (pp. 162–181). London: Routledge.
Gee, J. (1996). *Social linguistics and literacies: Ideology in discourses.* London: Falmer.
Gee, J. (1999). *An introduction to discourse analysis: Theory and method.* New York: Routledge.
Halliday, M. (1978). *Language as social semiotic: The social interpretation of language and meaning.* London: Edward Arnold.
Holland, D., & Quinn, N. (1987). *Cultural models in language and thought.* Cambridge: Cambridge University Press.
Jackson, R., & Denson, H. (2001, August 23). A call to action. *St. Louis Post Dispatch*, p. C3.
Jonassen, D. (2000). Revisiting activity theory as a framework for designing student centered learning environments. In D. Jonassen & S. Land (Eds.), *Theoretical foundations of learning environments* (pp. 89–122). Mahwah, NJ: Lawrence Erlbaum Associates.
Lareau, A. (1989). *Home advantage. Social class and parental intervention in elementary education.* New York: Falmer.
Lave, J. (1996). Teaching, as learning, in practice. *Mind, Culture, and Activity, 3*, 149–164.
Lave, J., & Wenger, E. (1991). *Situated learning: Legitimate peripheral participation.* New York: Cambridge University Press.

Luke, A. (2000). Critical literacy in Australia: A matter of context and standpoint. *Journal of Adolescent and Adult Literacy, 43*(5), 448–461.

Luttrell, W. (1997). *School smart and mother-wise: Working class women's identity and schooling*. New York: Routledge.

Morgan, M. (2002). *Language, discourse, and power in African American culture*. Cambridge, MA: Cambridge University Press.

Moss, B. (2001). From the pews to the classrooms: Influences of the African American church on academic literacy. In J. L. Harris, A. Kamhi, & K. Pollock (Eds.), *Literacy in African American communities* (pp. 195–212). Mahwah, NJ: Lawrence Erlbaum Associates.

Myers-Scotton, C. (1993). *Social motivations for code-switching: Evidence from Africa*. Oxford: Clarendon.

Pennycook, A. (2001). *Critical applied linguistics. A critical introduction*. Mahwah, NJ: Lawrence Erlbaum Associates.

Reder, S. (2002). *The state of literacy in America*. A report prepared for the National Institute for Literacy.

Rogers, R. (2002). Between contexts: A critical analysis of family literacy, discursive practices, and literate subjectivities. *Reading Research Quarterly, 37*(3), 248–277.

Rogers, R. (2003). *A critical discourse analysis of family literacy practices: Power in and out of print*. Mahwah, NJ: Lawrence Erlbaum Associates.

Rogers, R. (under review). Storied selves: A critical analysis of adult learners' literate lives.

Rogers, R., Light, R., & Curtis, L. (under review). Anyone can be an expert in something: Exploring the complexity of discourse conflict and alignment in a 5th grade classroom.

Sawin, P. (1999). Gender, context and the narrative construction of identity: Rethinking models of "Women's Narrative." In M. Bucholtz, A. Liang, & L. Sutton (Eds.), *Reinventing identities: The gendered self in discourse* (pp. 241–258). New York: Oxford University Press.

Sfard, A. (1998). On two metaphors for learning and the damage of choosing just one. *Educational Researcher, 27*, 4–13.

Smitherman, G. (2000). *Talkin' that talk: Language, culture, and education in African America*. London & New York: Routledge.

Stuart-Wells, A., & Crain, R. L. (1997). *Stepping over the color line: African American students in white suburban schools*. New Haven, CT: Yale University Press.

U.S. Census Bureau. (2002). *Racial and ethnic residential segregation in the United States: 1980–2000*. Washington, DC: Author.

APPENDIX A: INTERVIEW PROTOCOL

Exploring the Integration of Family Knowledge and Resources on Literacy Development

The questions are semistructured interview questions.

History With Schooling

This domain includes past and present experiences with school. This includes interactions and experiences with formal and informal teachers.

I am going to ask a set of questions that relate to your experiences with school.

Describe yourself as a learner.

Tell me about your school experiences.
Who was your best teacher? Why?
Who was your worst teacher? Why?
Tell me about your parents' involvement in your education.

Tell me about your reasons for returning to the ABE classroom?
Barriers to returning?
What are your goals for your own education?
How would you describe your learning in the classroom right now?
In what ways does your husband/partner support your continuing education?
How do you see yourself as a reader?

History With Children

I am going to ask a set of questions that relate to your children's education.

Tell me about your children.
Tell me about their classroom.
Tell me about their reading.
What do you remember as a "teachable" moment when they were young?
Tell me about your children as learners.

Involvement With Children's Education

This domain includes all of the ways in which the adult is involved in their children's education. It also includes the way in which their family was involved with their education.

I am going to ask a set of questions that relate to your involvement in your children's education.

Describe how you are involved with your children's education.
What do you think of your children as readers? As writers? As students?
What are issues/concerns you wish you knew more about?
What types of activities do your children like to do at home?
Are there any experiences that stand out where you interacted with the school on behalf of your children?
Do your children receive extra support in remedial reading, special education, support services?

Can you think of and describe a situation where you were recently involved with your child's learning?

Outside of School Literacy Practices

This domain includes the range of literacy practices that adults interact with outside of school. This may include activities, the types of texts involved, formal and informal teachers.

I am going to ask you a set of questions that relate to your use of literacy outside of school.

What type of reading and writing occur at home?
What are some of the traditions in your family? Tell me about them.
What is something that you are an expert at?
How do things get done around your home?
Describe a typical day in your house from when you get up to when you and your children go to bed.

Include Artifacts With the Interviews

Newspaper story
Generative themes from their lives
Reading documents (phone bills, bills, traffic tickets, bible)
Differences in reading styles
Note from the school
Report cards (how they are read)
Documents that have come home from the school that they have to negotiate

APPENDIX B: CDA CHART

Questions to ask in each (and across) domain of analysis:

Fairclough (1992) suggested selecting cruces or moments of crisis in the data as an entry point into the analysis. These are moments in the discourse when it is evident something is going wrong. Fairclough wrote, "such moments of crisis make visible aspects of practices which might normally be naturalized, and therefore difficult to notice; but they also show change in process, the actual ways in which people deal with the problematization of practices" (p. 230).

I. Genres:

What is the text for analysis? The object of this domain of analysis is to describe the organizational properties of interactions.

Microlinguistic analysis:

What are the microlinguistic aspects of this text?

Thematic structure of the text
Information focus
Cohesion devices (parallel structure, repetition)
Wording
Metaphors
Politeness conventions
Turn taking

II. Discourses/Interpersonal:

Luke (2000) defined *discourses* as, "systematic clusters of themes, statements, ideas and ideologies." These themes can be seen through the production, consumption, and distribution of texts and talk in conjunction with genre and style. Contradictions are a necessary part of discourses.

What voices/perspectives are represented?
What are the possible interpretations of this text?
Who are the possible audiences?
What resistant readings are possible?

III. Style/Ideational:

The purpose of this domain of analysis is to specify the social structures and processes and how people are drawn into such processes.

Active and passive voice
Modality (tense, affinity)
Often associated with modal verbs (*must, may, can, should*) and adverbs (*probably, possibly*)
Patterns of transitivity

Transitivity:

A property of language that enables humans to build a mental picture of reality, to make sense of their world and the "goings on" of doing, happening, feeling, and believing. These "goings on" are sorted out in the semantic system of language and expressed through the grammar of the clause. The reflective, experiential aspects of meaning is the system of transitivity. Transitivity specifies the different types of processes that are recognized in the language and the structures by which they are expressed.

Action

Action with dialogue
Action Passive
Action Active
Physical or cognitive action
(OR lack of action)
Modal construction

Affective—statement of want, desire, like, or need
(deficit affective)

State—statement of physical or mental being
Had

Ability—internal characteristic of something he can or cannot do
(lack of ability)
Have, got, am, get

Cognitive—think, thought, believe, remember statements

(Compiled from Gee, 1999, appendix; Fairclough, 1992, see chap. 8; Halliday, 1994.)

APPENDIX C: SUMMARY OF CONFIGURATION OF DISCOURSES

Across all of the domains, Natasha demonstrated a high value in education. Within the *history with schooling* domain, the most frequent configuration of discourse patterns was the Discourse of reading as defined by the school (e.g., reading as memorization, reading as concentration, reading as one on one) coupled with negative ability statements (style), negative cognitive statements (style), and a passive construction of self (style). Another network of practices within this domain was learning as defined by transmission and memorization (Discourse) coupled with a passive construction of self (style).

Within the *involvement with children's education* domain a frequent configuration of practices was the Discourse of reading as defined by the school (e.g., reading as memorization, reading as concentration, reading as one on one/individual) (Discourse). This Discourse was coupled with an active construction of self (style), and positive cognitive statements (style). In this domain, the discourse of learning was defined as transmission model rather than as observation, guided practice, and independent practice.

In the domain *family and community literacy practices*, the primary configuration of discourse practices included the Discourse of reading as purposeful coupled with an active construction of self (style). Similarly, the Discourse of learning in this domain was discussed as a process of observation, guided practice, and independent practice and was networked with an active construction of self and positive cognitive statements.

Chapter 4

Discourse in Activity and Activity as Discourse

Shawn Rowe
Washington University in St. Louis

CENTRAL CONCEPTS

Learning—The appropriation of culturally valued physical and psychological tools as part of participation in active, distributed meaning making.

Members' resources—Social and linguistic resources for signaling and interpreting identities and making meaning of texts (Fairclough, 1989).

Situation definition—A socioculturally particular type of activity or context that specifies what we are doing at a given moment or what we take to be the background against which our utterances and actions are to be interpreted.

Activity—An uninterrupted stretch of physical activity whether carried out by one or more people. Activity may be distributed among people and the physical and psychological tools they use. In addition, for purposes of analysis, activity can be broken down into subactivities and individual actions.

Utterance—A unit of analysis of speech that corresponds to any uninterrupted stretch of speaking by one or more people.

A basic claim of Discourse analysis (Gee, 1999), Critical Discourse Analysis (CDA; Fairclough, 1989), and dialogic approaches to conversation analysis (Linell, 1998) is that Discourse is constituted by both talk and actions working in concert.[1] This may be stated in either a weak or strong version. Linell (1998) argued for a weak version, describing talk as a type of action that "includes accompanying paralinguistic signals and embedding contexts" (p. 6). Gee (1999) made the case more strongly, drawing a distinction between discourse (with a small "d") and Discourse (with a capital "D"). Discourse (with a capital "D") includes both talk and action:

> To "pull off" an "X" doing "Y" (e.g., a Los Angeles Latino street-gang member warning another gang member off his territory, or a laboratory physicist convincing colleagues that a particular graph supports her ideas, or, for that matter, a laboratory physicist warning other laboratory physicists off her research territory) it is not enough to get just the words "right," though that is crucial. It is necessary, as well, to get one's body, clothes, gestures, actions, interactions, ways with things, symbols, tools, technologies (be they guns or graphs), and values, attitudes, beliefs, and emotions "right," as well, and all at the "right" places and times.
>
> When "little d" discourse (language-in-use) is melded integrally with non-language "stuff" to enact specific identities and activities, then, I say that "big D" Discourses are involved. (p. 7)

Two things, however, are missing from analyses like Linell's, Gee's, and Fairclough's. First, there is not generally a learning theory articulated in these kinds of discourse analyses. The result is that it is hard to describe just how people learn to recognize and use the right members' resources (Fairclough, 1989) and nonlanguage stuff necessary for getting particular identities right. Second, activity as part of discourse is usually ignored in both transcribing talk and analyzing it. The result is that, although analysts refer to activity in their discussion of talk, close analysis of the nonlanguage stuff of Discourse is not carried out. The two solutions I offer are to make some of the connections between CDAs and sociocultural approaches to learning (Rogoff, 1990, 1995; Wertsch, 1985, 1991, 1998) explicit and to demonstrate a way of transcribing and analyzing talk and activity simultaneously.

---

[1] In some senses, these are three different traditions in analyzing spoken and written texts with different histories, units of analysis, and purposes of analysis. In other senses, they share a great deal in common. Despite differences in their analytical styles and focal points of analysis, Gee and Fairclough both departed from traditional discourse analysis because of their insistence on the ideological saturation of the elements of language (a tradition that stems from Marxist and deconstructivist literary analysis and systemic-functional linguistics [SFL]). This makes them also consistent with Linell's work, which seeks to anchor conversation analysis in a dialogic or Bakhtinian approach to language in use that takes account of the ideological nature of all elements of language and the dialogic structure of all language in use.

SOCIOCULTURAL APPROACHES
TO LEARNING AND CDA

There are many approaches to learning that fall under the heading of *sociocultural*. What they all share in common are their roots in the work of Vygotsky (1978, 1981, 1986). The particular version of sociocultural approach that I draw on here is that outlined by Wertsch (1985, 1991, 1998). This approach sees development and learning in terms of the appropriation and mastery of physical and psychological tools as part of participation in collective and individual activities (Vygotsky, 1978, 1986; Wertsch, 1985) during which individuals engage in what Wertsch (1985) called *strategic activity*, appropriating collective problem-solving procedures and cultural tools as part of "mediated activity" (Wertsch, 1991, 1998).

Traditionally, the primary, although by no means the only, tool of the collaborative problem solving that sociocultural theorists focus on is language. Although he did spend some time investigating other types of psychological tools, Vygotsky focused on language as the premier tool of psychological development. Language is ubiquitous to human activity—especially the kinds of group activities on which discourse analysts and sociocultural theorists focus. Yet it is certainly not the only semiotic system or mediational means at work in learning. As Gee argued earlier, learning to perform a given identity in any given activity is much more than getting the language right. From a sociocultural perspective, we can speak of all semiotic systems functioning as tools in the development of interpersonal communicative activity and individual cognitive activity. Taking into account how language shapes activity is important, but it is also important to find ways to talk about how the wider array of other semiotic systems operating as part of activity afford and constrain group learning activity as well as how activity shapes language use and interpersonal interactions. A sociocultural approach to learning and language in use thus addresses CDA's concern with transformation by focusing on the ways in which members' resources are privileged, appropriated, rejected, and deployed as part of participation in activity.

Yet sociocultural approaches to learning have often failed to recognize questions of inequity and authority in the distribution of mediational means. They have failed to recognize, as Linell (1998) suggested, not only cooperation, negotiation, and shared activity, but also fragmentation, complementarity, and struggle, which characterize much of interpersonal activity. Of particular importance in this regard is the idea that cultural tools, including language, are often unequally distributed throughout a group and a society. Critical approaches to discourse bring to a sociocultural approach to learning recognition of the ideological saturation of cultural tools and their potential for re-creating and/or subverting particular orders of Discourse (Fairclough, 1989). A critical approach to language, psychology, and activity is a crucial, but often neglected, addition to any sociocultural project that seeks to highlight the structure and realization in everyday activities of the inequitable distribution of power, authority, and valued cultural and physical resources that shape the institutions we all inhabit.

DISCOURSE AS TALK AND ACTIVITY

For a combined sociocultural and CDA analysis to work, however, the analyst must be able to describe not only language in use (the purview of Discourse analysis), but also activity as it develops (the purview of sociocultural analysis). Discourse and conversation analyses of all kinds generally relegate activity to the background of analysis, citing it solely as something that accompanies talk. Nevertheless, even those linguists who do not work directly with language in use (and language in use with Gee's nonlanguage stuff) generally recognize that activity and talk are generally interrelated. The psycholinguist Clark (1996), for instance, created a discourse continuum moving from activities that are mostly linguistic to those that are mostly nonlinguistic:

1. telephone conversations, newspaper items, radio reports, novels
2. face-to-face conversations, tabloid items, TV reports, science texts
3. business transactions, plays, movies, coaching demonstrations, apprenticeship lessons, bridge games
4. basketball games, tennis matches, two people moving furniture, making love
5. playing a string quartet, waltzing, playing catch. (p. 50)

Most analyses of language in use cover only a tiny part of this spectrum. Yet a great deal of activity, especially learning activity as Clark's continuum suggests, occurs at the place where talk and action co-occur. Precisely because interlocutors' actions are such a strong part of establishing relevant contexts for making sense of utterances, they must be taken into account.

Despite the importance of capturing the co-occurrence of talk and action to understand meaning making and learning, most transcription techniques used by discourse and conversation analysts completely ignore activity. At the most, the analyst adds some parenthetical information to *disambiguate* the referent of certain deictic expressions for the reader or to explain the result of some talk. For example, look at the following transcript from a science classroom taken from Lemke (1990):

Transcript 1: Carbon

27 *Teacher:* Ron?

28 *Ron:* Boron?

29 *Teacher:* That would be—That'd have uh . . . *seven* electrons. So you'd have
30   to have one here, one here, one here, one here, one here . . . one
31   here—Who said it? You?

32 *Student:* Carbon.

33 *Teacher:* What's—

34 *Students:* Carbon! Carbon!

35 *Teacher:* Carbon. Carbon. Here. Six electrons. And they can be anywhere
            within those—confining—orbitals. This is also from the notes
            from before. The term orbital refers to the average *region*
            transversed [sic] by an electron. Electrons occupy orbitals that
            may differ in size, shape, or orientation. That's—that's from the
            other class, we might as well use it for review. (pp. 17–18, 20)

Lemke explained that this is a conversation between a teacher standing at the blackboard on which a chalk Atomic Orbital Diagram is drawn. As the teacher talks, he gestures at the diagram and a periodic table hung on the wall. The drawing and table are more than mere props of the teacher's and students' dialogue, and they are more than mnemonic devices for the students. At the least, they serve as part of preparing contexts (Lemke, 1990) within which particular questions and statements make sense. When students miss these preparations, they might not even understand what is expected of them as interlocutors, much less the science content of the talk (Lemke, 1990). In terms of our discussion, the students are expected not only to learn to talk about atoms and their orbitals in the correct way, but also to recognize and use such diagrams and tables in the correct ways as well to perform adequate identities as science students. Because science talk is a gateway to further education as well as career choices, such simple routines as this one are important as apprenticeship activities.

When we employ turn taking as the unit of analysis and fail to include any description of the activity that co-occurs with the talk and contextualizes it as part of the transcript, some parts of the talk become virtually meaningless to the analyst (i.e., pointing out electrons—"one here" or referring to the diagram "that's from the other class"). If we are interested in how the mediational means (like diagrams), talk, and activity work together as a distributed system, with how both talk and action shape each other over the course of an activity, and thus with how people learn to use the linguistic and nonlinguistic stuff that makes up Discourse, then we need a different kind of transcript.

GETTING TALK AND ACTIVITY TOGETHER FOR ANALYSIS

Transcript 2 (Rowe, 2002) shows a different kind of transcript: In this case, the participants are interacting with a particular kind of mediational means (a hands-on exhibit) in an interactive science museum. Such hands-on activities are almost ubiquitous in U.S. science museums now, and they are a large part of many science classrooms as well. This exhibit consists of a 2-meter inclined plane. The plane is made up of two sets of railings down which two wheels roll. Each wheel has an axle at its center. When the wheel is placed in the ramp, its axle is actually the part that rolls on the rails. In this way, the wheels spin around their axles as they move down the ramp. Each wheel is further equipped with three movable weights placed evenly around the axle. Each weight can be moved to one of three positions from close to the center of the wheel to close to the outer edge of the wheel. Adjusting the position of the weights affects the movement of the wheels by distributing mass differently around the rotating axles.

To try to understand how small groups of adults and children organize their activity around this exhibit and make meaning out of it, and how that contributes or not to the re-creation of particular orders of Discourse, it is necessary to see how activity contextualizes talk and vice versa. Thus, the transcript includes both talk and actions; further, it visually shows the relationships between utterances and actions, between utterances and other utterances, and between actions and other actions by including a person's actions and utterances in one box of the table. Each box contains two lines of text—the first is a transcription of talk, the second of action. This procedure allows the analyst to literally see how action and utterance are related to each other in creating contexts within which those actions and utterances have meanings.

Transcript 2: Rolling

1

B	
	walking to right end of ramp; takes right wheel, carries to top Places wheel
M	
	Approaches right top, puts hand on right wheel

2

B	holding wheel with M	Releases wheel

W		approaches right top

M	**1) You see how you can move these weights That makes it go faster or slower**
	with B moves two weights takes hand off Steps back from ramp one step

3

B	walks to bottom, rolling wheel back up picks up wheel carries to top

W	**2) Pick it up Sonny, carry it up** **3) Now if you put it in**
	walks halfway down ramp follows B back to top

M	**[unint] they say**
	standing two steps away

4

B	places wheel	adjusting weights

W	**a different place**	**4) I think this one's been**
	leans over B holding wheel, touching weights	

M	**That's what affects the speed**
	pushes weight in place steps back steps back further

5

B	**5) I wanta move down that one**
	looks at M

W	**there a while [unint] change them**
	steps back

M	**That's what affects the speed**
	steps up pushes weight in place

6

B	Releases wheel Follows down hand on ramp leaning on ramp, walks to bottom, rolls

W	steps back farther	leaves

M	steps back steps back farther	walks down

7

B	
	wheel part way up, turns and walks away
W	
	from top of ramp, talking to researcher
M	
	ramp past B and toward different exhibit

(Adapted from Rowe, 2002.)

Inspired by Bakhtin's (1979) concept of polyphony and a microgenetic approach to the development of activity (Rowe & Wertsch, 2002; Vygotsky, 1978), and to capture the relationships among actions and talk carried out by multiple agents as they develop over the course of an activity, I have used the musical score as the model for constructing the transcripts. The transcript is read from left to right as a musical score is read. In this particular case, there are seven segments on the page representing just over 1 minute of activity and talk. When the reader reaches the end of one segment (the right-hand margin) he or she returns to the beginning of the next segment immediately below it (the left-hand margin).

Agents (B—a boy around 10 years old, M—a man in his late 40s, and W—a woman in her late 40s) are listed in order of their appearance at the exhibit. As new agents enter the setting, a new box or cell is added for them. Each box or cell contains two lines. The bottom line details the agents' actions. Just above that in the same box is a line that details the agents' talk. Boldface type separates talk from action. Within this kind of microgenetic analysis of activity, it is important to capture the development of activity and talk across time (Wertsch, 1991). However, because the actual time at which an action or utterance is begun and ended is less important than the relative position of that action or utterance with regard to other actions and utterances, the transcript is not broken down into equally spaced time units. Thus, the transcripts capture both talk and action as they develop over the course of an activity within a group. They also visually represent which actions and utterances are co-terminus and which are co-constructed.

Any transcript is already an abstraction for a particular purpose, and one of the challenges of any transcription procedure is determining what level of detail should be included in the representation of both talk and actions. The level of detail is usually determined by the purposes of the analysis or the theoretical assumptions underlying it. In this case, for instance, not every action is described. There is no attempt to include individual movements such as "takes wheel with right hand" or "looks upward and to left." Some analyses require this level of transcription detail. The transcript is the result of hours of transcribing multiple videotaped interactions and comparing the interpretations of multiple researchers. Over the course of the work, certain categories of activity recur (such as walking to the top of the ramp, taking the wheels, placing the wheels). Although these may exhibit a great deal of variety in how they are carried out, for my purposes it is more important to note whether they did or did not occur rather than exactly how they occurred.[2]

Yet there are also theoretical assumptions underlying the transcript, and I turn to some of those now because they are important for the claims I make about what is going on in the transcript. There are basically two claims that arise from the dialogic and sociocultural approach to language and development that I am trying here to integrate with a critical approach to discourse analysis: (a) the unit of analysis for language in use is the utterance, and (b) activities are often distributed among multiple agents.

THE UNIT OF ANALYSIS FOR LANGUAGE IN USE IS THE UTTERANCE

Within a dialogical approach to language, the utterance (rather than the phoneme, morpheme, word, phrase, or sentence) is the basic element of language in use. Bakhtin (1986) rather loosely defined the *utterance* as "the change of speaking subjects" (p. 71). Because his model was dialogue between speakers, the "change of speaking subjects" that Bakhtin was interested in has some analogies to turn taking as it is described by contemporary conversation analysts (Linell, 1998). From the point of view of analyzing individual contributions to dialogue, the change of speaking subjects or turn taking is a natural unit of analysis. Yet such a unit becomes problematic when there are multiple speakers (and sometimes even in dyads) when, for instance, conversational partners complete each other's sentences, speak simultaneously, or immediately latch one speaker's words onto another's without salient break. These examples represent the *co-construction of dialogue* by multiple participants. Unfortunately for the discourse analyst using turn taking as the basic unit of analysis, such cases are more the rule than the exception in some activities and among some groups.

In such cases, and generally from the point of view of analyzing how discourse contributes to group activity, it makes more sense to treat any *uninterrupted stretch of speaking activity* as one utterance even if it is distributed among multiple speakers. For reasons that become clear later, I am quite interested in just those places where multiple speakers construct one utterance. I call these *co-constructed utterances*. Thus, I define the *utterance* as an

---

[2]See Rowe (2002) for discussion of how the categories were developed and changed over the course of the study.

"uninterrupted stretch of speaking" and the *co-constructed utterance* as an "uninterrupted stretch of speaking activity involving more than one agent." Not every utterance that includes more than one recognizable voice is co-constructed. As Bakhtin (1981, 1986) noted, multiple voices almost always co-exist within one speaker's utterance. Such utterances are polyphonic or heteroglossic (Bakhtin, 1979), but are not co-constructed. My definition of co-constructed utterances tries to take account of utterances that might involve more than one speaking agent, but only one voice. Like the Greek Chorus who speak in one voice, these are potentially cases of co-construction that are not heteroglossic (Bakthin, 1981, 1986).

In terms of the transcript, this means that when utterances are numbered for reference or coding, not every individual contribution is separately numbered. Rather, when two or more people co-construct an utterance, it is numbered and coded as one utterance. For example, Utterance 3 (W: "Now if you put it in a different place"; M: "that's what affects the speed") is one utterance co-constructed by two speakers (M and W). The two voices are latched without break. W begins the utterance with a statement that ends with rising intonation, and M completes the utterance.

Co-Constructed Talk and Situation Definitions

In Transcript 2, utterances are co-constructed as part of explicitly formulating a situation definition for the activity. A situation definition is a socioculturally particular type of activity or context that specifies what we are doing at a given moment or what we take to be the background against which our utterances and actions are to be interpreted. Here is the first link between sociocultural approaches to learning activity and CDA. Not everyone in every situation has the authority to define the situation. That authority is negotiated on the ground as part of activity, but it may be couched in terms of talk about content. In Utterance 3, M and W seek and provide information about the way the exhibit works. They also work to define the situation in a particular way that explicates "what's going on" at this given moment. In this case, "what's going on" is something like MOVING THE WEIGHTS (Rowe, 2002).[3] This way of defining the situation contrasts with, for example, what we call RACING, where two participants roll the two wheels simultaneously as part of a competitive game to see which one will reach the bottom first. The co-constructed utterance works this way by indexing a particular context within which each other utterance and action has meaning potential. Thus, such co-constructed utterances are part of establishing and maintaining intersubjectivity (Rommetviet, 1974)—that is, a tempo-

---

[3]Throughout the rest of the chapter, SITUATION DEFINITIONS are presented in ALL CAPS.

rarily shared version of the social background against which what we say and do can make sense to interlocutors.

As the example in *Transcript 1: Carbon* suggests, learning to recognize and use such cues as these to understand the situation is part not only of learning to interpret what is said and what is expected of us as interlocutors, but it is also part of "pulling off" a particular social identity. It is the ability to manipulate particular members' resources to be recognized as a particular kind of who doing what (Gee, 1999). In that sense, M and W are pulling off identities as the kind of people who go to museums and know what to do with exhibits there—that is, you do not simply play with them, you experiment and observe the results.

Yet utterances alone do not make up the particular constellations of members' resources that make up particular Discourses. That brings us to the second theoretical claim underlying these transcripts. As the transcript shows, such co-constructed utterances are combined with co-constructed actions as well as part of defining the situation and performing particular identities.

ACTIVITIES ARE OFTEN DISTRIBUTED AMONG MULTIPLE AGENTS

For purposes of analysis, I have borrowed Gee's (1999) three-part terminology of activity, subactivity, and action.[4] An activity is a bounded sequence of doing something with a more or less recognizable beginning and end. In the case of *Transcript 2: Rolling*, and from the point of view of the observer, the activity is something like "Doing an interactive museum exhibit." Similarly, in the case of *Transcript 1: Carbon*, the activity is something like "Using a diagram to review a lesson" in the classroom. Both of these activities are in turn made up of particular subactivities that are shaped by the physical and social constraints and affordances of the exhibit (rather heavy wheels on an inclined plane) and the classroom (chalk of different colors; a diagram left over from a previous class) and of the setting (a free-of-charge, public museum, on the one hand, and a secondary school science classroom in a public school, on the other hand).

In *Transcript 2: Rolling*, there are several identifiable subactivities that have to do with the nature of the exhibit and setting. These include, approaching the exhibit, reading the label, setting up a roll by moving the

---

[4]These categories are consistent with those of activity theory—activity, actions, and operations (Leont'ev, 1978), stemming from Vygotsky's work. Leont'ev's (1978, 1981) version of activity theory is also consistent with CDA as it makes the links between activity and identity explicit.

wheels to the top of the ramp, rolling the wheels, solving a variety of technical difficulties with the operation of the exhibit, adjusting the weights, and exiting the area. Some of these subactivities are mandatory (approaching, setting up a roll), whereas others are optional (reading the label or rolling the wheel or adjusting the weights). Last, solving physical problems with the exhibit is mandatory when they occur, but might not be part of any given group's activity. In addition, other subactivities are not necessarily part of the activity as dictated by its physical nature, but are elements of how people interact as they use the exhibit and shape the way the activity is socially distributed. These include things like establishing participation, directing activity, or explaining the activity.

These subactivities are in turn made up of particular actions. Any number or type of actions can be used as part of setting up or explaining the activity. For example, as part of setting up, sometimes a participant simply drags the wheel from the bottom of the ramp to the top before releasing it. Another person might set up by lifting the wheel out of the ramp and carrying it to the top and placing it in the ramp. Still another person might bring the wheel to the top, place it in the ramp, and then roll it backward slightly to reorient the weights. Each of these actions can be coded, but for my purposes here the categories I use in Transcript 2 generally belong to the level of subactivities rather than actions or activities.

Co-Constructed Activity and Situation Definitions

For my analysis of activity, I treat the activity in an analogous way to utterances. Thus, one subactivity or one action is any uninterrupted stretch of physical activity. It is immediately obvious that an action, subactivity, or activity can be distributed among multiple agents. Two students who work together to assemble a balance beam for an in-class experiment are in this sense engaged in one subactivity with roughly identifiable boundaries (a beginning and an end). More important for the current discussion, an action or subactivity may be begun by one participant and completed by another. Two students—one of whom picks up weights of different sizes and hands them to another student who places them on the balance beam—may complete the subactivity of putting weights on the balance beam, which in turn may be part of several activities (measuring the unknown weight of another object, calibrating the balance) and may be made up of multiple actions (getting attention, putting the weight in one's hand, grasping the weight, etc.).

In the case of Transcript 2, there are two co-constructed subactivities. The first occurs at the beginning of the activity in Segment 1. B has approached the exhibit and taken one of the wheels to the top of the ramp. Before he can do anything else, M approaches, places his hand on the wheel, and says, "You see how you can move these weights" (Utterance 1) and moves two of the weights while the boy holds the wheel. M thus takes authority early on in the activity for defining it in a certain way—not only by what he says, but also by what he does. He and B co-construct the subactivity of moving the weights, and the activity is thus defined as MOVING THE WEIGHTS rather than simply ROLLING THE WHEEL or RACING. The second case of co-constructed activity further reinforces this situation definition. In Segments 4 and 5, B, W, and M all co-construct the activity of moving the weights. This group (as do many of the groups who use this exhibit—see Rowe [2002] for more discussion) co-constructs activities at just those points where they are defining the activity as a particular type (Segment 1) or when they are trying to solve a physical problem (how to move the weights in Segments 4 and 5).

LEARNING AS THE APPROPRIATION OF MEDIATIONAL MEANS FOR MEANING MAKING

By extending this analysis in more detail, we can address the critique that CDA includes no viable learning theory. Bringing together a sociocultural approach to learning activity, a dialogic approach to language in use, and a critical analysis of discourse, we can define *learning* as the appropriation of culturally valued mediational means or members' resources as part of participation in active, distributed meaning making. The key to understanding learning thus defined is analyzing how the appropriation of mediational means occurs across time and in interaction or does not occur.

In Transcript 2, the three participants are at the exhibit for 1 minute and 17 seconds. As soon as B brings the wheel to the top of the ramp, M approaches having read the label and puts his hands on the wheel with B. In his first utterance, M draws B's attention to the weights and explains the activity in terms of the situation definition MOVING THE WEIGHTS. The second half of this utterance is actually addressed to both B and W (who has joined them) and positions M as the interpreter of authority by presenting the situation definition as part of what "they say." He and B then co-construct the activity of adjusting the weights, and he steps away from the exhibit. W, however, steps in (physically and verbally) immediately, directing B's activity and behavior through a direct address (Utterance 2) and by physically approaching him. In this utterance and action, she contributes to the situation definition by addressing what it is not. It is not about ROLLING THE WHEEL (up or down the ramp), but about MOVING THE WEIGHTS, which she further makes clear in her part of Utterance 3. This utterance has the form of a statement, but is said with rising intonation that seeks a completion as a question or clarification of "what's going on." All three of them then participate in adjusting the weights. W initiates the adjusting by leaning over B, touching the weights, and seeming to explain their difficulty in moving them in Utterance 4. B then enlists M's aid with an utterance (5) and look, and W steps back. After M helps adjust the weights, W and M both move back further, allowing B to finish the subactivity. At the end of the next roll of the wheel, B again begins to roll the wheel back up the ramp before following M to a different exhibit.

In this short time, these three participants do quite a bit of work (both physically and in terms of what they say) to shape the situation definition. This is not PLAY, RACING, or ROLLING THE WHEELS, although the last seems to be B's preferred activity. Rather W and M define the situation as MOVING THE WEIGHTS to affect the speed. M and W's situation definition is cast in terms of a preferred or privileged way to do the exhibit, associated with the authority of the museum (i.e., with what "they say" about it). As already noted, they employ co-constructed subactivities and utterances to articulate the situation definition.

Note also how carefully M and W monitor and control B's actions. As soon as B places the wheel for the first time, M establishes his participation (and authority for defining the situation) by placing his hand on the wheel and adjusting the weights while drawing attention to the weights as the salient feature of the wheels and what you can do with them (make it go faster or slower) as the salient activity. He does not, however, attribute this to his own knowledge or observations, but to the authority of the museum. The second time B places the wheel, he has just been admonished for "breaking frame" by rolling instead of carrying the wheel back up to the top. As soon as he places the wheel, W establishes her participation in a more direct way than her Utterances 2 and 3 do by placing her hands on the wheel and trying to adjust the weights while talking about what happens when you do move them ("put it in a different place"). Thus, W and M do a lot of (literally) hands-on work to define what it is they are all three doing and how they should do it.

Once B's participation is established and a correct or preferred way of doing the exhibit is assured, they physically and verbally leave the activity up to B. This is consistent with teaching and learning or apprenticeship (Rogoff, 1990, 1995) activities of all kinds, where one participant who is positioned as an *expert* scaffolds the participation of another participant who is positioned as a *novice*. The expert gradually transfers authority for doing the activity to the novice, who appropriates the tools, procedures, and goals of the activity or rejects them. In this case, although B is the first to approach the exhibit, M takes control immediately of the situation, and W enters the scene at just the point where B seems to be taking too much authority (ROLLING THE WHEEL back up the ramp instead of conforming to the situation definition of MOVING THE WEIGHTS). Eventually, both M and W remove themselves from the activity: a full transfer of authority over the doing of the exhibit to B. In this case, he does not pursue it for long, but seems to have his own definition for what's going on as he begins again ROLLING THE WHEEL back up the ramp just before exiting. He thus rejects the situation definition of MOVING THE WEIGHTS once authority for doing the activity has been physically and verbally transferred to him. He does not seem to have appropriated the situation definition as defined by the adults.

As a result of all this work, one situation definition predominates. There is little chance for an alternative situation definition to be activated. Rather, the adults work hard to limit the possible situation definitions by presenting their preferred one as authoritative and by working to direct the child's participation in a way that is appropriate to the situation thus defined. Once the child seems to have appropriated that situation definition, the adults relinquish verbal and physical control over directing the activity and eventually exit the exhibit area. Yet the child then turns to a different kind of activity for a short period. He has rejected the preferred way of contextualizing the activity by rejecting the preferred members' resources handed to him by his parents.

APPROPRIATING DISCOURSES, THE BIGGER PICTURE

In the case presented in *Transcript 1: Carbon*, it is clear that a particular, privileged school Discourse is being negotiated and enforced by both the teacher and students (and that is in fact part of what Lemke goes on to discuss). Yet the same kind of thing is happening in *Transcript 2: Rolling*, too. In the case presented in Transcript 2, a particular way of interacting with the exhibit is privileged and deployed by M and W as part of organizing their own activity and directing B's participation in it. Yet their privileging this particular situation definition has implications beyond their own, local activity. In the science museum, this particular way of interacting with the exhibit is associated with a socially privileged Discourse—that of science. The exhibit label presents this activity as being about "The Scientific Method" and what scientists do. M and W reproduce at the level of this one group's interactions this wider social privileging of a particular order of discourse (Fairclough, 1989) or social language (Bakhtin, 1981)—that of the scientist.

Looking just at the talk, however, does not give the analyst many clues as to how this Discourse is privileged, how much work M and W do to privilege it, or how B appropriates or rejects it. What participants say and do are equal parts of understanding how they create a situation definition that privileges or rejects particular social languages and orders of Discourse. The microgenetic analysis I demonstrate allows us to analyze privileging, appropriating, and rejecting particular members' resources and mediational means as part of activity. This sort of microgenetic analysis of course does not demonstrate how or if participants appropriate these social languages in a really deep sense so that they become part of their everyday performances of identity. That requires analysis of the same agents' participation in a wide variety of interactions over time to see whether and how they appropriate and deploy privileged and nonprivileged ways of acting and speaking. It also does not demonstrate how certain ways of speaking and acting and those who use them come to be privileged or nonprivileged. That is precisely what CDA offers to sociocultural approaches to learning: analysis of the histories, social affordances, and constraints of the particular Discourses people appropriate and reject as part of learning.

Reflection and Action

1. Using Transcript 2 as a model, transcribe the actions and talk of a group involved in an activity and try to describe the situation definition you bring to what they are doing as well as the possible situation definitions they are working from.

2. Walk through a museum that has some interactive exhibits.

   (a) Interact with or watch others interacting with the exhibits without reading any labels. Analyze what kinds of activities are suggested by or made possible or impossible by the object and its context.

   (b) Walk through the same museum again reading labels. What sorts of activities and meanings do they promote? How do they coincide with or conflict with the actions suggested by the object and its context?

3. Look back at Transcript 2. What sort of members' resources can we assume the participants have to participate in the activity the way they do? What does a critical discourse approach say about where these come from? How do they become privileged in one context and not in another?

4. Try to imagine an example of two or more people engaged in the same activity, but with different, even competing situation definitions.

5. Do participants in an activity necessarily have to share a situation definition that has something to do with learning for learning to occur?

   (a) If your answer is yes, is it always necessary to consciously define what we are doing as learning for learning to occur?

   (b) If your answer is no, to what extent do you think participants' situation definitions can be different before they are unable to continue interacting?

6. Critical discourse analysts are concerned with those points where the reproduction of inequalities in talk and activity can be disrupted. How can analysis of activity be a part of the analysis and challenging of such social reproduction?

RECOMMENDED READINGS

Besides the basic works by Fairclough, Gee, and Linell listed in the references, the reader interested in other ways to link the analysis of discourse to the reproduction of social inequities should consult *Social Semiotics* (Hodge & Kress, 1988) and *Discourse Strategies* (Gumperz, 1982).

In addition to the works by Wertsch detailed in the reference list, *The Guided Mind: A Sociogenetic Approach to Personality* (Valsiner, 1998) and *Cultural Psychology: A Once and Future Discipline* (Cole, 1996) provide comprehensive extensions of Vygotsky's work. *Everyday Cognition: Development in Social Context* (Rogoff & Lave, 1984) offers a variety of viewpoints on communicative and cognitive development from a sociocultural point of view.

Last, for those interested in more analyses of learning activity in museums and other informal learning environments, *Perspectives on Object-Centered Learning in Museums* (Paris, 2002) offers a variety of methodologies and theoretical approaches.

REFERENCES

Bakhtin, M. M. (1979). *Problemy poetiki Dostoevskovo* [Problems of Dostoevsky's poetics]. Moskva: Sovetskaya Rossiya.

Bakhtin, M. M. (1981). *The dialogic imagination: Four essays by M. M. Bakhtin* (C. Emerson & M. Holquist, Trans.; M. Holquist, Ed.). Austin: University of Texas Press.

Bakhtin, M. M. (1986). *Speech genres and other late essays* (V. W. McGee, Trans.; C. Emerson & M. Holquist, Eds.). Austin: University of Texas Press.

Clark, H. (1996). *Using language.* Cambridge: Cambridge University Press.

Fairclough, N. (1989). *Language and power.* London: Longman.

Gee, J. P. (1999). *An introduction to discourse analysis: Theory and method.* New York: Routledge.

Lemke, J. L. (1990). *Talking science: Language, learning and values.* Westport, CT: Ablex.

Leont'ev, A. N. (1978). *Activity, consciousness, and personality.* Englewood Cliffs, NJ: Prentice-Hall.

Leont'ev, A. N. (1981). The problem of activity in psychology. In J. Wertsch (Ed.), *The concept of activity in soviet psychology* (pp. 40–71). Armonk, NY: M. E. Sharpe.

Linell, P. (1998). *Approaching dialogue: Talk, interaction, and contexts in dialogical perspectives.* Amsterdam: John Benjamins.

Rogoff, B. (1990). *Apprenticeship in thinking: Cognitive development in social context.* Cambridge: Cambridge University Press.

Rogoff, B. (1995). Observing sociocultural activity on three planes: Participatory appropriation, guided participation, and apprenticeship. In J. V. Wertsch, P. del Rio, & A. Alvarez (Eds.), *Sociocultural studies of mind* (pp. 139–164). Cambridge: Cambridge University Press.

Rommetviet, R. (1974). *On message structure: A framework for the study of language and communication.* Chichester: Wiley.

Rowe, S. (2002). *Activity and discourse in museums: A dialogic perspective on meaning making.* Unpublished doctoral dissertation, Washington University in St. Louis.

Rowe, S., & Wertsch, J. (2002). Vygotsky's model of cognitive development. In U. Goswami (Ed.), *Blackwell handbook of childhood cognitive development* (pp. 538–554). London: Blackwell.

Vygotsky, L. S. (1978). *Mind in society: The development of higher psychological processes* (M. Cole et al., Eds.). Cambridge, MA: Harvard University Press.

Vygotsky, L. S. (1981). The instrumental method in psychology. In J. V. Wertsch (Ed.), *The concept of activity in Soviet psychology* (pp. 134–143). Armonk, NY: M. E. Sharpe.

Vygotsky, L. S. (1986). *Thought and language* (A. Kozulin, Trans.). Cambridge, MA: MIT Press.

Wertsch, J. V. (1985). *Culture, communication and cognition: Vygotskyan perspectives.* New York: Cambridge University Press.

Wertsch, J. V. (1991). *Voices of the mind: A sociocultural approach to mediated action.* Cambridge, MA: Harvard University Press.

Wertsch, J. V. (1998). *Mind as action.* New York: Oxford University Press.

Reframing for Decisions: Transforming Talk About Literacy and Assessment Among Teachers and Researchers

Loukia K. Sarroub
University of Nebraska–Lincoln

CENTRAL CONCEPTS

Reframing—transition strategy by which the nature and direction of the talk are negotiated

Ethnographic analysis—analyzing mundane and unusual events in the lives of research participants and attempting to understand these events from their perspectives on their lived experiences

Discourse analysis—analyzing language beyond the sentence

Critical Discourse Analysis—analyzing language beyond the sentence for meaning in relation to power

Repair—strategy by which conversation participants negotiate agreement where there is intense disagreement

> *Discourse analysis is an inclusionary multidiscipline.*
> —Deborah Tannen (1989)

Education research in the 21st century can be characterized by at least four dynamic, interpretive movements that include the critical analysis of pedagogy, schools, and communities; the politics of representation; the textual analyses of literary and cultural forms; and the ethnographic study of the production, consumption, and distribution of these forms in everyday life. Although these issues are beyond the scope of this chapter (see

Denzin & Lincoln, 2000, for an extensive discussion), in large part the basis of these movements in the field of education grows out of a struggle
among researchers and educators to make sense of competing social and
political goals for children, their teachers, and the communities in which
these key players live. An example of this is the ideological and policy debates focused on the implementation of the right reading assessments in
U.S. schools during the last 30 years (Sarroub & Pearson, 1998). The
changes that have occurred as a result of ideological stances toward the
teaching of reading have often undermined local and sometimes national
efforts at change. The work of researchers and educators who attempt to
critically represent everyday life in this political milieu becomes all the
more complicated and complex in the research process. My aim in this
chapter is to critically examine how a study group of elementary school
teachers and two university researchers made decisions about the type of
entries that should constitute the reading portion of an archival portfolio.
Through ethnographic and discourse analysis, I explore how one group
meeting served to transform the actors in the group, reconstitute previously agreed-on agendas, and shift authority in the group. This study took
place in the mid- to late 1990s, at a time when the accountability movement in the United States was gaining national prominence at all levels of
political life. The case of this study group (the Alternative Assessment
Study Group) exemplifies a grassroots effort at change at both personal
and institutional levels.
    To understand how a group of researchers and teachers made decisions
that would eventually transform not only their practice, but also the ways in
which they understood themselves in the process, I adopt ethnographic
and discourse analysis strategies as I analyze the talk. In this instance, I leave
out the term *critical* because, like Deborah Tannen, by the analysis of discourse I only mean analyzing language beyond the level of the sentence. Of
course to do so implies an objective stance that may deny social and political characteristics embedded in the talk and, more important, the analysis.
In the field of education, discourse analysis embodies a critical agenda
aimed at both understanding and improving the status quo. This double
entendre—critical as vital and critical as ideologically analytical—allows for
discourse analyses that draw on various disciplinary traditions. Whether
one studies involvement strategies (the main focus of the case I present in
this chapter), form–function relationships, turn taking, and so on, the analysis is driven by the researcher's questions and frame of reference. This
stance reflects the dialectical relationship between discourse and the social
practice (see Fairclough, 2001) for making decisions in the context of reform in school. Studying how people talk beyond the sentence level is discourse analysis. Critical Discourse Analysis refers to *how* and *why* people talk
and interact the way they do in their everyday lives. It means understanding

the relationship among talk, interaction, and power. In education, CDA is a window into the relationships among teachers, researchers, children, parents, communities, and government.

Of course the notion of transformation in this chapter's title implies change within this dialectical relationship. As such *transforming* denotes both my own and the study group's conscious efforts at reflexive change through talk from week to week. Transformation implies change in practice. As Hanks (1996) so aptly put it, practice denotes the point at which three things converge: form (talk), activity, and ideology. These three aspects of practice call for different types of analyses, and I think that a critical discourse and ethnographic lens is particularly salient in this enterprise because it values the insider's worldview. For example, in the process of making decisions, the Alternative Assessment Study Group employed involvement strategies that served to create functional and interpersonal involvement (Tannen, 1989). Involvement in making decisions was certainly challenging for the study group because of its internal diversity in terms of grade-level expertise, professional status, and background experience, and negotiating decisions became the group's primary function as it struggled to make the portfolio meaningful to each individual's work. As Rogers suggests (chap. 11, this volume), both Gee and Fairclough's version of CDA assumes that meaning and the potential for meaning beyond the status quo are main aims of CDA. Uncovering what people mean in various contexts is really at the heart of transformation and learning. In the rest of the chapter, I offer a way to think about and analyze talk that captures the spirit of discourse analysis in a critically minded way.

THE SETTING

To document our decision-making process, I audiotaped discussions and took notes during the meetings. In addition, I observed the teachers' classrooms and wrote field notes to get a better sense of how alternative assessment could be implemented in their work. These observations also allowed me to understand the teachers' perspectives in the decision-making process as they used various classroom examples to make sense out of the demands of the portfolio.

Before describing our discussions and the conversation that I think is indicative of the decision-making process, I want to first relate how our study group came to be and then describe the physical context within which we met. Ron, a professor at a large midwestern university, wished to develop alternative assessment measures in schools to better engage both students and teachers in their own learning. Through personal and professional contacts, he met with teachers (K–5) at Arnold Elementary School at the beginning of the 1995–1996 academic year. I agreed to participate in this study and accompanied Ron every other week on Mondays to talk with Arnold's teachers and principal. Initially, Ron's main contact at Arnold was a teacher (Rhonda) who was in charge of the literacy program for the entire school. However, after the second meeting, university researchers were told that she had left her job. Teachers who were interested in implementing the portfolio into their assessment repertoire attended the meetings. The teachers and principal endeavored to make this project a school-wide goal.

In the mid-1990s, Arnold Elementary School was a professional development school located in Miller. This means that since 1983 teachers at Arnold have worked in alliance with Miller University studying ways to improve teaching, learning, and teacher education. Ongoing projects at Arnold included the Archival portfolio, the development of inclusion teams, and a strong commitment to teacher education. Of Arnold's 284 students, 58% were male and 42% were female. Minority students composed 71% of the population at Arnold (57% African American, 2.5% Asian/Pacific Islander, 11% Hispanic, 29% White, .007% American Indian). Arnold was a Title I school and was designated by the state as a school with a significant number of at-risk students: 48% of the eligible (Grades 1–5) students received free or reduced lunch. Arnold was a highly sought after school of choice: 41% of Arnold's students attended as students in the schools of choice programs. Arnold Elementary was the most highly requested school of choice for minority parents in the Miller area. Its mission statement was prominent in the school handbook description:

> At Arnold, all people are teachers and learners. The curriculum consists of important ideas and skills including the students' own questions and interests. All students find acceptance and support for learning in their unique ways. Our professional culture encourages mutual support, professionalism, and collegiality.

During each meeting, the study group sat around three tables pushed together in the media center. Animal crackers were usually passed around, and all of us took notes on what was being said. I briefly describe each of the participants in our assessment group next (see Fig. 5.1).

Participants

Ron was a professor at Miller University and conducted nationally recognized research in reading and literacy.

I (Loukia) was a graduate student at the time of this project. I mediated between Ron, who expected me to be organized and ready with the recording equipment, and the teachers, who welcomed me into their classrooms for observations. Both Ron and I found the observations to be helpful in our conversations with the teachers.

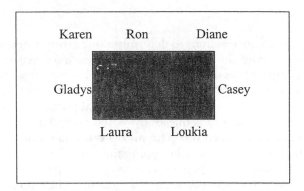

FIG. 5.1.   Alternative assessment study group.

Gladys was a fourth-grade teacher who was enrolled in a PhD program at the local university, although she said that she did not have the time to work on her graduate program. She was outspoken and dominated most of our conversations. At the same time, she was thoughtful and very interested in assessment, although she did not want to "reinvent the wheel" when the group talked about rubrics.

Laura was a second-grade teacher who was soft spoken, but who added much insight to the assessment issue because she had attended conferences and was aware of recent research in reading.

Diane was a second/third-grade combination teacher who worked closely with Rhonda before she left. Diane asked many questions of the other teachers during our conversations. She was the only one who looked thoroughly at the materials that Ron and I passed around the table. Diane was also very outspoken and had definite ideas about what worked and did not work in her classroom.

Karen was a new fifth-grade teacher at Arnold. She did not speak much at our meetings, but always brought a huge jar of animal crackers to share with everyone. She was struggling to find ways to teach genres more specifically in her classroom—a goal that Arnold had for its students before they graduate.

Casey was a second-grade teacher who replaced Rhonda after the winter break. I had the chance to be in meetings with her twice. Casey was very soft spoken. When she talked, she addressed the topic with examples from her own experience at her previous school or from her master's work.

Peter was the principal at Arnold. He did not attend most of our meetings or attended for only a short time. He thought it important that teachers talk about their work together because he felt there should more cohesiveness and carryover from grade to grade. When he commented during meetings, it was usually to reinforce and support teachers' comments.

ANALYSIS

In examining the conversations to determine our group's decision-making process, which would ultimately influence the teachers' classroom work, I chose to concentrate on our fourth meeting. This meeting was a turning point for our study group because we finally *acted* or engaged ourselves and made decisions about the contents of the archival portfolio. This active engagement led me to ask several questions: When do we know what decisions have been made and agreed on? Who makes those decisions? Are high involvement, high intensity, and overlapping talk ways through which conversational participants voice agreement or disagreement? How is turn taking affected? Whose proposition is taken into account when there is an established authority? How are decisions negotiated within this study group? I turned to Davies and Harré's (1990) work on positioning and Goffman's (1981) explication of footing to construct what occurred during out meeting. In addition, I found Florio-Ruane and de Tar's (1995) analysis on reframing quite useful as I attempted to explore turn taking and floor uptake through Edelsky's (1981) work. I return to these ideas and concepts as I analyze the discourse.

For the first time during this conversation, each teacher identified herself and her position on certain issues. This self-identification included making decisions based on personal experience in the classroom. As Davies and Harré (1990) pointed out, "positions are identified in part by extracting the autobiographical aspects of a conversation in which it becomes possible to find out how each conversant conceives of themselves and of the other participants by seeing what position they take up and in what story, and how they are then positioned" (p. 48). In turn, Ron's own position as facilitator was quite clear in the discussion of assessment issues. As "animator," "author," and "principal," Ron often occupied multiple social roles (Goffman, 1981, p. 147). Davies and Harré summarized these speaker roles as follows. The "animator" is he or she who speaks. The "author" is he or she who is responsible for the text. The "principal" is he or she whose position is established by what is said. All three of these roles can be identified in any one person.

This inhabiting of a multiplicity of social roles was also available to the teachers, but I think that the speaker role of "principal" was mediated by implicit (to the teachers) political and/or status constraints. In other words, because Rhonda's absence left her position as the literacy liaison between Arnold and the university open, the teachers in our study group began to realign themselves in terms of the goals they intended to pursue within the project. Much more was at stake than assessment issues, particularly for Gladys and perhaps for Diane, who had worked closely with Rhonda. At the time this conversation took place, I was not aware of the political undercurrent. In the data I present in this chapter, I think that the politics at Arnold Elementary only play a marginal role during the decision-making process.

Having read and analyzed the transcription of the entire or speech event, I noticed that certain discursive patterns developed in the talk. The speech event began and ended with procedural talk. For example, the meeting started with people seating themselves, wondering where everyone else was, and talking about e-mail communication. The meeting ended with people talking about when we would meet next and what would be on the agenda. Procedural talk is characterized by high involvement and overlapping talk, in which almost everyone participates in getting ready to engage in the day's agenda or constructing a future agenda (Tannen, 1989). Florio-Ruane and de Tar (1995) called what I named *procedural talk* at the beginning of the meeting as *topic finding*. I hesitate to use their term because the agenda for this meeting had already been decided at the previous meeting. The remainder of the speech event embodies one discursive pattern that I call *reframing*, within which *sharing* and *topic shifting* occur subsequently as co-patterns. By reframing I mean that during talk there are transitions in which "the nature and direction of the talk are negotiated" to sustain the conversation (Florio-Ruane & de Tar, 1995, p. 22). Furthermore, reframing involves a change in a participant's alignment or footing where the projected self and what is said is at issue (Goffman, 1981). Davies and Harré countered this notion by suggesting that Goffman "takes for granted that alignments exist prior to speaking . . . , rather than that alignments are actual relations jointly produced in the very act of conversing" (p. 55). I tend to agree with Goffman's notion of footing because it seems reasonable to suggest that alignment, footing, or positioning are relational conceptualizations of group talk. By its very nature, *relational* presupposes a priori experience as well as the present, co-constructed experience of the group. As I mentioned before, political undercurrents may influence the co-constructed footing of group members. In addition, reframing is a way to seek consensus or agreement and/or a way to summarize what has been said. In part, topic shifting is implicit in the sense that a topic shift denotes that the previous topic has ended and/or been decided. Of course who shifts topics is a key element in the reframing. For the participants in this study group, reframing also initiated sharing. By sharing I mean that members of the group disclosed past experiences in the classroom as a way to validate the reframing. Consequently, reframing was dependent on the sharing. In the analysis of the conversation, reframing and all of its components are indicative of the decision-making process that took place.

In examining the talk, I found that Ron did most of the reframing and all it entails and that the teachers usually shared after he reframed. Topic shifts were also usually made by Ron, but Gladys and Diane each shifted topics two and three times, respectively. I sometimes used examples from their classrooms to explain to the teachers what Ron asked them to consider, but my participation was minimal. The following table quantifies the

Reframing and Shifting Topics During 1 hour 45 minutes

	Reframes	Shifts Topics
Loukia	2	0
Ron	12	4
Diane	0	3
Gladys	0	2

reframing and topic shifting for the entire speech event. I reframed twice at
the beginning of the discussion because I was the one who had notes from
the previous meeting and who had typed the agenda for this meeting. Appendix A shows the entire transcribed timeline of our meeting.

Although the timeline helped me shape a framework for what was happening during the conversation, one specific segment (Side B, counter
numbers 176–338) alerted me to the negotiation and decision-making process. In this 11-minute segment of the discussion, teachers are highly engaged and in conflict with one another and with Ron when he takes up only
a part of what Diane shares, logging instead of genres.

Ron	(176)Well, I think it could come up in the, in things like what do, what does this writer assume, you know, about this particular group of people or something like that, yea. (Pause) So, so far in reading, we have uh, response to informational text, and response to literature as common entries. Anything else occur to you? Uh, there's uh, uh . . .	Reframing
Diane	At one time, and I don't know if that's still important, we felt that at least by the end of when they left this school, **that they should be** exposed to all the genres. This is a place for that. And I don't necessarily think all the, I mean, **we can't keep track of all the books.** We did that and I don't ever want to do that again.	Proposition from teacher; backchannel noise of agreement Logging is a marginal proposition
Ron	Laughs.	
Diane	Um, but I would think it would be important because, I, it seems to me that first year we found out you had some gaps and the kids left the school without—	Shares proposition

Gladys	Being exposed.	
Diane	Being exposed to—	
Ron	Did someone here tell me, was it another school I was at, that they had computer programs where kids could enter their books that they were reading?	Responds not to main proposition but to marginal proposition
Gladys	(192) OH! There's hypercard.	
Ron	Yea.	
Laura	Gladys does that.	
Elena	That's your book log, right?	
Gladys	Uhum.	
Ron	Computerized book log. Uh, and I don't know if you wanna get into that but if you did want to get into that—	Proposes shift from genre to log
Diane	*I don't, but go ahead.*	
Laura	Laughs.	Disagrees
Diane	My kids, I have my kids—	
Gladys	Well, now wait a minute. Let me tell you what's going on with that!	Asks for turn
Diane	But I also, some read, you know, a book that takes two minutes so they can write the title down.	

At the beginning of the 11-minute segment, Ron reframed by summarizing what had been decided so far and asked the group to share any new entries for the portfolio. Ron was the established authority figure in the group, yet in reframing he adopted a type of talk that distanced him from his status as the expert on assessment in the group to make sharing all-inclusive. He used in this segment and throughout all meetings a modal verb such as *think*, and in the entire discussion he often *hedged* by using the first-person plural pronoun to be inclusive. "For one thing, hedges and qualifiers introduced in the form of performative modal verbs (I 'wish,' 'think,' 'could,' 'hope,' etc.) become possible, introducing some distance between the figure and its avowal" (Goffman, 1981, p. 148). Ron's footing as he reframed aligns with Harré and Van Langenhove's (1991) assertion that "when a person is engaged in a deliberate self-positioning process this often will imply that they try to achieve specific goals with their act of self-positioning" (p. 401). Ron was looking for something specific when he asked the teachers for more ideas. When Diane replied with a primary proposition of students being exposed to all the genres and the marginal proposition of logging books, Ron immediately took up the marginal proposition because important element of the portfolio is to show breadth in reading. Gladys, who had been logging books in fourth grade for a long time, also took up Diane's marginal proposition, and this led Diane to say that she was not interested in computerized logging of books after Ron shifted the topic to logging. Logging books became the primary topic on the floor when Diane's main proposition was dropped. Essentially, Diane gave up her space on a floor that had been co-constructed by the group without her. In doing so, she acknowledged that she was not interested in logging, but that the conversation could go on without her or her primary proposition. In effect, Diane took a turn, but did not have the floor because her primary proposition was not taken up by the group.

Edelsky (1981) defined the notion of *conversational turn* as "an on-record 'speaking' (which may include nonverbal activities) behind which lies an intention to convey a message that is both referential and functional" (p. 403) and *floor* as "the acknowledged what's-going-on within a psychological time/space" (p. 405). Diane's position was that she shared in her turn and did not get the floor and then gave up the floor when asked by Ron if she was interested in computerized logging. The next section of the 11-minute segment includes an intense disagreement between Gladys and Diane concerning their goals for reading. Here Diane attempts to regain her space on the floor by reintroducing the importance of including genres in the assessment project.

Gladys	Yea, hypercard, the problem with it is Shelly had her own program and we couldn't boot it in. So we've asked Linda to order it for the school so it'll go on the server, so that means that everybody in the school can have access to hypercard and then the kid starts his own disk and that disk could move with him right through kindergarten all the way through 5th. Just the same way— (raises her voice and yells this out because of backchannel talk)	Long turn Backchannel consensus]]
Diane	(206)I don't want them spending time typing it all the titles of the books they read. I want them to spend time writing and other things—	]] Overlapping talk]]
Laura	Don't have enough time, no.	]
Gladys	Is this something, ok, but is this something that—	]]
Diane	(interrupts)No, what I think is important, well, I don't, I think it's important that kids read. I think it's important that they have their choice reading and all that. I don't think it's	

	necessarily important that I keep track of all that. What I think is important is keeping track of what I INSTRUCT THEM IN, WHAT I KNOW THEY HAVE BEEN EXPOSED TO.	Emphatic
Gladys	Yea.	
Diane	(213) I mean, because they write down that they read *Sarah, Plain and Tall,* does not mean they read *Sarah, Plain and Tall.* (Sarcastic) I hope that's what it means, but I happen to know the truth with the a lot of the kids that age what it means, but if I have done x amount of trade books—	}Overlapping talk } } } } } } }High intensity
Gladys	Yea.	}
Diane	And I'm in instruction and I know that we've talked about the author's meaning, the way they wrote and all of that, I think that's, might be important.	} } } } } }
Gladys	Then, what about—	}
Diane	Not necessarily a list of books.	}
Gladys	Well—	}
Diane	Even then, I don't even think I need to write down all the books.	} }High involvement
Gladys	Ok, I, we may use it for our— *(makes time-out sign, looks around for help).*	} }
Everyone laughs at the tension.		}
Diane	—For historical fiction—I can go into a portfolio—	} }
Gladys	(221) Upper grades, they can do that, they can even do that during silent reading or whatever. How about this? Ah, I think you've done this, and we had space on, I don't know, we had space on our grade cards. You list books kids had read and I've never done it. I just typed it up and it's not listing books kids have read. What I put down are books we have done together or in small group for each quarter of the marking period. I've used that consistently for the last several years. It goes in their permanent record. Why couldn't we flip that into portfolio? And, I mean, and that will—	} } } }Compromise } } } } } } } } } } }

Diane	(230)I guess what I wanted is to make sure they've had all the genre. That's more important to me. Like I take a book that I really want to do some things with it, and uh, (more in a stage whisper), "she read that last year. So, books are like friends, we'll do this book again"—	Back to initial proposition (shift)
Gladys	(233)I'm saying, Diane, we can label it, we can create our own page that would follow, but that could be an entry per year. The genre, the books that have been attended to either in small group or large group or read aloud and separate them—	Compromise
Diane	If I remember correctly, we did that. We did that when Rhonda was here. That was part of that first piece of that study. I still have my copies. There's hundreds of books listed, especially for some of the lower levels where you do someone reading aloud—	
Everyone talks at once.		

In this excerpt, Diane shifted back to the importance of tracking genres and argued with Gladys about what she thought was important in her classroom. This part of the segment shows high involvement, overlapping talk, high intensity, and a lot of backchannel talk (side conversations and movement that are not part of the floor). Diane interrupted Gladys so many times that Gladys was forced to look around the table at the group with an exasperated expression and made a time-out sign. By the end (233), Gladys attempted to reconstruct the floor to include Diane as a participant on the floor. In effect, Gladys did some repair work on the original uptake of Diane's suggestion about genres. Sacks et al. (1974) commented that repair exists for "dealing with turn-taking errors and violations" (p. 723). This is a mechanistic view of repair work in conversations. I would like to suggest that in this segment of talk, in which there is high involvement and high intensity, interruption and turn violations fit the norms of social practice of school meetings for these teachers. I take repair to mean that the participants, principally Gladys, are negotiating agreement where there is intense disagreement. The repair work is a way for the group to make decisions without excluding or keeping the floor from being available to everyone. This view of repair is closely related to Florio-Ruane and de Tar's use of the concept. At this point, Gladys and Diane seemed to enter into an implicit consensus about what is important in their practice.

At the end of the segment, Ron reframed by offering a compromise that accounted for both logging and genres (breadth and depth). By this time Gladys had shifted her position and the topic back to genres instead of logging, and, as stated earlier she and Diane stood firm on the issue of genres. Ron reframed one last time without resolving the logging issue. The following quantifies the number of reframings and topic shifts in the 11-minute segment. I also created a timeline to capture the sequence of discursive moves made by Ron, Gladys, and Diane.

Reframing and Shifting Topics During 11 Minutes

	Reframes	*Shifts Topics*
Loukia	0	0
Ron	4	2
Diane	0	1
Gladys	0	1

11 minute Timeline

Ron	*Diane*	*Ron*	*Diane*	*Ron*	*Ron*	*Gladys*	*Ron*
Reframes (176)	Shares	Shifts (Gladys uptakes)	Shifts (230)	Reframes compromise (261)	Reframes (283)	Shifts (299)	Reframes (338)

To recapitulate what occurred in this segment is to denote what made it different from the rest of the speech event. Ron reframed by summarizing and asking for more ideas. Diane shared the importance of genres, and Ron shifted to uptake the part in her sharing about logging books. Gladys took up the logging by talking about hypercard. Diane entered again by shifting the topic back to genre. Gladys did some repair work at this point (not on timeline), and Ron reframed by suggesting again that breadth was important. Ron reframed again and compromised by suggesting that depth (genres) was also important, but that we should still try to get at breadth (logging). Gladys shifted back to genres in a move to support Diane. Ron reframed one more time, but the issue remained unresolved.

DISCUSSION

What is unique about this segment is that it is an atypical example of the decision-making process that occurred during the entire speech event and even during the three previous meetings. First, two teachers dominated the floor. Second, turns were short and overlapped. Third, there was much backchannel talk throughout. Fourth, even if Diane and Gladys disagreed with each other, Gladys shifted her position from supporting Ron to that of supporting Diane. Fifth, this was the first time a participant other than Ron or I had shifted the topic. Finally, the discourse can be characterized as intense and involved because the teachers had something at stake. As Goffman (1959) perceptively pointed out, "when the individual appears before others his actions will influence the definition of the situation which they come to have" (p. 276). What Ron had not been aware of before this meeting is that in years past Diane had attempted to have her students log all of their books because all the teachers had been doing so. She found that logging was not productive; she was never sure what her students actually learned or understood or even if they had read the books they logged. To Diane, what mattered most was the instruction that she had control over— what she thought she was teaching. Also one of Arnold Elementary's goals as a professional development school had been to emphasize genres in the curriculum because the students were often unprepared in that area when they reached junior high school. Interestingly enough, Karen had said earlier in the conversation and in the previous meeting that she needed to improve her teaching of the different genres at the fifth-grade level and that the assessment project was a way to do this. In retrospect, it is quite evident, although I did not interview each teacher, that each group member came to the meeting with an agenda based on previous professional and personal experiences. The conflict that arose between logging and genres reflected a series of past experiences that needed to be taken into account.

How were decisions negotiated within this study group? After Ron and I left Arnold Elementary that day, we were pleased with how engaged the whole group had become over the course of the meeting. It was not until I reread over the transcript many times that I started to think of engagement as positively and/or negatively driven. In a sense, the reframing that took place in the speech event centered on finding the right answers for building an archival portfolio. We as researchers attended the meeting with many presuppositions regarding the types of evidence and documentation that were necessary about students' lives in school for the successful implementation of the portfolio. What we did not take into account, at least in this instance, was that Diane had tried to gather that type of evidence, logging books, in the past and had not been successful because it was not instructionally helpful to her or educationally relevant to her students. In Diane's case, sharing was extremely important because she wanted to reinforce her classroom teaching by implementing the most appropriate portfolio possible. In a group of six people with different perspectives and agendas, this was a difficult task. Ron's reframing enforced positive engagement, but the lack of uptake of the primary proposition initiated conflict or negative engagement that resulted in repair work and supportive coalition from the teachers in the group. In the end, the group moved on to a different topic, and the logging versus genre controversy remained unresolved. In attempting to make decisions, our study group utilized reframing to achieve its goals. Yet because reframing entails a complicated and complex process, decision making proved to be difficult.

Although I based my analysis on 11 minutes of talk, the implications drawn about the decision-making process in a group of researchers and teachers in an intervention study are consequential. First, one could argue that through conflict people are able to verify their own positions regarding certain matters and that conflict is productive. In that sense, CDA is crucial to the understanding of reflexive modes of expression in talk. However, as researchers, and knowing what the normative aspects of portfolios are, we should have done some preliminary work to find out what had worked for the Arnold Elementary teachers in the past and what would not be constructive for them before going into this meeting. In other words, more ethnographic fieldwork might have provided insight during this particular meeting. Taking account of the school culture and teachers' prior experiences with assessment, standards, and evidence could have helped us negotiate through positive instead of negative engagement. Second, this short segment effectively illustrates the difficulty of listening and hearing accurately when high involvement and overlapping talk occur. Is it possible for a study group to know what its members are feeling and saying in that situated moment? Diane found that the floor did not belong to her after her initial sharing, but she argued her way onto it by giving an autobiographical account of past experiences. This instigated Gladys' shift of perspective, and a new floor was co-constructed. Ron had to make his way to it. Perhaps all of this floor construction suggests that conversations are developed through co-construction, but I would like to argue that we must become better listeners and customize our research knowledge to individual schools and individual teachers. In the same vein, teachers should help in the customization process by being more open and confident about their experiences. As Fairclough (2001) pointed out, "social actors within any practice produce representations of other practices, as well as ('reflexive') representations of their own practice, in the course of their activity within the practice" (p. 2). For instance, some teachers have been using alternative assessment measures for years, but just never called it "alternative assessment" or "portfolio." To assume that researchers can just hold meetings in a *tabula rasa* setting is far too presumptuous. Of course Ron and I did not do that, but we could have been better listeners and could have avoided those uncertain and uncomfortable moments. Finally, I think positive engagement means that power and authority in any one person are not driving the decision-making process. As I stated earlier, Ron was explicitly inclusive in his discourse throughout the meeting although he was the established authority. Ironically, perhaps this made for easier eruption of conflict. In any event, when teachers did not agree with Ron's direction, they disagreed, took the floor, and even formed support structures among themselves. Thus, power was distributed easily among the group because Ron's reframing actions from the beginning (and in previous meetings) allowed for that possibility.

Following this analysis, I am left with some questions. I wonder how far one can extend implications drawn from CDA across phenomena such as the intricate world of researcher–teacher collaboration during the research process. I argued that researchers and teachers can learn from an 11-minute segment, but to what end? Is it possible to say more about how researchers and teachers across school sites and intervention studies can learn from this analysis? As I noted earlier, the relationship between discourse and social practice is a dialectical one, and CDA both transforms the phenomenon studied and privileges the actions and individuals whose social practices are meant to transform the world around them. The case of this study group shows that, "we need a way of describing practice as production . . . inflected with value" (Hanks, 1996, p. 13). The study of talk, the activity in which it is embedded, and the value(s) ascribed to it is by no means an easy task. A critically minded discourse analysis in conjunction with ethnography begins to help us understand how to get at meaning produced by our everyday practices in education. As a researcher and educator, one of my goals is to find patterns of communication that have relevance for those people and situations that I study.

Reflection and Action

Discourse Analysis Activity

These two activities, adapted from the work of Florio-Ruane (1996), are stages among many of the analysis of discourse. My students and I use these activities in combination with others to make sense of talk and interaction in a variety of settings.

Cataloguing and Analyzing Taped Discourse Data

1. Inventory all your data, including tapes (video/audio), field notes, interview transcripts, work samples, and so on.

2. Identify one complete activity for which you have taped data (e.g., whole lesson, meeting). Listen to/view the taped activity, stopping as often as necessary to make a running catalogue of its contents according to counter number on the tape recorder (or real-time readout). (Note in the catalogue the counter numbers for parts of the tape that stand out to

you—i.e., where something happens, where things change, where there seems to be discomfort, etc. Briefly note contents of the tape at these points, trying to stick with descriptions of speech and related behaviors rather than making interpretations of their meaning or judgments of their quality.)

3. Listen to/view that segment of tape once without stopping. Summarize your impressions of the interactional behaviors recorded in this segment of tape. These behaviors may include speech, intonation, prosody, movement, use of space, and so on. Initial questions you might ask include: What is going on? Who are the participants? What is being done and said? To whom? By whom?

4. As you review the tapes and your completed catalogue, make a preliminary analysis in terms of your research questions. Pay special attention to questions such as the following:

   a. Based on the patterns you are noticing in the data as well as information from the readings and your knowledge of the wider social context of these data, what analytic categories do you see as potentially useful in making sense of the discourse data?

   b. How have your initial questions and impressions changed as you catalogued the tape?

   c. How might someone else (e.g., participant or researcher with different questions) catalogue the tape differently?

   d. What parts of the tape would you like to revisit for a closer look and why?

5. Link this initial analysis to the one or two main research questions with which you started and revise those questions as appropriate. List several more focused questions about language, social life, and teaching/learning you would like to answer by analyzing this segment of tape.

Selecting, Transcribing, and Analyzing a Segment
of Conversation From Your Data Set

1. Identify one focused research question addressable by analysis of discourse and related to the "big questions" motivating your research.

2. Revisit the catalogued round of activity you identified and develop a timeline in which you attempt to note transitions between various phases of the activity/talk (speech events) and the transitions between them.

3. Based on this timeline, locate one or several segments for transcription and close analysis. Explain why you chose this segment(s) and how it relates to the questions about discourse that you are attempting to address.

4. Review the segment repeatedly being careful to start the tape before the segment begins and play it more until after the segment ends (i.e., pay attention to transitions).

5. Transcribe the talk in the segment(s). (If you are using videotape, in addition to the transcript you may want also to find ways of documenting the use of space, gaze, posture, and movements of participants.)

6. In making the transcript, think about the conventions you would like to use. At a minimum, you should note as best you can who is speaking and show when speech is overlapping. In addition, depending on your data and the analysis you craft, you may also want to note pauses, rising or falling intonation, and so on.

7. Use constructs from your reading of theory to help you "read the transcript closely"—turn taking, form–function relationships, strategies for conversational involvement.

8. Write a timeline (identifying clearly the segment you are analyzing and its relation to other parts of the round of activity you catalogued).

9. Include the transcript (with conventions explained) and other documentation you may have made to help you with your analysis (e.g., charts or diagrams).

10. Show and explain your work-in-progress to interested colleagues for feedback.

RECOMMENDED READINGS

Coulthard, M. (1993). *An introduction to discourse analysis*. Essex: Longman.

Kramsch, C. (1998). *Language and culture*. Oxford: Oxford University Press.

Street, B. (Ed.). (1993). *Cross-cultural approaches to literacy*. Cambridge: Cambridge University Press.

Schiffrin, D., Tannen, D., & Hamilton, H. (Eds.). (2001). *The handbook of discourse analysis*. Oxford: Blackwell.

REFERENCES

Davies, B., & Harré, R. (1990). Positioning: The discursive production of selves. *Journal for the Theory of Social Behavior, 20*(1), 43–63.

Denzin, N., & Lincoln, Y. (2000). *Handbook of qualitative research* (2nd ed.). Thousand Oaks: Sage.

Edelsky, C. (1981). Who's got the floor? *Language in Society, 10*(3), 383–421.

Fairclough, N. (2001). The dialectics of discourse. *Textus, XIV*, 231–242.

Florio-Ruane, S. (1987). Sociolinguistics for educational researchers. *American Educational Research Journal, 24*(2), 185–197.

Florio-Ruane, S. (1996, Spring). *Course syllabus on discourse analysis*.

Florio-Ruane, S., & de Tar, J. (1995, February). Conflict and consensus in teacher candidates' discussion of ethnic autobiography. *English Education, 27*(1), 11–39.

Goffman, E. (1959). *The presentation of the self in everyday life.* New York: Anchor.

Goffman, E. (1981). *Forms of talk.* Philadelphia: University of Pennsylvania Press.

Hanks, W. F. (1996). *Languages and communicative practices.* Boulder: Westview.

Harré, R., & Van Langenhove, L. (1991). Varieties of positioning. *Journal for the Theory of Social Behaviour, 21*(4), 393–407.

Sacks, H., Schegloff, E., & Jefferson, G. (1974). A simplest systematic for the organization of turn-taking for conversation. *Language, 50,* 696–735.

Sarroub, L. K., & Pearson, P. D. (1998). Two steps forward, three steps back: The stormy history of reading comprehension assessment. *The Clearinghouse, 72*(2), 97–105.

Tannen, D. (1989). *Talking voices: Repetition, dialogue, and imagery in conversational discourse.* Cambridge: Cambridge University Press.

APPENDIX A: TIMELINE OF ENTIRE CONVERSATION—1 HOUR AND 45 MINUTES

Side A of Audiotape

- (4) Preliminary talk and procedure talk
- (110) Framing of meeting's business (Loukia)
- (162) Long turns: Frames meeting (Ron)
    - -Mitigating and exercising authority
    - -use of 1st person plural
- (139) Teacher sharing
- (207) Framing (Loukia)
    - -teachers share
- (238) Decision-making process starts (Ron)
    - -teachers share
    - -long turns as Ron redirects
- (279) Teachers share (Diane)
    - -Loukia contextualizes with observation from Diane's classroom
    - -Ron reframes
- (345) Teacher solidarity
- (455) Ron reframes
    - -teachers share
- (427) Suggestion from Loukia
    - -no take-up
    - -Ron shifts topic
- (482) Diane clarifies topical shift for all the teachers
    - -Ron reframes and summarizes
- (522) Topical shift (Gladys)
    - -takes up Loukia's suggestion
    - -teachers share
- (550) Ron reframes and adds Loukia's suggestion
    - -Gladys & Loukia share

(605) Ron reframes and makes topical shift
(632) Teachers share
(654) Ron frames consensus
            -teachers share off-topic
(683) Loukia on topic with classroom example

Side B of Audiotape

 (10) Ron reframes
 (17) Teachers share
 (55) Teacher solidarity—disagreement w/Ron's suggestion
(128) Decision made (Gladys)
            -Ron reframes
(143) Loukia contextualizes Ron's frame
(176) Ron reframes
            -Diane shares about genres
            -Ron shifts topic to logs
            -Gladys takes up logs
            -Diane does not agree
            -Gladys compromises
(230) Diane shifts back to genre
            -teachers share and focus on genre
(261) Ron reframes logging—long turn
(283) Ron reframes genre
(299) Gladys shifts topic and disagrees with logging—long turn
(338) Ron reframes and makes topic shift
            -teachers share
(376) Ron ready to summarize
            -Diane shifts topic and reframes
            -teachers share
(422) Ron reframes w/Diane's suggestion—topic shift
(437) Postmeeting procedure talk—Peter is present

Learning as Social Interaction: Interdiscursivity in a Teacher and Researcher Study Group[1]

Cynthia Lewis
University of Iowa

Jean Ketter
Grinnell College

CENTRAL CONCEPTS

Socially situated identities—We use this term as defined by Gee (1999) to mean the different social positions that people enact or perform in particular settings. *Identity* is usually associated with a stable, internal state of being. Adding *socially situated* to the term foregrounds the fluid, socially constructed notion of identity that informs our study.

Interdiscursivity—This term refers to the presence or trace of one discourse within another. Interdiscursive language rearticulates already existing discourses. Often in our research interdiscursivity occurs when one participant appropriates and reconstructs discourses associated with other participants. This process involves a generative reconstruction of a discourse rather than a recapitulation or imitation. It is a process that we associate with learning.

Dialogic discourse—Based on the work of Bakhtin, we use this term to represent the ways in which speakers are always in the process of addressing and answering previous and future utterances across time and space. As Bakhtin (1981) put it, "The word in language is half someone else's" (p.

---

[1]This study was funded by a National Academy of Education/Spencer Foundation Postdoctoral Fellowship that the first author received in 2000 and by an Arts and Humanities grant from the University of Iowa's Obermann Center for Advanced Studies.

293). Applied to our research, a dialogic conversation is one in which there is an awareness of other utterances and social meanings.

Communities of practice—We use this term as defined by Wenger and Lave to mean the informal social systems that develop over time as people engage in a shared enterprise. These shared practices create and reinforce the tacit and explicit expectations and worldviews held in common by the community. Thus, participants in a community of practice learn collectively as they interact.

Liberal humanism—This term refers to the modernist philosophy that places human beings as individuals at the center of social activity and aims to validate the dignity of all human life wherever it occurs. This ideology also emphasizes the bond formed among human beings by our common traits and problems. For our purposes, we refer to the ideology's focus on these common human abilities and traits and on the belief that individual access to opportunity determines how free a society is.

Critical multiculturalism—Critical multiculturalism aims to move beyond a recognition and legitimizing of cultures—or what some think of as a celebration of difference. Instead advocates of critical multiculturalism seek to understand first how assumptions about such characteristics as race, class, and gender lead to oppression. In addition, critical multiculturalism examines both how power structures provide a dominant group's control of social institutions and how cultural practices naturalize the dominant group's advantage by attributing it to individual achievement.

In this chapter, we closely examine the interactions of a long-term teacher and researcher study group focusing on the reading and teaching of multicultural literature in a rural middle school setting. Over the 4-year span of the study, the group included 10 members—all White females—the two of us as researcher-participants and eight teachers of Grades 5 to 9. The purpose of the group was for participating teachers to read and discuss multicultural young adult literature in ways that would help them make decisions about whether and how to teach these works in their community (see Appendix A for book list). To do this, our work together over the years focused not only on issues related to the teaching of literature, but, more important, on our individual and collective assumptions about race, identity, and multicultural education in terms of how these assumptions shape decisions about text selection and teaching approaches.

This study builds on earlier phases of our research that examined how our discussions of multicultural young adult literature were shaped by community contexts and constructions of racial identity (Ketter & Lewis, 2001; Lewis, Ketter, & Fabos, 2001). In this work, we identified the fixed practices in which all members of the group engaged—practices that seemed to create barriers to our learning and dialogue. We came to see how these practices were created and reinforced by the sociopolitical contexts of the particular setting.

For this phase of our longitudinal study, we were interested in understanding the nature of learning over time among members of the study group. In addition, we wanted to know how interaction patterns in the group sustained or disrupted fixed discourses in ways that shaped the group's learning.

REVIEW OF LITERATURE

Three areas of scholarship inform this research: sociocultural theories of learning, critical theories of language, and critical multiculturalism as it relates to the reading and teaching of multicultural literature. Our theoretical framework views learning not as primarily a mental act, but as a social act dependent on interaction among people and their tools and technologies (Gee, 1999; Lave, 1996; Rogoff, 1995; Wenger, 1999). Based on her research on learning communities outside of schools, Lave (1996) argued that learning is about constructing "identities in practice" (p. 157). Wenger (1999) also viewed learning as arising from the identity work that occurs through participation in communities of practice, communities "created over time by the sustained pursuit of a shared enterprise" (p. 45). Identities practiced in such communities are always a work in progress shaped by individual and collective efforts to create coherence through participation in varied social contexts. Gee's (1996, 1999) social and critical theory of language leads to similar conclusions. He referred to shifts in "socially-situated identity" (1999, p. 86) that mark the kind of changes associated with learning, thus articulating a conception of identity as it connects to learning, which is central to this study. Explicitly connecting a theory of language with a theory of learning, Hicks (1996) asserted that learning involves the learner in *appropriating* and *reconstructing* the discourses within his or her social world. Grounding her use of the term *appropriation* in the work of Bakhtin (1981, 1986), she argued that his emphasis on the dialogic nature of utterances supports a generative use of the concept of appropriation. Central to Bakhtin's theory of language is the sociocultural constitution of utterance, with a speaker's utterance embedding prior and anticipated utterances. Hicks argued that this process represents a rearticulation rather than a recapitulation of existing discourses.

This theoretical argument is important to our study because we are interested in examining what Fairclough (1992) referred to as *interdiscursivity*, defined as the presence or trace of one discourse within another.[2] According to Fairclough, interdiscursive texts can lead to dynamic rearticulations of otherwise stable discourses. In this way, such hybrid discourses have transformative potential that, in our view, connects language to learning. Related to Fairclough's notion of interdiscursivity is Wenger's description of the interdiscursive demands placed on anyone who enters a new community of practice whose discursive practices may conflict or contrast with those of another community in which the participant has been a long-time actor. All communities of practice bring with them unarticulated but shared knowledge—ways of acting and generic expectations that prescribe or make convenient certain ways of writing, thinking, and speaking and preclude others. Hence, those who join a new community of practice often initially operate on the boundaries of that community—a boundary where the participants must negotiate with intersecting and often conflicting discursive practices (Wenger, 1999). Wenger argued that these boundary locations are exactly where new knowledge is produced and identities can be transformed.

An examination of how the teachers and researchers in this group are challenged to rearticulate and reconstruct available and often conflicting discourses, including each other's, has implications for what it means to learn in a professional development community. Moreover, such a view corresponds to recent research on professional development that underscores the benefits of teachers forming learning communities that provide intellectual renewal (Grossman, Wineburg, & Woolworth, 2001), productive conflict (Achinstein, 2002), and the structures necessary to form critical relationships (Gallego, Hollingsworth, & Whitenack, 2001). In their study of a long-term learning community of English and social studies teachers, Grossman, Wineburg, and Woolworth (2001) found that, whereas group members initially shared their individual content expertise, more substantial learning over time was evident when individual perspectives and epistemological positions were internalized by other members.

Beyond these features of professional development, Lawrence and Tatum (1997) argued that White teachers engaged in professional development related to multicultural education must examine their own racial identities to be effective educators. This argument is particularly compelling in light of the demographic statistics (Henke, Choy, Chen, Geis, Alt, & Broughman, 1997), which reveal the persistence of a majority White teaching force, suggesting the need to examine issues of racial identity in teacher education and professional development. Moreover, as Sheurich and Young (1997) main-

---

[2]Fairclough's use of the term *interdiscursivity*, also referred to as *constitutive intertextuality*, draws heavily from Kristeva's (1986) use of the term *intertextuality* in her explication of Bakhtin's (1981, 1986) dialogic theory of social languages and genres.

tained, the epistemology of racism constitutes the conditions on which knowledge is enacted and evaluated within dominant institutions such as public schools. Indeed many theorists of race and ethnicity argue that White people rarely see their Whiteness as a racial category, but instead normalize Whiteness and the privilege it represents (Fine, Weis, Powell, & Mun Wong, 1997; Haymes, 1995; McIntyre, 1997; Roman, 1993; Thompson, 1997). In her study of White teachers' responses to workshops on multicultural education, Sleeter (1993) found that the teachers typically denied that racial identity was a significant factor in their teaching. White teachers do not expect to examine Whites as a racialized group when attending workshops or classes on multicultural education. Instead preservice and practicing teachers are accustomed to focusing on groups they perceive as "other"—groups about which they want information. In this way, race and ethnicity are marked as "foreign," and teachers are positioned as cultural tourists (Kincheloe, Steinberg, & Chennault, 1998; Purves, 1997).

According to many scholars, reading multicultural literature in ways that consciously consider the cultural and sociopolitical influences that shape authorship and interpretation can challenge a reader's perception of self and other (Florio-Ruane, 2001). By examining how social structures limit or enhance different cultural groups' access to power and authority, readers also come to see how cultural identities are forged (Cai, 1997; Hade, 1997). Fang, Fu, and Lamme (1999) argued that multicultural literature "should be considered sociocultural and political texts (Taxel, 1992) for fostering students' understanding of the historical and material forces underpinning the construction of cultural identities" (p. 270). Yet teachers are rarely taught to read children's and young adult literature as political texts nor are they encouraged to read bibliographic resources with a critical eye (Harris, 1993).

The meanings and purposes that teachers assign to the teaching of literature influence and reflect how young adult literature functions politically and theoretically in any context, but these political and theoretical functions are often disregarded in curricular conversations (Barrera, 1992; Harris, 1993). Our initial study of our teacher–researcher study group found, for instance, that as we attempted to engage with multicultural literature and bond with one another, we enacted personal, professional, and group affiliations that served to sustain particular norms of Whiteness even as we attempted to disrupt them (Lewis, Ketter, & Fabos, 2001).

METHODS AND ANALYSIS

Given our current research focus on learning over time, we have found it useful to combine a view of learning grounded in the literature on communities of practice with social and critical theories of language. Doing so has provided us with the theoretical and methodological tools to better understand how our interactions produce and at times disrupt a particular set of discourses. Whereas earlier phases of this research used ethnographic tools to help us fully understand the context of this rural school district and community related to the teachers' responses to multicultural texts, this study employs Critical Discourse Analysis (CDA) to help us understand the longitudinal nature of our learning. Using CDA, we studied key transcripts over the 4-year period to examine the ways that participants took up particular worldviews, patterns of talk, and systems of thought as they related to multicultural literature and to the meaning and purposes of multicultural education. Teaming CDA with ethnographic research allowed us to establish invaluable contexts for the sort of knowledge CDA extracts from texts.

Although eight teachers participated over the 4 years of the study, five teachers formed the consistent core of the study group. These language arts and reading teachers teach fifth-, sixth-, and eighth-grade students at a middle school that has an all Euro-American faculty and two administrators who are both White males. The student body of the middle school is over 94% Euro-American, and 25% of the students receive free or reduced-cost meals. We researcher-participants are White, middle-class women who have both taught language arts and reading in the public schools before going on to work at the university and college where we are now respectively employed. We acted as participant-observers in the study group and saw ourselves as viable contributors to the process of text selection and procedures for discussing the texts. We secured funds to purchase one class set of multicultural books for each participant teacher and to pay for the books we read for all but 1 year of the study.

To establish the ethnographic context for the CDA used for this part of the study, we called on the wealth of data we collected and coded using the NUD*IST qualitative research program over the past 4 years. The ethnographic context included a careful analysis of our own positions within the study group and community related to status, affiliation, and ideological stances. Data included audiotaped sessions of the literature discussions, audiotaped interviews with participants and 11 community informants, written responses to surveys, an audiotaped focus group discussion of group dynamics, and both observational and reflective field notes. After each session, we recorded our observations and analyses separately to ensure that they were first articulated without the influence of the other researcher. We also taped several key research meetings in which we examined how our roles as researchers and participants played out in the literature discussions (Alvermann, Commeyras, Young, Randall, & Hinson, 1997).

To analyze the group's interactions in this phase of the study, we used a method of CDA suggested by Fairclough (1992) and Chouliaraki and Fairclough (1999). Specifically, we examined 15 transcripts taken from the entire span of the study (six from the first 2 years and nine from the last 2 years). It was important that we analyze more transcripts from the latter part of the study given our research focus on change over time. We chose the transcripts that were most salient to our research question about learning and social interaction. The ones that struck us as having the most potential in this regard were transcripts that included segments in which we either sustained or disrupted discourses that had become fixed interactional positions taken up repeatedly by members of the group. We reasoned that to understand learning over time, we would need to closely examine segments of talk that contained statements and ideological positions that repeatedly surfaced in the transcripts and compare those segments to others that moved us beyond these reified positions. Given our long-term involvement with this study group and our multilayered analyses of the transcripts, we were able to use the knowledge gained from earlier phases of this research to locate the transcripts containing such segments. For instance, in our earlier work (Lewis, Fabos, & Ketter, 2001), we identified statements and ideological positions in our talk that reinforced norms of Whiteness through the use of language that universalizes across experiences. This insight—the result of both qualitative coding procedures and tools of discourse analysis—was useful to us as we selected the 15 transcripts to be closely examined in this new phase of our research.

Once we identified the 15 transcripts, we divided each transcript into episodes, with each episode representing a series of turns that all relate to the same topic or theme (Florio-Ruane, 2001; Marshall, Smagorinsky, & Smith, 1995). We then examined each episode to identify first its prominent discourses. Chouliaraki and Fairclough (1999) defined *discourse* as "the construction of some aspect of reality from a particular perspective . . ." (p. 63). However, in our efforts to identify prominent discourses in the transcripts, we found it useful to draw on Luke's (2000) definition of *discourse* as "systematic clusters of themes, statements, ideas, and ideologies [that] come into play in the text" (p. 456). In this vein, we searched the transcripts for regular clusters of themes, statements, and ideologies. Again this process was aided by our extensive involvement in the study group and its surrounding community as well as our previous analyses of the transcripts. Identifying the recurrent and somewhat fixed themes, statements, and ideologies present in these transcripts led us to formulate the coding categories for discourse listed in Appendix B.

One prominent discourse that frequently surfaced was the discourse of liberal humanism and individual choice or circumstance taken up by the teachers. In our analysis of the transcripts, we found that this discourse was often paired with a discourse that we researchers espoused—that of critical multiculturalism with a focus on systems or structures of inequality. Because CDA requires an in-depth examination of language in use, we have limited the focus of this chapter to these two discourses as they repeatedly surfaced over time. We decided to focus on the intersection of these two discourses because they represent an epistemological conflict that was central to our discussions and persisted over time. The discourse of liberal humanism represents the individual as unified, coherent, and possessing freedom of choice. The discourse of critical multiculturalism represents the individual as a socially, culturally, and historically produced subject. The intersection of these discourses often suggested conflicting worldviews that had implications for how we interpreted and evaluated multicultural texts. Once intersections of the two discourses were located in the 15 transcripts, we chose episodes for close analysis that would be most salient to our research questions.

We cross-coded these episodes using the categories of genre and voice as defined by Chouliaraki and Fairclough (1999) as follows:

(1) Genre is "the language (and other semiosis) tied to a particular social activity . . ."
(2) Voice is "the sort of language used for a particular category of people and closely linked to their identity. . . ." (p. 63)

An analysis of genre included an analysis of participant structures with regard to turn taking. We established the other categories for genre by considering all the features of our activity setting. Given the overarching genre of *book group*, we made repeated passes through the transcripts to identify norms and expectations that were established in this social and linguistic setting—a process that led us to formulate the codes for the category of *genre* that appear in Appendix B. Most of the coding categories listed under *voice* (Appendix B) are adapted from Fairclough (1989, 1992) and Chouliaraki and Fairclough (1999), who suggested that these features of language are particularly salient to issues of power and identity in the construction of social reality.

We theorized that CDA would help us discover how our fixed discourses (liberal humanism and critical multiculturalism) persisted through or were interrupted by the interaction patterns we enacted as the group evolved. Focusing closely on genre, discourse, and voice in these portions of text allowed us to identify subtle processes not readily apparent in more holistic readings of text. Underlying our analysis is the assumption that fixed discourses are most likely to be interrupted when more dialogic (Bakhtin, 1981) conversations occur. These moments may be marked by hybridized discourses—discourses that indicate shifts in the socially situated identities of the participants and in which newly constructed perspectives or ideologies are embedded.

FINDINGS

We begin this section with a brief discussion of the overarching discourses and genres that characterized our conversations about multicultural literature. We then move to a more nuanced analysis of transcripts from the early and middle years of our study to reveal the ways in which our binary discourses and interaction patterns evolve over time. This chapter covers a span of study group years from June 1997 to April 2000.

Overarching Discourses and Genres

Across the 15 transcripts, there is a tendency on the part of the middle school teachers to see the inequity characters experience in novels (and real life) as resulting from individual choices or circumstances rather than from structural or systemic forces. Public schools have long been and continue to be institutions that define as democratic a championing of individual achievement and individual responsibility, and thus discount countertheories charging that institutions and their established cultural practices oppress and disempower the poor, immigrants, and people of color (Spring, 2000). According to numerous studies, this view is typical of White preservice and practicing teachers (Beach, 1997; Fang, Fu, & Lamme, 1999; Naidoo, 1994; Rogers & Soter, 1997; Sleeter, 1993). The teachers also demonstrated a related tendency to attribute the cause of the character's oppression to poor parenting or abnormal social practices, rather than to structural barriers or institutionalized racism—a move that Bonilla-Silva (2001) labeled "biologization of culture" (pp. 147–149). We argue that the liberal humanist discursive practices reinforced and reinscribed through the teachers' participation in their public school's community of practice conflicted with the more social constructionist practices typical of our institutions and the research community of practice in which we are active members. For example, the transcripts suggest a tendency on our part to see the inequities depicted in these novels as examples of structural racism and to focus on the social or cultural rather than the individual experience. This finding is in keeping with research on perceptions about racism conducted by Gee (1999), in which teachers' responses focused on individual acts and professors' responses focused on institutional racism.

From the beginning, this group was a hybrid social and linguistic activity or genre: part book group, part professional development, and part academic seminar. It was a site on the boundary between conflicting communities of practice that challenged all participants to search for coherence and stability in the face of our shifting identities as teachers and readers. From the academic community of practice, the group borrowed from a seminar format, with we researchers leading the discussion of texts. As a book group, it was part informal discussion similar to book groups meetings held in people's living rooms, where in fact we did meet on several occasions. As professional development, the talk frequently focused on how the books might be used in a classroom or whether they were appropriate for a particular age level or group of students—topics not typical of adult book group discussions and more likely to occur in workshops or seminars meant for the continuing education of practicing teachers.

In our earlier study, we found that the middle school teacher participants viewed us as having a kind of outside authority they did not, and we viewed the middle school participants as having an insider authority arising from their daily interactions with students and other teachers. In keeping with the seminar genre (seminar leaders), we were commonly the speakers who introduced a topic or began the discussion, particularly in the early years of the study. We had a tendency to make what we call *teacherly moves*, although we did not consciously plan these moves. Included in this category were probing questions, requests for elaboration, intertextual references, and the citing of authorities (e.g., scholars, children's book authors, colleagues).

As researchers connected to the university, we often felt as if we were looked on for expertise at the same time that our expertise was viewed as impractical or erudite. We brought to the group an orientation toward critical multiculturalism that shaped the discussions in ways that were alternately taken up, ignored, or resisted. We used verbal and nonverbal cues to signal our shifting affiliations and statuses. We would look down when saying something that we believed might sound too academic or politically radical, for instance, and we often adjusted our vocabulary so that it would not be mired in the jargon of our disciplines. We stumbled over sentences that we would have spoken articulately in our university or college settings, not intentionally, but because our hyperawareness of power and status relations within the group troubled our speech. We assume that the teachers may have been doing some of the same, working out their own issues related to status and power among themselves, much as one of the teachers put it when she talked about feeling intimidated by another teacher in the group based on their long history of professional relations. Although we usually were not conscious of these performances at the time, they repeatedly surfaced during our independent analyses of transcripts and in our reflective field notes.

The Early Transcripts: Polite Opposition

Our early book discussions reveal the emergence of the two intersecting and often opposing discourses: liberal humanism and critical multiculturalism. We begin with an excerpt from our discussion of *An Island Like You:*

Stories from the Barrio (Cofer, 1995), our third book discussion in the first year of the study. A theme that runs through this collection of short stories about life in a Puerto Rican community in Paterson, New Jersey, is that of adolescents trying to find a comfortable identity in the face of competing views of who they are or should be, some stemming from their own community and some imposed by normative definitions of beauty and success mired in Eurocentric institutions and sensibilities. In this excerpt, Cynthia initiates a turn in which she tries to illustrate that racism and oppression have cut this barrio off from the rest of the country, but this move is resisted by Denise, who identifies with what it must feel like to be an individual in the barrio:[3]

> Cynthia: It's interesting what you said about the universality of it, too, because I think that is so much there, and that's why it's such a good book to use with kids. At the same time, it's called "An Island like You" and I know that's a reference to the grandparents, but I think it's also sort of a claustrophobic sense of being apart from the rest of the world that so many of the characters feel. The barrio is sort of a part of the rest of the world. . . . There's this universality, but there's also this incredible difference.
>
> Denise: And the poem at the beginning says "alone in a crowd." And, you know, I think that's something kind of like an island, I mean you're the only one who feels that way or the only one that thinks that way or the only one who's had that experience, and you don't connect with people.

This exchange was characteristic of many early exchanges in which either Cynthia or Jean made a statement to focus on how the race or ethnicity of the characters marginalizes them. In this case, Cynthia was offering a response to an earlier comment made by Denise suggesting that the stories are about common, universal experiences. Here Cynthia began by affirming Denise's stance, but quickly moved to what is, in effect, an argument against Denise's view that the characters' experiences are universal. Denise responded by indirectly asking us to identify with the experience—one we presumably all have had—of being a lone individual in the midst of others who do not understand the individual's experience. She used *you* in a way that works to persuade her listeners to identify with the lone individual as

---

[3]The following conventions are used in the presentation of transcripts: [text] indicates descriptive text added to clarify elements of the transcript; *text* indicates overlapping speech; ( ) indicates unintelligible words; . . . indicates extracts edited out of the transcript; / indicates interrupted or dropped utterances.

she does ("you're the only one," "you don't connect"). Her take on the book title and poem that serves as the book's prologue was a decidedly psychological one, whereas Cynthia's was sociological and cultural.

Perhaps most interesting is the language used to signal agreement despite the disagreement at the root of the exchange. Cynthia began by affirming Denise's earlier comment valuing this book for its universality and suggested that it is these universal qualities that make it a good book to share with kids. This being only our third book discussion, Cynthia voiced her disagreement in a manner that was likely to be palatable and fairly indirect. Couched in an overall sense of affirmation and a wanting to claim any particular authority, she introduced her disagreement with the phrase "at the same time," which suggests that the two discourses can co-exist, side by side, with no contradiction, rather than a phrase such as "on the other hand," which would point to the incompatibility of the two discourses. Similarly, Denise initiated her response to Cynthia's comment with the conjunction *and*, which suggests a continuation of Cynthia's idea and an implicit agreement. However, she quickly shifted to her focus on the individual, using the pronoun *you* and the repetition *only one*, which created a bond with her listeners by pulling them into the experience of the lone individual.

Later in the same discussion, we can see the same dynamic at work, this time between Denise and Jean:

Denise: But, I think that self-esteem—and going back to some of the characters in this book—is such a vital thing for students. I just see kids with low self-esteem that are, really have big problems.

Jean: And it's interesting since self-esteem issues arise out of racism they experience, you know, a lot these kids, like the Mateo boy, and, um, Luis and Arturo, to some extent, especially, I think, and the girls too.

Here again the teacher, Denise, in the exchange was focusing on the individual psyche of the characters (and, by association, her students), whereas the researcher, Jean, was focusing on the structure of racism as it affects self-esteem. Again we see Jean begin her turn with the appearance of agreement ("And it's interesting since self-esteem"), but then shift quickly into the discourse of structural inequity (racism).

In terms of genre, we coded Jean's initial clause, "And it's interesting," in two categories: *politeness/etiquette* and *teacherly move*. She avoided disagreeing with Denise in any direct way as she might have had she known her better or not been concerned about appearing to be in control of the discussion. She did not begin her turn with something on the order of "It's important to understand that the lack of self-esteem arises out of the racism these characters experience"—a statement that would have made her sound like a teacher who is correcting Denise's response. Yet we believe that beginning her turn with "And it's interesting" represented another kind of teacherly move—one that we have both often used with our own students when we want to detract from our own power by affirming the student's point even as we disagree. This is a way of "honoring a response" of a speaker while arguing against it or restating it to make a different point. Such moves are beyond mere politeness or attempts to downplay difference because the teacher is attempting to refine or reinterpret an idea for the participant who presented it.

We are not suggesting that our use of language (the teachers' or our own) was an intentional ploy to achieve a certain affect—we doubt this was the case. It is the form and function of the text that is of interest to us—and how the form and function constructs and is constructed by the situated identities of the speaker. That is, we are interested in how social identities are achieved through moment-to-moment interaction and how these interactions are shaped by particular identities. The process, as Fairclough (1992) and Gee (1999) made clear, is dialectic.

In our discussion of *Scorpians* (Myers, 1988), the sixth book our group read together, similar dynamics were at work. When discussing *Scorpians*, a book about an African-American youth caught up in a gang to which he does not want to belong, all of us worked to connect at an emotional level perhaps to offset the effects of the opposing discourses we espoused. Here again Jean began with a comment that pointed to structural inequity as it is passed on from generation to generation. In contrast, Denise responded through identification with the boy who suffers in the story. By this point in our discussion, it had already become clear that our discourses about the literature differ; therefore, we worked to agree at an emotional level. All of us agreed from the start of this discussion that the characters in the stories suffer—that they are forced into situations that present difficult if not impossible choices even if we disagree about the context that creates that suffering:

Jean: But you just see this, I kept thinking about this kind of trap that doesn't seem to, it doesn't seem to be different from generation to generation. And one of the poignant things about this book that I thought was very well done was because it wasn't overdone, but two times she talks about when, when the older son was born . . . how she has all this hope.

Denise: Yes. There was just no hope. I mean, how, there was no way out. There was just no way out, you know, and even this kid that picks on him at school. He doesn't want to fight with this kid. He just wants to ignore him. He wants him just to go away. And yet, he's not, you know, that, the other kid is not going to allow that to happen, and so then, what do you do if you're that kid? And you're constantly being picked on. And how many of our kids are victimized like that? And then they end up striking back and then they get in trouble and then they get a reputation and then people expect them to be bad. Just like all his teachers.

Cynthia: Right. Such a cycle.

Affective bonding is clear in this exchange through our direct reference to the emotional nature of our responses to the work. In Jean's turn, she referred to the *poignancy* of the mother's hope when her older son is born, and Denise spoke of empathizing with the students who get in trouble and then cannot shake their bad reputations. This was an emotional issue for Denise, whom we have found to be the consummate child advocate—always seeing the best in her students and believing that kids have enormous capability to respond to literature in deep and thoughtful ways. When Jean co-taught with Denise on several occasions, she found that Denise often raised the concern that teachers make judgments about students based on what other teachers say or what they know about the students' families. She often spoke with outrage about a situation in which a teacher told one of her students that he was too "dumb to make it to college."

The use of intensifiers, repetition, and pronouns also signifies emotionality or affective speech. For example, in her turn Denise used intensifiers such as *just* and *constantly* to index her empathy with the character. She also switched to *you* in the fourth line, indicating her own empathy with the character she imagined and also to include the others as participants in her distress about how the boy is victimized. She referred to the victims she imagines as *our* kids, including all the participants as caregivers or guardians of the kids she described.

Cynthia affirmed her response with agreement and restatement. "Right. Such a cycle." Although her response echoed Denise's response with the intensifier *such* and affirmation of her feelings, she was also returning to Jean's initiating turn in the episode focusing on the structural forces at work, passed on, in cyclical fashion from generation to generation. In contrast, Denise focused on individual experiences and choices in her analysis of the victim's experience.

This pattern repeats itself in another turn between Denise and Cynthia. Cynthia had just asked whether the lack of hope in the book would make it too difficult to share with adolescents. Sarah's response initiated the following exchange:

Sarah: You don't, you wouldn't want to be preachy about it and say, *"Look you guys, this is what could happen to you if you don't toe the line.*

Denise: *I think the, I think the, uh, no,* I think the value of the book is for kids to see what other kids in other subcultures are going through. Every day of their life. I think we're so removed from that here. I mean that. Maybe we're not.

Cynthia: Yes. And it makes those, those, these kids seem very human and very. And to have, they have ethics and morals and /.

Although Sarah sounds as if she would not want to use the book as a cautionary tale, she often talked about young adult literature in just those terms, believing that it should present kids with moral and ethical truths by which they can live. She tended to view students as incapable of getting beyond surface responses to texts and often asked group members how she could help her fifth-grade students "dig deeper" under the surface of the literature they read. This is in contrast to Denise, who, as described earlier, had every confidence that her eighth-grade students could think deeply and thoughtfully about the books they read. In response to Sarah, then, Denise somewhat tentatively offered her belief about the value of teaching this book. Although she seems to second-guess herself at the end of this turn ("Maybe we're not"), she uses intensifiers like *every day*, *so*, and *I mean* to express her distress that these other teens, who are "in other subcultures" do not have the advantages Denise sees her students enjoying. Cynthia's first response with "Yes." Again she affirmed Denise's response at an emotional level, but then presented a different argument in that she emphasized the way that the characters in the book can be normalized rather than viewed as other. Features of voice here are interesting because Denise uses othering pronouns—*they* and *we*—and Cynthia began by repeating this pattern, but then changed it: "those, those, *these* kids."

In this excerpt, Denise signified the other adolescents for whom she would like her students to have empathy. This way of viewing the other can lead to a moral judgment or paternalism or a desire to protect the innocence of the adolescents in this community. Although it is tempting for us to read her remarks in this way, we would like now to offer an alternate reading—one that is more generous and in keeping with Denise's strong affinity for her students and general advocacy for youth. Asked to come up with a reason for teaching this book to kids in her community, and wanting to emphatically divorce herself from any sense of this book as a cautionary tale, she made what we believe to be an attempt to situate the characters in this book within an unjust system of oppression and inequity. She referred to this system through her use of the word *subcultures*, which marks a movement away from viewing the characters as individuals who make what appear sometimes to be bad choices. Cynthia's response can be read as a shift to a focus on the kids rather than the structures that shape them.

This exchange is an example of interdiscursivity as defined earlier—a trace or presence of one discourse within another. In this case, one can read the discourse of the individual in Denise's remark (the individuals who are her students can learn from what the other individuals experience every day) and the discourse of structural inequity in Cynthia's remark (the underlying assumption being that it is necessary to represent as human those who have been systematically represented as "other" and as malevolent). Embedded in each of these remarks, however, are alternate discourses: an understanding about the structural nature of subcultures in Denise's remark and an understanding about the importance of foregrounding the individual, with moral and ethical dilemmas, in Cynthia's remark. This pattern of interdiscursivity becomes more pronounced in later transcripts, and we argue that such hybrid language opens spaces for learning as we have defined it—the appropriation and reconstruction of discourses within one's social world. Fixed practices are most likely to be interrupted when more dialogic conversations occur, resulting in subtle shifts in the social identities of the participants.

The Middle Transcripts: Interdiscursive Moments

In our analysis of transcripts from the middle years of this study, we found marked changes in the categories of genre and voice as they intersected with the discourses of liberal humanism (individual) and critical multiculturalism (structural forces). To demonstrate these changes, we focus this section on a lengthy exchange from our discussion of *American Eyes: New Asian American Short Stories for Young Adults* (Carlson, 1994), which took place in April 2000. This collection of short stories by Asian American writers explores issues of assimilation and acculturation among young Asian Pacific Americans. We focus on two episodes from the book group discussion. We include nearly the entire episode in each case to make some points about the structure of participation.

We begin with an episode that starts with Carol, a teacher who taught gifted education and had been a member of the group for a little over 2 years at the time of this discussion. Carol is unique in the group because she had experience teaching in a rural south Texas community with a population of working-class Latinos. Her experience was often reflected in her analysis of a character's motivation and, in particular, her perceptions of the conflicts those from a minority culture experience in schooling and society at large. At this point we were discussing a story about a first-generation Japanese adolescent who revisits Little Tokyo in Los Angeles, where his recently deceased father had taken him many times as a child (Oba, 1994):

Carol: And it's so funny, too, I think all the way through that that, um, all the way through the book, the trade-off that they have to be an American and not give up whatever culture is offered, whatever their culture offers them. I'm not explaining this right, but each one of them has kind of a different way, like, like, when you were talking about that seeing ghosts, you know, calling back his uncle, and accepting that he would really appear, and the boy who went back, tried to go back to that Japanese part, yeah, yeah, to find the different stores and everything and they were gone, and, I don't know /

Sarah: Oh, that was sad.

Cynthia: And he wasn't accepted in the store [restaurant]

Carol: Right. Exactly. Exactly. When he sat there waiting for him

Sarah: Yes ( )

Cynthia: That was sad.

Sarah: Um-hmm. It was.

Sarah: Was that the story where they repeated this phrase a couple times, "If you lived here you'd be home"?

[All affirm]

Sarah: There's something about that phrase.

. . .

Cynthia: His father has died, right, and his mother is filling her life by making origami. That's a great image.

Sarah: All over the house.

Carol: And she left the neighborhood, too, so it's like there aren't any connections back with that neighborhood anymore.

The episode started with Carol struggling to explain her sense that these characters are caught between American and their ancestral cultures. One could argue that Carol's use of the word *American* reveals an experiential value (Fairclough, 1989) or ideological stance toward first-generation ethnic minorities that marks them as immigrants or non-Americans and assumes White people as unmarked Americans. Yet in the context of her entire turn, it seems more likely that the phrase *American culture* refers to dominant American culture, and that Carol is interested in how this individual's life is shaped by a larger sociocultural framework. In another interdiscursive moment, this speaker turn holds traces of both discourses under discussion—the individual and the structural. Given that before Carol's turn we had been discussing something entirely different (nuclear family narratives), Carol took control of the topic—a move not typical of the teachers in the early transcripts.

Also related to the genre of *book talk*, Carol claimed a particular stance at the same time that she seemed either unwilling to claim it or unsure of herself. She began this rather serious statement about the characters' cultural positioning with the seemingly contradictory "And it's so funny, too," perhaps as a way to undercut the seriousness of what she was about to say. A few sentences later, she undercut her claim to authority by stating, "I'm not explaining this right." We found that when teacher participants in the group began to frame their responses in terms of the discourse of structural forces, they did so with some degree of inarticulateness, using more filler words and sometimes apologizing for their manner of speaking ("I'm not explaining this right"). This inarticulate voice was far from ineffective, however, because it signaled a shift in discourse as participants constructed new perspectives. Carol did not simply appropriate a way of thinking more associated with Cynthia or Jean. Instead she reconstructed this worldview in her own way—one that centered as much on the individual as it did on the social constitution of the individual.

We include most of the turns that were part of this episode because they reveal both the animated, collaborative talk that we displayed by this time in our group's evolution and because this series of turns serves as an extended example of interdiscursive talk that weaves in and out of both discourses. For instance, although all of the turns add a bit of detail to create a sense of immediacy and sadness about the predicament of this individual adolescent boy, three of the turns reinforce the structural nature of his predicament. Cynthia reminded others that the boy was not accepted as more than a tourist in one of the Japanese restaurants he entered, searching for a past he had lost. Carol agreed and added an image of the boy waiting to be acknowledged in the restaurant. Finally, Carol underscored the lack of cultural affiliation the boy experiences. Throughout this set of cohesive turns, we follow up on each other's comments, almost finishing each other's sentences and building on previous turns.

The next episode followed directly after the one just discussed. It too represents an instance of interdiscursivity, but one that works quite differently than the first episode. Sarah began by asking a question about White privilege, but did so from a position of dominance that served to marginalize those whom she refers to as "people who are different":

Sarah: I wonder how many white people are aware in their day to day life how much other people are trying to be like them? You know, people who are different. I never think of that until I read these stories and see about how important all these things are—the language, the hair color, all of those things—that striving for those things, that we don't even think about it. Why, why do people feel they have to be just like that in order to be of worth?

Cynthia: Yeah, I don't see them as striving for it, I see them as (pause) *wanting*

Sarah: *envy?*

Cynthia: the privilege that comes with *that*

Sarah: *Oh, okay.*

Cynthia: and the power that comes with these things and feeling like they're completely denigrated and treated with prejudice because they don't have it. That seems like it's more directed towards *us* than towards the *self* to me, but what do others think?

It was difficult for us to be generous in our response to Sarah's initial turn in this episode, coming as it did nearly 3 years into the study group at a time when we had hoped we had progressed beyond such comments. In our view, her first sentence was inscribed with the very White privilege her comment, at some level, sought to challenge. Moreover, by indexing White people as *them*, she seemed not to acknowledge her own implication in this system of privilege. Later in the turn, Sarah used repetition of an article (*the* language, *the* hair color, all of *those* things) to refer to characteristics of White people that she believes are seen as desirable. Her use of *the* and shift from *these things* to *those things* further serves to distance her from this system of privilege.

Indeed there are some characters in *American Eyes* who measure themselves against Eurocentric standards of beauty. However, they do so with an awareness of the power differences that privilege these standards. One can read into Sarah's turn the now familiar discourse of liberal humanism (and the individual psyche). She was concerned that this striving toward White characteristics could be damaging to one's self-worth.

Cynthia channeled her frustration into a response that directly opposed Sarah's discourse of Whiteness, attempting to disrupt the way that Sarah conflated White privilege with what she perceived as the desire to be White. Even as Cynthia paused to consider the best way to finish her sentence about not seeing people of color as "striving" to be White, Sarah jumped in to finish Cynthia's sentence with the word she thought would fit—*envy*— further revealing her belief that White people serve as objects of desire for people of color.

Earlier in the life of our book group, as is evident from our analyses of genre and voice in the exchanges included in the section on early transcripts, Cynthia most likely would have made her point less directly. For instance, she might have found some common point of agreement before moving on to disagree or, possibly concerned about sounding too authoritative, she might have found herself pulling back—speaking inarticulately, using filler words, half-spoken sentences, and seeming not to want to claim her position. Such was not the case by this time in the study group, however, and so after a quick affirmation ("yeah"), she explicitly stated her opposition, claiming her position, in part, through the use of repetition ("I don't see them as striving for it, I see them as . . ."). She continued to draw on the features of book talk genre that we labeled as *teacherly moves* and *disagreement* for several turns, strongly stating her position. Finally, having had control of the floor for three turns, Cynthia opened the floor to others in a teacherly manner ("But what do others think?"). She spoke those words, as teachers sometimes do, as if she were completely open to other perspectives, but we now suspect that everything about her words and intonation suggested otherwise. Vocabulary such as *privilege, power, completely denigrated,* and *prejudice* make the discourse of critical multiculturalism clear, and this discourse, it seemed to us when we first analyzed this episode, stands in stark contrast to Sarah's discourse of liberal humanism and self-worth.

However, as we have read and reread Sarah's words, placing them in the context of our historical understanding of Sarah and her position in our group, we have come to see her contribution differently. Sarah was reared in a midwestern town where she lived in what she described as a "working class town with much prejudice, including [her] parents." Many times in our years together, she commented, often derisively, about the way her home community would have treated a particular character. She was proud of her participation in this group, calling it a *class*, and reporting that her friends, family, and fellow teachers asked her questions about why she belonged to the group and what its value was to her. She kept count of the books we read and shared short articles and bibliographic entries about multicultural literature taken from teaching magazines. This year, the fifth year of the study, the group is continuing their monthly meetings without us. Sarah, who just retired from teaching, is organizing and audiotaping the meetings and leading the book-selection process.

Sarah's role in the group was often tentative. Her turns were often questions, asking for advice or elaboration, usually directed to Cynthia or Jean. She also had a habit of echoing the end of someone's sentence and then nodding her agreement. She represented herself in interviews as someone who did not know as much about interpreting literature as others in the group (because she was elementary trained and the others were trained in secondary English). Her social identity as a member of this group was tentative and insecure, whereas her social identity as derived from participation in the group was elevated. She often referred to the strong bonds we had developed as a collegial learning community.

This history of identities, relationships, and connections (Gee, 1999) moved us to re-see Sarah's turn about *other people* striving to be like White people. In the context of Sarah's evolution in this group, we began to realize that the lens through which we interpreted Sarah's words was shaped by the way our academic discourse community talks about race. Thus, we did not consider that Sarah's words could be read as an awareness of Whiteness as a race rather than a taken-for-granted norm. As she put it, "I never think of that until I read these stories and see about how important all these things are—the language, the hair color, and all of those things—that striving for those things that we don't even think about it." Here she moved in a new direction, tentatively considering the construction of race in relation to self and other, before the next sentence, when she returned to a focus on the psychology of individual self-worth. This move was in keeping with research findings (Helms, 1990; Lawrence & Tatum, 1997), suggesting that becoming aware of one's own Whiteness is an early stage of White racial identity development.

Although Sarah could be said to "other" those who are "different," she also represents White people as other in her first sentence. Later in the turn, she used the pronoun *we* to refer to White people, but in the first sentence, she referred to White people with the pronouns *their* and *them*, setting herself apart from those White people who live their lives day to day naturalizing race. However, she had begun to denaturalize race, and reading the literature under discussion has helped her to do so. Sarah's way of representing the discourse of structural inequality was different than ours. She embedded the discourse within a story—the story of her thinking and reading processes.

After Cynthia asked what others thought, hoping, at the time, that someone else would challenge Sarah, Carol continued the episode with a turn that displayed a common feature of the book talk genre—the personal story.

Carol: I think it is whatever that country puts up as their ideal. I know that my friend who came from Bolivia had, has, fair skin and, um, golden eyes, and dark hair. And his skin is not, and he would be my color—he's not, like, very fair. And he was looked down upon, I mean literally, to the point where he was carrying a knife in school to scare them away, because he was not dark. So, it's just, he wasn't Indian enough looking.

Denise: He didn't fit in. That must be a sad state of affairs.

Carol: Right, and he was looked upon as a foreigner even though he was Bolivian. And his mother came from Chile.

Here, as in the case of Sarah's turn, the personal story is being used in ways that are quite different than one might expect. Rather than feeding into the discourse of the individual, Carol told a story from which listeners were expected to extract significance: It is the larger structures of privilege that determine who will be marginalized, and those structures are somewhat arbitrary (changing from country to country). Perhaps having read Sarah's comment as a privileging of Whiteness, Carol's story served to contest that privilege. Some readers might suggest that her discourse is too quick to assume that the structure of power and privilege is arbitrary rather than historical, political, and economic. However, coming on the tail of Sarah's comment, it serves an important purpose in this local scene—to gently challenge within the framework of story. Carol sticks with this position in her last turn despite Denise's attempt to focus on the individual circumstance of Carol's friend ("He didn't fit in.").

THE INTERSECTION OF GENRE, DISCOURSE, AND VOICE

In the early transcripts, the individual/structural binary was constructed through generic features of talk in our book group, such as politeness and affirmation. We researchers denied our authority even as we controlled most topics and made indirect teacherly moves. Although our talk was constituted in a range of social languages, those social languages emerged out of the discourses we brought to the table from our respective social worlds (e.g., liberal humanism for the teachers, critical multiculturalism for us). We tried to bridge these binary discourses through elements of voice that would downplay them—using pronouns, filler words, and intensifiers that created bonds and promoted affect. In the middle transcripts, the individual/structural discourses were less distinct. Elements of genre intersected with these discourses in ways that blurred their boundaries. For instance, the use of personal story, an often-cited feature of book talk genre (Florio-Ruane, 2001; Long, 1986; Marshall, Smagorinsky, & Smith, 1995) that serves to accentuate the individual, here instead provided a form through which teachers gave shape to the structural.

Although we researchers still at times resorted to teacherly moves as a feature of our book talk, we did so with more explicitness, making our agendas clear (a feature that is even more accentuated in later transcripts). Disagreements among members were more explicit as well. For instance, one teacher disagreed so strongly with Jean's statement that racism was the root cause of an African-American character's incarceration that she strongly retorted, "Now wait, wait, wait! You think that's what he's thinking? Or is that what *we're* reading into it." More often during this middle period, a teacher participant would challenge another teacher's reading of the text more effectively than we did because the teacher's use of hybrid discourses (individual/structural) was accomplished through the use of a familiar and affective genre such as personal story.

In the first phases of this longitudinal study, we analyzed transcripts of literature discussions with a firm conception in mind of what it means to critically engage with multicultural texts. We had defined critical engagement as an awareness of how texts are shaped by the ideological power relations within which they function. Specifically, we were looking for evidence that readers could analyze how texts position readers, how readers position texts, and how readers function within sociopolitical contexts (Lewis, Ketter, & Fabos, 2001). Cynthia presented a paper, for instance, that used Hall's (1993) theoretical work on encoding and decoding to consider whether the teacher privileged dominant codes in the literature they read or whether they read against the dominant code to construct an alternative frame of reference (Lewis, 2001). What has now become clear to us is that this conception of critical engagement was closely aligned to our own ways of reading and our own academic backgrounds in critical multiculturalism, and that defining learning or growth according to such a standard was antithetical to a more dialogic view of learning.

Along these lines, we have become less interested in defining our talk according to some standard of what it means to read critically and more interested in the ways that the participants have taken up each other's discourses in talk about texts and what this might have to say about how identities are constructed in practice. As is evident from the data shared in this chapter, our conception of this learning community is hardly utopian. Differences in status, power, affiliation, and ideologies shaped our conversations in ways that made them tense at times. Yet this tension is inevitable, we would argue, in dialogic interaction. Following Bakhtin, we see dialogic interaction as constituted in an awareness of other utterances and social meanings, but these meanings and utterances can exist in opposition in ways that can be productive, yet profoundly uncomfortable. Holquist (1993) underscored the centrality of this tension to Bakhtin's work:

> Bakhtin was at great pains never to sacrifice the tension between identity and difference that fueled his enterprise. He always sought the minimum degree of homogenization necessary to any conceptual scheme. . . . (p. 307)

We want to make some claims about growth in this long-term study group without homogenizing the relationship between identity and difference in our quest for evidence of learning or transformation. To do so we have shared particulars of our conversations that represent what Florio-Ruane (2001) called "education at the 'point of contact' " (p. 148). Our use of CDA to analyze these points of contact longitudinally has allowed us to articulate a theory of learning as social interaction that has implications for the professional development of teachers in long-term learning communities. Our analyses of the data point to the central role interdiscursivity plays in learning. If we view learning as the appropriation and reconstruction of one's social world, it stands to reason that interdiscursive language would be critical to this process: It is through the presence of one discourse in another that a generative rather than a fixed appropriation becomes possible. In this vein, the members of our study group take up each other's genres, discourses, and voices over time in ways that create rather than replicate, thus opening spaces for new ways of constructing a teaching and learning self.[4]

Reflection and Action

1. Using Luke's (2000) definition of *discourse* as "systematic clusters of themes, statements, ideas, and ideologies [that] come into play in the text" (p. 456), identify other recurring patterns of discourse across the data exemplars in addition to or instead of the fixed pair highlighted in this chapter. How might you convince a reader that the discourses you have identified are salient to the study?

2. Homing in on a data exemplar of your choice, provide an alternative analysis of the intersection of discourse, genre, and voice. What implications are suggested by this alternative analysis?

3. This chapter argues that interdiscursivity plays a central role in learning, defined as the appropriation and reconstruction of one's social world. Given the veracity of this argument, what have the researcher-participants in the book group learned?

RECOMMENDED READINGS

Bonilla-Silva, E. (2001). *White supremacy & racism in the post-civil rights era.* London: Lynne Rienner.
Chouliaraki, L., & Fairclough, N. (1999). *Discourse in late modernity: Rethinking critical discourse analysis.* Edinburgh, Scotland: Edinburgh University Press.

---

[4]We are interested in studying how the teachers' learning in the study group might shape their work with each other and with their students now that we have left the site. Currently the study group is continuing without us—a group that includes five of the core teachers plus two new teachers. The teachers have agreed to provide us with audiotapes of their discussions, which will allow us to study instances of interdiscursivity as they occur without our participation. We are also interested in how our study group may have shaped discussions of multicultural texts in the teachers' classrooms. To this end, we are currently analyzing interviews with the teachers that speak to this subject as well as the artifacts and narratives related to their teaching that the teachers brought to our study group meetings. In addition, Jean has taught three collaborative units with Denise in her eighth-grade classroom. The data from this collaboration provide more information about the role of interdiscursivity in learning as it plays out in the classroom context.

Holland, D., Lachicotte, W., Jr., Skinner, D., & Cain, C. (1998). *Identity and agency in cultural worlds*. Cambridge, MA: Harvard University Press.
Mahalingam, R., & McCarthy, C. (2000). *Multicultural curriculum: New directions for social theory, practice, and policy*. New York: Routledge.

REFERENCES

Achinstein, B. (2002). Conflict amid community: The micropolitics of teacher collaboration. *Teachers College Record, 104*, 421–455.
Alvermann, D. E., Commeyras, M., Young, J. P., Randall, S., & Hinson, D. (1997). Interrupting gendered discursive practices in classroom talk about texts: Easy to think about, difficult to do. *Journal of Literacy Research, 29*, 73–104.
Bakhtin, M. (1981). *The dialogic imagination: Four essays* (M. Holquist, Ed.). Austin: University of Texas Press.
Bakhtin, M. (1986). *Speech genres and other late essays* (C. Emerson, Ed.). Austin: University of Texas Press.
Barrera, R. B. (1992). The culture gap in literature-based literacy instruction. *Education and Urban Society, 23*(2), 227–244.
Beach, R. (1997). Students' resistance to engagement with multicultural literature. In T. Rogers & A. O. Soter (Eds.), *Reading across cultures: Teaching literature in a diverse society* (pp. 69–94). New York: Teachers College Press.
Bonilla-Silva, E. (2001). *White supremacy & racism in the post-civil rights era*. Boulder, CO: Lynne Rienner.
Cai, M. (1997). Reader-response theory and the politics of multicultural literature. In T. Rogers & A. Soter (Eds.), *Reading across cultures: Teaching literature in a diverse society* (pp. 199–212). New York: Teachers College Press.
Carlson, L. (1994). *American eyes: New Asian American short stories for young adults*. New York: Holt & Company.
Chouliaraki, L., & Fairclough, N. (1999). *Discourse in late modernity: Rethinking critical discourse analysis*. Edinburgh, Scotland: Edinburgh University Press.
Cofer, J. O. (1995). *An island like you: Stories of the barrio*. New York: Puffin.
Fairclough, N. (1989). *Language and power*. New York: Longman.
Fairclough, N. (1992). *Discourse and social change*. London: Polity.
Fang, Z., Fu, D., & Lamme, L. (1999). Rethinking the role of multicultural literature in literacy instruction: Problems, paradox, and possibility. *The New Advocate, 12*, 259–276.
Fine, M., Weis, L., Powell, L. C., & Mun Wong, L. (1997). *Off White: Readings on race, power, and society*. New York: Routledge.
Florio-Ruane, S. (with de Tar, J.). (2001). *Teacher education and cultural imagination: Autobiography, conversation, and narrative*. Mahwah, NJ: Lawrence Erlbaum Associates.
Gallego, M. A., Hollingsworth, S., & Whitenack, D. A. (2001). Relational knowing in the reform of educational cultures. *Teachers College Record, 103*, 240–266.
Gee, J. P. (1996). *Social linguistics and literacies: Ideology in discourses* (2nd ed.). London: Taylor & Francis.
Gee, J. P. (1999). *An introduction to discourse analysis: Theory and method*. New York: Routledge.
Grossman, P., Wineburg, S., & Woolworth, S. (2001). Toward a theory of teacher community. *Teachers College Record, 103*, 942–1012.
Hade, D. D. (1997). Reading multiculturally. In T. Rogers & A. O. Soter (Eds.), *Reading across cultures: Teaching literature in a diverse society* (pp. 233–255). New York: Teachers College Press.

Hall, S. (1993). Encoding, decoding. In S. During (Ed.), *The cultural studies reader* (pp. 90–103). New York: Routledge.

Harris, V. J. (1993). Literature-based approaches to reading instruction. In L. Darling-Hammond (Ed.), *Review of research in education* (pp. 269–297). Washington, DC: American Educational Research Association.

Haymes, S. N. (1995). White culture and the politics of racial difference: Implications for multiculturalism. In C. E. Sleeter & P. L. McLaren (Eds.), *Multicultural education, critical pedagogy, and the politics of difference* (pp. 105–128). Albany, NY: State University of New York Press.

Helms, J. E. (1990). Toward a model of white racial identity development. In J. E. Helms (Ed.), *Black and white racial identity: Theory, research, and practice* (pp. 49–66). New York: Greenwood.

Henke, R. R., Choy, S. P., Chen, X., Geis, S., Alt, M. N., & Broughman, S. P. (1997). *America's teachers: Profile of a profession, 1993–94.* U.S. Department of Education, National Center for Education Statistics.

Hicks, D. (1996). Contextual inquiries: A discourse-oriented study of classroom learning. In D. Hicks (Ed.), *Discourse, learning, and schooling* (pp. 104–144). New York: Cambridge University Press.

Holquist, M. (1993). Answering as authoring: Mikhail Bakhtin's translinguistics. *Critical Inquiry, 10,* 307–319.

Ketter, J., & Lewis, C. (2001). Already reading texts and contexts: Multicultural literature in a predominantly white rural community. *Theory into Practice, XI*(3), 175–184.

Kincheloe, J. L., Steinberg, S. R., & Chennault, E. (Eds.). (1998). *White reign: Deploying whiteness in America.* New York: St. Martin's Press.

Kristeva, J. (1986). Word, dialogue and novel. In T. Moi (Ed.), *The Kristeva reader* (pp. 34–61). Oxford: Basil Blackwell.

Lave, J. (1996). Teaching, as learning, in practice. *Mind, Culture, and Activity, 3,* 149–164.

Lawrence, S. M., & Tatum, B. D. (1997). Teachers in transition: The impact of antiracist professional development on classroom practice. *Teachers College Record, 99*(1), 162–178.

Lewis, C. (2001). *Critical engagement: Multicultural literature in a rural context.* Paper presented at the annual meeting of the National Academy of Education, Berkeley, CA.

Lewis, C., Ketter, J., & Fabos, B. (2001). Reading race in a rural context. *International Journal of Qualitative Studies in Education, 14*(3), 317–350.

Long, E. (1986). Women, reading, and cultural authority: Some implications of the audience perspective in cultural studies. *American Quarterly, 38,* 591–612.

Luke, A. (1995/1996). Text and discourse in education: An introduction to critical discourse analysis. In M. Apple (Ed.), *Review of research in education* (Vol. 21, pp. 3–48). Washington, DC: American Educational Research Association.

Luke A. (2000). Critical literacy in Australia. *Journal of Adolescent and Adult Literacy, 43,* 448–461.

Marshall, J. D., Smagorinsky, P., & Smith, M. W. (1995). *The language of interpretation: Patterns of discourse in discussions of literature.* Urbana, IL: National Council of Teachers of English.

McIntyre, A. (1997). *Making meaning of whiteness: Exploring racial identity with white teachers.* Albany, NY: State University of New York Press.

Merriam, S. B. (1988). *Case study research in education: A qualitative approach.* San Francisco: Jossey-Bass.

Myers, W. D. (1988). *Scorpions.* New York: HarperCollins.

Naidoo, B. (1994). Through whose eyes? Exploring racism thought literature with white students. In D. Graddol (Ed.), *Researching literacy and language in social context* (pp. 62–81). Avon, UK: Multilingual Matters.

Oba, R. (1994). Home now. In L. M. Carlson (Ed.), *American eyes: New Asian-American short stories for young adults* (pp. 25–33). New York: Holt.

Purves, A. C. (1997). Introduction: The grand tour and other forays. In G. Cruz, S. Jordan, J. Meléndez, S. Ostrowski, & A. C. Purvis (Eds.), *Beyond the culture tours: Studies in the teaching and learning of culturally diverse texts* (pp. 1–8). Mahwah, NJ: Lawrence Erlbaum Associates.

Rogers, T., & Soter, A. O. (1997). *Reading across cultures: Teaching literature in a diverse society.* New York: Teachers College Press.

Rogoff, B. (1995). Sociocultural activity on three planes. In J. V. Wertsch, P. Del Rio, & A. Alvarez (Eds.), *Sociocultural studies of mind* (pp. 139–164). New York: Cambridge University Press.

Roman, L. G. (1993). White is a color! White defensiveness, postmodernism, and anti-racist pedagogy. In C. McCarthy & W. Chrichlow (Eds.), *Race, identity, and representation in education* (pp. 71–88). New York: Routledge.

Scheurich, J. J., & Young, M. D. (1997). Coloring epistemologies: Are our research epistemologies racially biased? *Educational Research, 26*(4), 4–16.

Sleeter, C. E. (1993). How white teachers construct race. In C. McCarthy & W. Crichlow (Eds.), *Race, identity, and representation in education* (pp. 157–171). New York: Routledge.

Spring, J. H. (2000). *Deculturalization and the struggle for equality: A brief history of the education of dominated cultures in the United States.* Boston, MA: McGraw-Hill.

Taxel, J. (1992). The politics of children's literature: Reflections on multiculturalism, political correctness, and Christopher Columbus. In V. J. Harris (Ed.), *Teaching multicultural literature in grades K–8* (pp. 1–36). Norwood, MA: Christopher-Gordon.

Thompson, A. (1997). For: Anti-racist education. *Curriculum Inquiry, 27*(1), 7–44.

Wenger, E. (1999). *Communities of practice: Learning, meaning, and identity.* New York: Cambridge University Press.

APPENDIX A: BOOK LIST

Date Read   *Book Title and Author*

6/19/97   *Hold Fast to Dreams*, Andrea Davis Pinkney
7/16/97   *Warriors Don't Cry*, Melba Patillo Peale*
8/6/97   *An Island Like You*, Judith Ortiz Cofer
9/22/97   *Journey to Topaz*, Yoshiko Uchida
11/05/97   *Last Summer with Maizon*, Jacqueline Woodson
12/01/97   *Scorpians*, Walter Dean Myers
1/20/98   *The Watsons go to Birmingham: 1963*, Christopher Curtis
2/17/98   *Behind the Bedroom Wall*, Laure E. Williams
4/07/98   *Jip, His Story*, Katherine Paterson
5/05/98   *Growing up Native American*, Patricia Riley (Ed.)
7/22/98   *Growing up Native American**
8/31/98   *Toning the Sweep*, Angela Johnson
9/23/98   *Bless Me Ultima*, Rudolfo Anaya
10/26/98   *Bless Me Ultima*, Rudolfo Anaya
12/07/98   *Novia Boy*, Gary Soto
4/10/99   *Playing in the Dark*, Toni Morrison* (our only text meant for adult readers)
5/16/99   *Sugar in the Raw*, Rebeca Carroll

6/28/99	*Annie John*, Jamaica Kincaid
8/11/99	*Seedfolk*, Paul Fleischman
9/29/99	*Circuit: Stories from the Life of a Migrant Child*, Francisco Jimenez
11/01/99	*True North*, Kathryn Lasky
12/18/99	*Power*, Linda Hogan
1/31/00	*Farewell to Manzanar*, Jeanne Houston
2/28/00	*Monster*, Walter Dean Myers
4/03/00	*American Eyes: New Asian American Short Stories for Young Adults*, Lori Carlson (Ed.)
5/09/00	*Cool Salsa*, Lori Carlson (Ed.)
8/07/00	*Oh Freedom, Kids Talk about the Civil Rights Movement with the People Who Made It Happen*, Casey King, Linda Barrett Osborne, & Joe Brooks
9/12/00	*From the Notebook of Melanin Sun*, Jacqueline Woodson
10/25/00	*If It Hadn't Been for Yoon Joon*, Marie G. Lee
12/05/00	*The Birchbark House*, Louise Erdrich
1/16/01	Discussion of article, "Reading Multiculturally," Daniel Hade
2/28/01	*Like Sisters on the Homefront*, Rita Williams-Garcia
4/25/01	*The Skin I'm In*, Sharon G. Flake
6/28/01	*Buried Onions*, Gary Soto
8/01/01	*So Far from the Bamboo Grove*, Yoko Kawashima Watkins

*Designates that the discussion of this book was not successfully audio-taped.

APPENDIX B: CODING CATEGORIES

1. Genre
   Language tied to a particular social activity (Chouliaraki & Fairclough, 1999, p. 63)—in this case, a book group.
   1. topic control (note when a new topic is initiated and when it shifts)
   2. participant structures (turn taking—overlap, interruption, etc.)
   3. encouragement and affirmation or agreement (encouraging someone to talk; affirming what someone says)
   4. not wanting to claim something (e.g., "I don't know if this makes sense or not" or "I would never do this, but")
   5. politeness/etiquette
   6. humor
   7. personal stories
   8. page reference/evidence from text

9. teacherly moves
10. disagreement
11. attention to literary devices
12. seeking affirmation

2. Discourse
    1. *"Construction of some aspect of reality from a particular perspective" (Chouliaraki & Fairclough, 1999, p. 63); "Systematic clusters of themes, statements, ideas, and ideologies [that] come into play in the text" (Luke, 2000, p. 456.)*
        1. Adolescence
            1. Universal
            2. Adolescent as other
            3. Developing child/maturity
            4. Adolescent as needing protection
            5. Adolescent as savvy
            6. Adolescent as gifted
        2. Feminism/gender
        3. Good parenting/bad parenting or good/bad families
        4. Critical multiculturalism/structural inequity
        5. Liberal humanism/individual choice or circumstance
        6. Teacher
            1. Overworked
            2. Beleaguered
            3. Under surveillance
            4. Teacher knowledge/lack of knowledge
        7. Capitalism
        8. Popular culture
            1. Corrupting
            2. Useful
        9. YA lit. as moral guide
        10. Whiteness
        11. Book group as useful
        12. Racism/prejudice/social class divisions
    2. *The way the perspective is put forth*
        1. reference to book or author (or other person) as authority
        2. personal experience

     3. teaching story

     4. reference to another form of popular culture

     5. reference to specific section of book under discussion

     6. reference to book group history or members' particular frameworks

3. Voice

Language used for a particular category of people and closely linked to their Identity (Chouliaraki & Fairclough, 1999, p. 63). The way we use language to present ourselves in relation to others in the group and outside the group, or in relation to the text.

    1. Pronouns (particularly places where we shift within our own utterance or where the pronoun shifts from speaker to speaker; note all uses of We and You)

       1. affect

       2. cognition

       3. othering

       4. bonding

    2. Modality (should, would, could, may)

    3. Qualifiers

    4. Inarticulateness (e.g., not completing sentences), fillers, or apologizing

    5. Passive voice/active

    6. Register (word choice associated with various statuses and identities)

    7. Kinds of questions

       1. Probing or asking for elaboration

       2. Asking what someone thinks

       3. Asking what to do

       4. Asking to challenge

       5. Asking to speculate

    8. Repetitions

    9. Irony

  10. Intensifiers

  11. Strong statement (lack of fillers, many intensifiers, affect laden)

Cultural Models and Discourses of Masculinity: Being a Boy in a Literacy Classroom

Josephine Peyton Young
Arizona State University

CENTRAL CONCEPTS

Discourse—I use big "D" Discourse in the tradition of James Gee to mean ways of reading, writing, acting, valuing, dressing, and so on to be recognized as a certain sort of person. In this chapter, I am interested in particular Discourses of a popular male athlete and male literacy student.

Critical Discourse Analysis—I use Critical Discourse Analysis to study the big "D" Discourses and understand the social practices of the Discourses of masculinity and being a male literacy student. Critical discourse analysis includes an analysis of power, status, and language. Like Gee (chap. 2, this volume), I do not abbreviate critical discourse analysis as CDA. I do this to differentiate it from Fairclough's (1995) CDA approach.

Cultural models—In this chapter, cultural models serve as an analytical tool or thinking device during Critical Discourse Analysis. Cultural models are storylines or folk theories that tell members of a particular Discourse what are relevant and typical ways of being or doing. An example of a cultural model, *boys will be boys*, is prevalent within many different Discourses of masculinity. Cultural models do not just exist in people's heads, they are shared through interactions with other people, media, and texts (Gee, 1999).

Learning—In this chapter, I take learning to mean changes in social practices and ways of being (Discourses) over time. For example, a boy learns how to be a male of a certain sort as he interacts in his social contexts.

147

Theories about masculinities (e.g., Connell, 1995, 1996; Jackson & Salisbury, 1996; Martino, 1999) suggest that there are multiple Discourses (Gee, 1996) or ways of being and doing masculinity. Discourses of masculinity are constructed and reconstructed within social contexts such as family, school, sports, and workplaces and they change throughout history and cultures. These theories recognize that masculinities and femininities are constituted in relation to one another, and that some Discourses of being masculine hold more social status and power than others within particular social contexts (Connell, 1995, 1996; Jackson & Salisbury, 1996; Reed, 1999). Often, however, Discourses of masculinity are represented as stable and non-negotiable. For example, *machismo*, a concept associated with Hispanic masculinity, has been represented as a rigid set of practices such as domination of women, aggression, confrontational behavior, and a strict division of labor in the household (Klein, 2000). Recent research (e.g., Klein, 2000) found that there are varying degrees of machismo and Hispanic men are far more complicated and diverse than the generalized concept of machismo might suggest. Still the beliefs associated with the ideals of machismo linger and serve to perpetuate rigid stereotypes about Hispanic men.

Critical Discourse Analysis allows for the study of the Discourses of masculinity. In this chapter, I adapted Gee's (1999, chap. 2, this volume) guidelines for critical discourse analysis while using Fairclough's work (1995, chap. 10, this volume) to inform my interpretations. I (a middle-class White female) explored through critical discourse analysis how Chavo's (a middle-class Hispanic 18-year-old male) constructions of masculinity shaped his participation in school literacy practices and the way that school literacy practices and classroom contexts, in turn, shaped his understandings of what it meant to be a boy in a literacy classroom.

Chavo was aware, as early as middle school, of the different Discourse of masculinity (e.g., popular male athlete, nerd, skater) that existed at his school. To be recognized as a member of the popular male athlete Discourse—a Discourse to which he aspired—he took steps to hide his good grades and learned ways to pass English courses without reading the required texts. Chavo's story is not unique among adolescent boys. What is unique was his ability to articulate the practices of masculinity and literacy that he believed would help others recognize him as a certain kind of young man. Chavo was 1 of 21 adolescent males who participated in a narrative inquiry that explored what was happening with and to them in a variety of literacy classrooms in the southwestern United States (Young, Hardenbrook, Esch, Hansen, & Griffith, 2003). My purposes in highlighting Chavo's literacy stories are twofold: (a) to complicate simplistic notions of male stereotypes, and (b) to make visible the ways in which critical discourse analysis can allow us to understand the multiple Discourses that inform our beliefs and understandings of masculinities and literacy participation.

During the year-long study in which Chavo was a participant, I, along with four other researchers, observed in seven adolescent literacy classrooms (e.g., English, reading, humanities, and writing) and selected three male focal students from each site to observe and interview. We interviewed these male students and their teachers and parents about their literacy and gender beliefs and practices. We also wrote weekly field notes about the literacy class in general and the ways that the focal students participated in it more specifically. I was solely responsible for the data collection at the site where Chavo was a participant, and I conducted the analysis independently for this chapter.

Meant to add to the growing body of research about boys, masculinities, and literacies, the purpose of the study (Young et al., 2003) was to gain an understanding of what it is like to be a boy in an adolescent literacy classroom. This research was timely given the resurgence of concern over boys' achievement, especially literacy achievement, in schools (e.g., Beaupre, 2003; Lesko, 2000; Smith & Wilhelm, 2002; Young & Brozo, 2001). These concerns rose to near panic status in the United States after the rash of school violence in late 1990s, statistics showing declines in school achievement (Hedges & Nowell, 1995) and male college attendance (e.g., Fonda, 2000; Goodman, 2002) were publicized, and boys' high school reading and writing standardized test scores fell (Beaupre, 2003). For example, Sommers (2000) suggested that we are waging a "war against boys" (title), and Faludi (1999) wrote about betraying our boys and men. Our study was particularly concerned with the trouble some boys seem to be having in the area of school literacy. For instance, boys are three to five times more likely than girls to be placed in learning/reading disabilities classes (National Center for Education Statistics, 2000). Boys in elementary through high school score significantly lower than girls on standardized measures of reading achievement (Hedges & Nowell, 1995), and boys are less likely than girls to take advanced placement (AP) examinations (National Center for Education Statistics, 2000).

Some educators, journalist, and lawmakers are calling for quick fixes that rely on equal opportunity approaches to curriculum (Skelton, 1998). Solutions include returning the so-called femininized literacy classrooms back to the boys by hiring more male teachers, providing all-male classrooms, more male literacy role models, and using more *boy books*, which focus on stereotypical male interests (Brozo, 2002; Scieszka, 2003). These calls for reform tend to narrowly define masculinity and do not take into account the long history of the *boy problem* in schools (Tyack & Hansot, 1990). They also tend to reinforce stereotypical gender roles by pitting boys' literacy needs against girls' and promoting a "boys will be boys" ideology (Kimmel, 2000, p. 7). In addition, these solutions have not adequately addressed the social complexities inherent in Discourses of masculinity and

school literacy practices. It is my intention to highlight some of these complexities through the analyses presented in this chapter.

MASCULINITIES

Discussions that theorize masculinities are taking place within literacy education (e.g., Hinchman, Payne-Bourcy, Thomas, & Olcott-Chandler, 2002;
Martino & Meyenn, 2001; Rowan, Knoeble, Bigum & Lankshear, 2002;
Young, 2000; Young & Brozo, 2001). These discussions about the practices
of masculinity enable us to explore the ways that race, ethnicity, and social
class complicate the picture of boys' literacy achievements and school behaviors (Kimmel, 2000). It makes visible the practices of masculinity and includes masculinity in our discussions about gender (Kimmel, 2000). Discussions of masculinity also make visible the influence of social contexts and
diversity on how boys do and think about gender and literacy and inform
our thinking about the ways boys participate in school literacy.

Certain social practices and Discourses of masculinity come with more
social status, potential power, and social goods than others. R. W. Connell
(1987) used the term "gender order" (p. 91) to describe the hierarchies
present between and among the different ways of being masculine and
feminine. He theorized that the Discourses of masculinity interact with institutional and societal relations to negotiate and construct hierarchies
and differences. These differences and hierarchies are known as the gender order and are influenced by race, class, age, and sexual orientation. In
addition, the gender order is not static; it is constantly changing and creating relations of power between men and women and among men. The
gender order describes the political nature of Discourses of masculinity
and is important to keep in mind when thinking about boys and literacy
because it works to limit the way boys and men participate in literate activities in and out of school. For instance, boys and men who strive for membership in a more dominant Discourse (one that defines a *real man*) may
adopt particular literacy practices that they believe will identify them as a
member of that particular *real man* Discourse. These practices might include liking books with action-filled plots, identifying with male characters not female ones, and selecting books and other texts written by and
about men; or they might include withholding all participation in school
literacy practices. In other words, boys who wish to be viewed as a boy of a
certain sort (e.g., jocks, nerds, skaters, gays) will read (or not read), write
(or not write), and so on like others who claim membership in that particular Discourse of masculinity.

CRITICAL DISCOURSE ANALYSIS METHOD

This research depicts stories recalled by Chavo, his mother, and his humanities teacher of Chavo's lived literacy experiences. The stories were told to me during individual semistructured interviews with Chavo, his mother, and his teacher, and they reflect my observations in Chavo's senior-level honors humanities classroom over a 6-month period and my informal observations of him in the sports arena for several years. As I constructed the stories for this chapter, I used four analytic tools suggested by Gee (1999, chap. 2, this volume) for Critical Discourse Analysis. According to Gee, a critical discourse analyst may use all or selected analytical tools or tools of inquiry as "thinking devices" (p. 37). The four tools I used were (a) Discourses, (b) social language, (c) situated meanings, and (d) cultural models. Although all of these were useful in helping me understand the Discourses that influenced Chavo, because of page limitations, I focus primarily on cultural models for this analysis.

One of the analytical tools suggested by Gee (1999, chap. 2, this volume), the notion of Discourses, was used to frame my study. I sought to identify the Discourses in which Chavo, his mother, and teacher were members and understand how these Discourses informed their ways of thinking, speaking, reading, acting, and so on. The other analytical tools assisted me in this process and offered questions to guide my thinking about the data. The questions, adapted from Gee (1999), helped me look closely at the words, how they were put together, and what they might mean within Fairclough's (1995) three social contexts—local (the interview), institutional (school and family), and societal (Discourses of school literacy and masculinity).

The analytic tools, *social language* and *situated meanings*, assisted my analysis. Social language is the way a person speaks or writes to enact a particular identity (e.g., Chavo's use of the phase *it sucks* when he described the humanities class to his teammates so that he appeared to be a certain kind of guy). As I read the data, I asked questions such as the following adapted from Gee (1999) to determine how Chavo used language to represent himself in different social contexts: What social language did Chavo use in his conversation during the interview? How did this social language represent him? What sorts of discourse patterns indicate this?

Along with these questions, I also asked questions to help me understand the situated meanings given to spoken or written words in specific contexts (local, institutional, and societal) by the speaker/writer and the listener/reader (e.g., different meanings are constructed during an interview and an informal chat). For instance, I asked myself to consider what were the possible situated meanings of Chavo's words given that his words were spoken during a formal interview with a university researcher, within the institution of school, and from the point of view of his particular Discourse of masculinity.

In addition, I considered how social language and the situated meanings constructed during the interviews influenced the way participants used language to represent themselves and their ideas. For example, during an interview, Chavo told me that the humanities class "isn't motivational." He used language that defined him as a student within the context of a formal interview with a professor. Using the terms *isn't motivational* helped me to recognize him as an experienced student—one who knew the lingo of school and one who blamed the course for his disinterest. One reasonable meaning that I could infer from this statement was that Chavo did not like the class, but he did not want to come out and tell me this during the interview. Perhaps he was unsure if I would report back to his teacher or mother. Perhaps he did not want me to think less of him as a student, so he blamed the course. Interestingly, in speaking about the same class to a soccer teammate who was considering signing up for it the following year, I overhead Chavo tell him that the course "sucked." The term *sucked* in this context helped his teammate recognize him as a fellow teenage athlete who did not like English courses, especially this one. As with *isn't motivational*, the terms *class sucked* also placed the blame for his disinterest and dislike for the course on the course, but in more popular terms. In both instances, Chavo used social language to enact a particular kind of identity within different social contexts—one as a student talking to a professor, one as a fellow male athlete.

Cultural model is the fourth and major analytical tool used during my analysis. Cultural models helped me make visible and understand how Chavo's constructions of masculinity shaped his literacy practices and how, in turn, his literacy practices shaped his understandings of what it meant to be a boy in a literacy classroom. Cultural models are everyday storylines or theories that help individuals determine what is normal and typical within a particular Discourse. It is the beliefs, values, and attitudes held that inform what we say and how we act, read, and interact. Cultural models (Gee, 1999; Strauss & Quinn, 1997) are not static; they change as we read, experience, observe, and adapt to new situations, and they mean different things to members of different Discourse communities. For example, the cultural model, *boys will be boys*, means something slightly different to mothers, young boys, adolescents, coaches, and teachers. Using cultural models as a tool of inquiry led me to ask interpretive questions such as: What cultural models were relevant to Chavo, his mother, and his teacher? How consistent are the cultural models throughout the study? How do cultural models relevant to Chavo, his mother, and his teacher reproduce, transform, and create Discourses and the social practices associated with being male in adolescent literacy classrooms?

To construct stories about Chavo's literacy practices, I first read and re-read the data many times and asked the questions of the data related to the analytical tools of Gee's (chap. 2, this volume) critical discourse analysis guidelines. I selected snippets from the interview transcripts and observational data that seemed to answer my research question about what it was like for Chavo to participate in literacy classrooms and how his constructions of masculinity might have shaped his participation in school literacy. I organized the transcripts into lines and stanzas as defined by Gee (1999). Each line consisted of a single idea unit or a small piece of information, and a set of connected lines that were about a theme, perspective, topic, or image was considered a stanza. In other words, I left large portions of the transcripts intact and did not rearrange the lines of the transcripts. I titled each stanza to help me determine themes and perspectives of the speakers. The following is a stanza I titled, *Chavo Used to Read*. It represents an idea unit represented by a snippet of intact transcript.

Chavo Used to Read

In sixth grade, ah,
we had a list of all the honors' books and
I had my mom go pick up like four or five of those during the summer.
In sixth grade and
I read them all
and then seventh and eighth grade
I just, I don't know, I just decided not to do that anymore.

I then constructed a 27-stanza narrative that wove together transcripts from interviews I conducted with Chavo, his mother, and his teacher. Using Chavo's transcripts as the foundation for each stanza, I selected transcripts from Chavo's mother and teacher that informed Chavo's words. Breaking the text up in this way and asking the analytical questions of the data allowed me to make hypotheses about the cultural models of the speaker. I then separated the stanzas back by speaker in an effort to represent different perspectives about Chavo's literacy and masculinity.

In the following, I present stories about Chavo's literacies and masculinities in the words of Chavo's mother, teacher, and Chavo. I constructed stories using the word-for-word transcripts of the interviews with his mother, his teacher, and Chavo. I took out sound representations such as "um," "ah," and false starts to make the text more easily read (Institute of Oral History, 2001). I also deleted my interview questions that stimulated these responses. I reorganized the stanzas for the purpose of connecting ideas or themes, but did not rearrange the lines within each stanza, thus leaving most of the transcripts intact. Then within each story of Chavo, I took apart the transcript again and looked carefully at the form and function of the words spoken by each participant. For example, to understand the cultural models that were relevant to Theresa, Chavo's mother, I found that her use of reported speech (dialogue used in retellings of events such as I said . . . , he said . . .) served as evidence to support the cultural models informing her beliefs. I then isolated the reported speech and organized it into stanzas. This microanalysis of the transcripts helped me see more clearly how Theresa perceived Chavo's literacy experiences and facilitated my interpretation of the function that reported speech played in Theresa's story of Chavo. Likewise, in Ms. Brown's story of Chavo, I found her use of two descriptive nominalizations (compound nouns used to name a certain kind of person, place, think—e.g., a literature kid or a man's man) and reported speech to be powerful in determining the cultural models important to her. For Chavo's story, I focused my analysis on his use of I-statements (e.g., I know, I read) during the microanalysis of his transcripts. In each case, I isolated the specific words (e.g., nominalizations or I-statements) and thought carefully about what they were telling me about cultural models and Discourse.

STORIES OF CHAVO'S ADOLESCENT LITERACY EXPERIENCES

In His Mother's Words

Chavo's mother, Theresa, is Hispanic and the mother of four sons. Chavo is the next to youngest. For many years, she stayed at home with the boys and participated in their school and after-school activities. She recalled that Chavo spent long hours putting puzzles together when he was preschool age, and that he loved to sit on her lap and be read to when he was young. He would snuggle up to her and ask her to read his favorite books. In fact he was so interested in reading at an early age that she taught him to read before he entered kindergarten. Later when he was a bit older, Chavo's father took over the nightly reading by reading aloud to Chavo and his three brothers from classical and popular novels.

Literacy was an important part of Chavo's household. Both parents are strong readers, and the family always deemed education an essential aspect of their lives. As young children, Chavo and the brother closest in age to him played creatively, much of the time without toys, making up their own stories and games. As they grew up, they played outside sports with the neighborhood boys and engaged in computer games together and alone. When Chavo entered high school and his younger brother was in middle school, Theresa went back to school to become a licensed social worker. Chavo saw her reading and studying during the years in which she pursued her master's degree. He also observed his Euro-American father, a public health physician and university instructor, studying his medical journals, writing a textbook, and grading medical student papers. Chavo was surrounded at home with literacy and never lacked literacy texts and tools—books, magazines, newspapers, computers, paper, and so on. In fact, Theresa reported that Chavo read the sports section of the newspaper every day. The following snapshot presented in Theresa's voice is a brief overview of her memories about Chavo's past school literacy participation.

Chavo Was Not Challenged at School

I.
Chavo was reading by the time he was in kindergarten,
And, so by the time he got to first grade,
He was in the top reading group.

He always did like rules and he always followed them.
It was important for him, too, for other kids to follow the rules.
And if they didn't, that's when he had a bit of a problem.

I think he had beautiful handwriting.
Chavo was one of the best printers,
But he worked really hard at writing so that it was done within the lines and by
    the rules.

And I think, in elementary school,
He was really fairly popular
    simply because he was hardly ever in trouble.
But I think that his love for reading was always there.
He did a lot of reading all the time.

II.
In middle school, they did a lot of group stuff.
Chavo was one of their better students,
Followed all the rules, did all the things he was supposed to.
He would end up doing all the work so that the group could end up getting a
    high grade.
He worked really hard.

I think towards the end of eighth grade, he wasn't being challenged enough
    in his classes.
And he got by.
Even his written work, I started noticing, [the work was] not the quality that it
    had been.
I could tell and I questioned him about it and said,
"Chavo, what is going on here?"
And he said, "Well, it doesn't matter. They don't care. I'm still getting A's."
So, I basically got the group of teachers together

and I said, "You know, you're losing him because he's not being challenged."
And, one of his teachers,
I think his English teacher actually said to me,
"He's still making very high grades."
And I said, "He may be doing that but I am telling you the quality of his work
    has really gone down."

III.
I tried to convince Chavo that he ought to go to St. Anthony's (a Catholic
    boys' prep school) so he would be challenged.
And instead, we compromised by taking honor's classes at the high school.
And he actually got into the [high school honor's] program
    and he did very well.

IV.
But I think that as time went on
    and he got interested in cross-country,
I think that he lost the interest [in academics].
It [running] was very, very satisfying to him.
I think a lot of that has to do with the fact
    that he was very much more interested [in running],
It is very demanding and it physically wears you out.
But I think the other half of that is that,
I don't think that he really had a challenge.
And all honor's meant was that it was more homework.
It wasn't necessarily more interesting.

   Being male has nothing to do with it

I think that with Chavo, because of his really deep love for learning,
I don't think that [being a boy] ever mattered to him,
    what anyone would say, or kid him about doing his homework, or being a
    good student.
He thrives on being a good student.
I mean, that is a really big thing for him to be able to accomplish.
But, when I think of him being male, I think that he very early figured out
    that, first of all that he loved to learn these things,
    but second of all, because of his rules, he knew that in order for him to play
    sports, he was gonna have to make the grades.
I think that made sense to him . . .
And I think the overall riding factor in that was that he does have a real huge
    love for learning.

Two cultural models seemed to inform Theresa's perspective about
Chavo's literacy and academic achievement. The first one, and perhaps the
most striking, was the cultural model that teachers are responsible for mak-

ing school challenging and motivating for all students. Chavo began school as a motivated student and always tried to do his best. He was a good student and knew that a good student followed the rules. He had a love for reading that was facilitated at home. Beginning in eighth grade, things started to change for Chavo. His mother believed that this was at least in part due to the fact that his teachers did not challenge him to achieve more than the status quo. He learned quickly by the middle school teachers' responses to his work that he could get an A without working very hard or even doing the same quality work he had produced in the past. Theresa went to the school to point out this observation and was greeted by a teacher who did not seem to understand her concerns because, after all, Chavo was still making As.

What Chavo did find challenging in high school was running cross-country. Cross-country challenged him physically and mentally. He ran long cross-country courses through the deserts of the Southwest, over terrain full of cacti, snakes, and rocks in hot August and September temperatures. Theresa observed her son running and perceived that running competitively was very satisfying and challenging for her son. He was animated after running and was a cheerleader for his teammates who ran slower than he.

The second cultural model relevant to Theresa's thinking about Chavo's literacy was that gender had nothing to do with his participation in school literacy and other academics. She believed that peer pressure from the other kids in school had nothing to do with Chavo's doing or not doing his work. The only thing about being male that may have influenced Chavo, according to his mother, was his respect for rules—specifically, the rule that stated he had to make good grades to play high school sports.

To identify and describe the cultural models that were relevant to Theresa, I looked closely at what she said and listened to how she said it. The tone of her voice changed as she told stories about Chavo's literacy. Her voice was warm with the memories of Chavo learning to read and becoming a reader and good student. When retelling about Chavo's middle school years, her voice reflected the anger and disappointment she felt about Chavo's experiences with some of his teachers. She spoke quickly and with much animation as she retold his middle school, emphasizing her belief that teachers had a responsibility to make school challenging and motivating.

Another way Theresa represented relevant cultural models was through her use of dialogue or reported speech within her interview with me. Reported speech served several functions (Myers, 1999), including giving evidence, making stories more vivid and interesting, and shifting the focus of attention from the speaker. As Theresa told stories about Chavo's past literacy experiences, she included reported speech that depicted her past experiences with Chavo and his teachers and provided evidence of the cultural models relevant to her. For example, when she described her meeting with his teachers, she selected speech that best represented her belief that teachers should present challenging learning opportunities for students (e.g., "You know, you're losing him because he's not being challenged") and her belief that the teachers did not believe in the same way (e.g., "He's still making very high grades"; "They [the teachers] don't care, I'm still getting As"). Her use of reported speech was powerful and served to emphasize and support her beliefs.

Reflection and Action

What sorts of texts, experiences, interactions, and institutions might have given rise to Theresa's cultural models identified earlier? How are these cultural models reproducing, transforming, or creating social, cultural, or institutional relationships and Discourses?

In Chavo's Teacher's Words

Chavo's honors humanities teacher was Ms. Brown. She was a 30-year-veteran English teacher and chair of the English department. Her passion for the humanities and teaching was evident in and out of the classroom. She was a humanities major in college until she realized she needed to broaden her field to English if she wanted a teaching position. She told stories of the Greeks and Romans with such intensity and excitement that often I forgot the write field notes about what her students were doing at the moment. I was enthralled by her stories and found her to be an engaging storyteller. Most notable was her desire for her students to love the humanities. She believed that humanities was more than literature—it was a world of ideas.

Many of the students in her class were leaders in the school and most were very high achievers. She expected high-quality written and oral participation from these students and usually got it. Ms. Brown was very proud of her students, and she believed that most had been raised as renaissance people. By this she meant that they were raised to believe they could be good at anything regardless of their gender. Because of this, she posited, gender was not a factor in determining how the students participated in this class. She believed that the boys participated "every bit as much as her girls," and she explained the lack of boys in the class (6 of the 25 students were male) as a consequence of other senior English course offerings such as regular senior English and creative writing. However, she held other notions about who were and were not humanities or literature kids that were not so visible.

Chavo Is Not a Literature Kid

I.
Nothing, I know nothing about Chavo.
I said to Chavo about a month or six weeks ago
I said "Chavo, I know you don't like this class."
I said, "You remind me so much of my daughter,
    she didn't like it either and I know your mother's making you stay in here."
I said, "but would you just smile at me once in a while."

II.
He must be so bored with this stuff.
He would never, you know, I don't know if Chavo reads on his own,
    but I would venture to guess if it's not a sports magazine or a soccer journal,
    he doesn't.
He is not a literature kid from my perspective.
He's gotta B in the class.
No, it's not an easy class.
And he does his work
But he doesn't love it.
It's not awful.
It's just not inspired.

III.
Chavo has never voluntarily participated in the discussions all year.
He has never opened his mouth unless I call on him
    and then he gets all spazzled.
So I don't do that anymore
    because I don't want to embarrass him.
I'm just trying to bring him in.
So, now I just wait, but he's been more jovial.
He's smiling a bit more.
But he is definitely not a humanities kid.

IV.
And I don't know if it's because he's a boy or not . . .
My daughter is not a boy, she's quite tomboyish (chuckle)
[she did not like the humanities class]
So I don't know whether that's just gender.
I'd say with my daughter, (laughingly) she had too many headers [soccer term
    for passing the ball with one's head] and maybe that's Chavo's problem.
No, he doesn't seem, not bright,
He's just not interested.

V.
It's not like there's not precedent,
    my two best discussers are boys.
It's not like he couldn't if he wanted to.
I don't know that it's a gender issue.

Unless all boys are interested in math and science and all girls are interested
  in literacy,
    but I don't think that's true anymore.
I just think that it's a Chavo issue.
I don't think it's gender . . .
He is my least enthusiastic student.

One of the cultural models that seemed relevant to Ms. Brown was that
not all kids were literature or humanities kids. Along with that model, like
Chavo's mother, Ms. Brown held the cultural model that gender had nothing to do with participation or enrollment in the honor humanities class. Ms.
Brown appeared to have a picture in her mind about who were and were not
literature or humanities kids. They could be male or female; in fact, she believed her best discussers were male. She also knew who were not literature
or humanities kids—her daughter, a tomboyish athlete, was not a humanities
kid, and neither was Chavo. Her belief that certain kids were or were not literature kids seemed strong and most likely influenced her interaction with
these students. For example, she stopped trying to get Chavo involved in class
after seemingly embarrassing him by asking him questions. She finally just
asked him to smile once and a while. She denied that being male might have
influenced how Chavo participated or that being male had anything to do
with the lack of boys in her class. She believed that Chavo's disinterest in the
class and his lack of participation was a Chavo issue, nothing more, and she
explained that the low number of boys enrolled in her class was due to the
number of senior English courses available.

To represent the cultural models relevant to her, Ms. Brown, like
Theresa, used reported speech to describe an interaction with Chavo and
as supporting evidence for the cultural model that some kids are not literature kids. Most powerful in her representation of cultural models is her
use of two descriptive nominalizations—literature kid and humanities
kid—during the interview. By describing Chavo as not being a humanities
kid or literature kid, she compiled lots of information into a compound
noun. It is hard to know the exact information that went into the creations
of nominalizations by Ms. Brown (Gee, 1999); we would need to know
more about Ms. Brown's expectations and experiences as an English
teacher to completely understand. We are left wondering what the exact
characteristics of a literature kid or humanities kid are, and characteristics
of not being one. All we really know is that Chavo was not a literature kid,
he was the most unenthusiastic kid in the class, and his work lacked excitement. Nominalizations tend to turn concretes into new abstract entities
(Fairclough, 1992), like literature or humanities kids. Using the nominalizations effectively named him without clearly defining the process or
attributes of being or not being a literature/humanities kid.

Reflection and Action

What sorts of texts, experiences, interactions, and institutions might have given rise to Ms. Brown's cultural models identified earlier? How are these cultural models reproducing, transforming, or creating social, cultural, or institutional relationships and Discourses?

In Chavo's Words

Chavo entered the senior honors humanities classroom with a face of stone each day. All expression of affect was erased from his face. He walked in and sat down quietly. His face told me (and his teacher) that he did not want to be 1 of the 6 males in a class of 25 high school honors students. His facial expressions were supported by his actions in the classroom. He rarely spoke in class or entered one of the many whole-group discussions. He slouched in his seat, looked down or around, and seldom looked at the teacher. Often he closed his eyes or put his head on his desk.

It was hard for me to believe that this was the same guy who was captain of the cross-country and soccer teams. My two sons were on the same high school soccer team as Chavo, so I had observed him for 3 years as a student athlete. He was a leader and motivator. He was a role model for the other guys on and off the soccer field. He quietly led through mutual respect, loyalty, and friendship. The difference in his demeanor in the classroom and on the soccer field intrigued me. After a few months of weekly classroom observations, I invited him to be part of the study. I wanted to investigate what it was like for Chavo to be a student in this high school literacy classroom and explore how his constructions of masculinity might have shaped his participation in it.

Athletes Don't Read Books

I.
In sixth grade,
We had a list of all the honors' books and
I had my mom go pick up like four or five of those during the summer.
I read them all.
And then seventh and eighth grade,
I just, I don't know, I just decided not to do that [read the summer honor's books] anymore.

Where the Red Fern Grows [was one of the summer honor books]
I couldn't put it down, like I'd go home and read . . .
But non-stop and then when it ended I seriously did not want the book to end.
I was so caught up in the characters
I felt like I knew 'em and stuff

II.
I think, I found sports more interesting [than reading] and doing stuff.
I mean like in a house full of guys
    you can always find some kind of athletic activity to do.
Whether it's playing basketball
    or Nintendo or the backyard swimming.
And especially where we live,
    there's always kids like in our neighborhood.
And then we'd ride bikes, play tag, all kinds of stuff.
So somehow I just lost reading as a priority.

III.
I think also once you get involved in sports
    like you're s'pose to be known as like an athlete.
It's just like a lot of the [athletes]
    really don't even want to like talk about reading or so don't even read.
So you just kind of get caught up into that somewhere along the line, I guess.

IV.
I still tried to get good grades,
    got straight As in middle school.
And I just wouldn't like be loud about it
    or brag about it.

V.
The kids just like to harass each other in middle school
Yeah, if he's a good athlete
    like he's better than other people
I get kind of mad about that.
And then also I, if he is good at something else,
I probl'y, I guess probl'y, I'd harass him now [in high school]

VI.
[The last book I read] was *Grapes of Wrath* [in 11th grade]
That's when I stopped [reading]
Because we had a quiz on it
And then I got like a D on it and I had read the whole book.
It was picky questions, really picky and that's a thick book . . .
I decided, I could just skip reading and get the same grade.
And that's when I totally stopped [reading].

We read current events every week in Economics.
I always read the sports page.

Guys Participate Differently than Girls

I.
Well, I don't participate in that class [honors humanities] at all.
I don't really want to,
and I probably won't want to for the rest of the year.

I mean I don't know, I don't feel uncomfortable around those people
  because I've been in the same class with them since sixth grade.
But it's just different, like, when I'm with the sports team or whatever, like
  that really motivates me and stuff like that.
This class isn't motivational.

II.
Ms. Brown thinks it's important that everyone is heard.
So sometime or another you have to participate.
I don't know, it [being called on] makes me feel kind of like, it puts me on the
  spot, really.
And it kind of makes me feel like I'm a little bit less,
  or kind of, I don't know, like she doesn't think I know the answer.
And that is usually the case.
I don't think she should be doing it.
I think that she's trying to make us feel involved.

III.
Since there are less of us [guys],
I feel overpowered by the women.
And our teacher is a woman.
I really think that she's like a big time supporter of women.
How it's their turn to get the spotlight, all this stuff.
She's always talking about women's rights.
And, I just think she's more, this might not be true,
I just see that she's more lenient towards the girls.
Like if they're all involved in after-school activities, not necessary sports but
  other stuff,
Well since they're involved in other stuff that's academically like more chal-
  lenging,
They seem to get a lot more exceptions.
They turn in work late.
I feel like I can't even ask her if I can turn in something late
  because it's dealing with a sport
  and I think she'll just tell me no.

IV.
They [guys in class] say how they feel.
All the girls just think whatever the teacher says they'll just do it.
Some of us [boys] speak out against that.
A lot of guys don't like to do the work, especially they're senior year.

V.
Well, the first semester like
I sat in the back of the room.
Which was, I don't know, I wasn't really with any of my friends or whatever.
And there's a bunch of girls back there
  and so I was like having to listen to them and everything.
And so I switched seats.

Now I'm sitting with Dave and Peter and Johnny.
And I think we all basically feel the same about that class.
[I'm] more comfortable around them cause they're my friends.
And then I don't know, it could be that they're males, you know,
   'cause over on the over side there wasn't (any males).
I was sitting next to a bunch of girls
   and I felt really uncomfortable.

These stories portray the cultural models relevant to Chavo's life that seem to guide the choices Chavo made about his participation in reading and being an athlete. One of the models was that male adolescent athletes do not read (or admit to reading) and they do not excel in school academics (or let anyone know if they did). Kids would harass you if they found out you were good in both, he believed. No one liked someone good in sports and academics. Chavo made decisions about his literacy practices based on this cultural model. Even after good experiences reading the summer honors books in 6th grade, Chavo decided not to participate in the honors summer reading again and said that somehow he lost reading. It appeared that he lost reading to outside play and sports, but not entirely. He read the sports page every morning, read current events, and he read at least some of the required books for school until he learned in 11th grade that reading the book was not necessarily linked to success on a test about that book.

Chavo was a good student and a good athlete. This presented a tension for him. As early as middle school, Chavo learned how to cover up that he was a good student to be identified as a male athlete. In middle school, he learned to keep his grades quiet. In honors humanities, he addressed this tension by acting bored and disinterested and refusing to participate in class discussions while quietly maintaining a B average. I am left to wonder how he earned the B without reading at least some of the required texts or paying some attention in class. Perhaps turning in all the written assignments and being present in class was enough. Perhaps he secretly read the materials. Perhaps not. Chavo did not openly participate in the humanities, nor did he think he ever would. His actions in class made it clear that the class was not motivating to him. Sports motivated him, the humanities did not.

Chavo believed that girls and guys participated differently in the humanities classroom. This belief was informed by the cultural model he held about male athletes, literacy, and school and contributed to the way he participated in the humanities classroom. In this particular class, there were significantly more females than male students. This fact probably fed into his belief that girls participated in humanities more than boys. He reported that he did not feel comfortable sitting among a "bunch of girls." Yet he sat in this location for almost an entire semester. The girls, he said, always agreed with the teacher, whereas the guys would speak out against the teacher's point of view or about a given assignment. Eventually, Chavo moved (there was never any restriction about where to sit) to sit by some of the guys. These guys questioned Ms. Brown, and Chavo perceived that they felt the same way about the class as he did. They were also athletes and wore their varsity letter jackets whenever the weather permitted. Interestingly, moving next to these guys did not change his participation in class discussions. However, I observed that Chavo did speak to the guys during class and worked collaboratively with them on certain assignments.

Another way Chavo thought the girls were different than the guys was the teacher's response to them. He perceived that the teacher was more lenient toward the girls about late assignments, for example, because they were involved in after-school activities that might not be related to sports. He never tested this belief and continued to believe that girls got more exceptions than the guys in the class without ever asking Ms. Brown for an extension himself. He perceived that the teacher honored academic and service after-school activities more than those that dealt with athletics.

In both stories, what was most apparent in the form of Chavo's words was the strength of his convictions and the personal responsibility he took for his views and actions. Chavo's use of strong *I-statements* (e.g., I think, I read; Gee, 1999, chap. 2, this volume) made more visible to me the cultural models that were relevant to him. In other words, how he answered my interview questions, the structure or form of his language, helped uncover what cultural models were relevant to him.

Whereas Gee and Crawford (1998) used I-statements to look at differences in the talk of middle-class and working-class youth, I found I-statements to be useful in uncovering cultural models. In the 119 lines of the selected transcript, Chavo used 53 I-statements. I categorized the I-statements based on the kind of verb that followed the pronoun, I. The vast majority of I-statements were either cognitive (16) or action (24) as defined by Gee (1999; Gee & Crawford, 1998). Following Gee (1999), I defined cognitive statements as statements made about his thinking and knowing. I-statements such as *I don't know, I decided, I think,* and *I guess* fell into this category. His cognitive statements provided information, knowledge, and opinions about his beliefs and experiences with literacy. They served to explain and state his opinions about his past literacy experiences and interactions.

Chavo used nearly twice as many action statements as he did cognitive statements. His use of action-oriented I-statements tell more about his historical story of being a male athlete who lost reading. His I-statements—such as *I had my mom, I read, I'd go home and read, I found, I'd harass, I stopped reading, I switched, I'm sitting*—paint a picture of Chavo as a young enthusiastic reader who gradually changed as he learned others' expectations of him as a male athletic and student and the social practices of the Discourse of male athlete to which he aspired. The action I-statements he used demonstrated how he took responsibility for his actions. Chavo's use of I-statements led me to believe that he perceived himself to be in control, that he consciously made decisions about his identity, and that he strongly believed that popular male athletes do not read (at least in public). He also believed that guys and girls participated differently in literacy classrooms.

When describing his experiences in the humanities class, much of his speech was laced with emotions and feelings as he reported his literacy experiences to me. Words and phrases such as *harass, uncomfortable, feel kind of on the spot, feel like I'm a little bit less, make us feel involved, feel overpowered by women, more comfortable,* and *I feel like I can't even ask her* exemplify the difficulties young men like Chavo may feel as they navigate the terrain of being male and participating in school literacy. It is interesting that he is so aware of and open about his feelings and emotions associated with being a male student in the class.

Reflection and Action

What sorts of texts, experiences, interactions, and institutions might have given rise to Chavo's cultural models identified earlier? How are these cultural models reproducing, transforming, or creating social, cultural, or institutional relationships and Discourses?

IN THE RESEARCHER'S WORDS

The Situated Meanings of Being Chavo

My story of Chavo is from the perspective of a White, middle-class university researcher, the mother of two of Chavo's teammates, and a past high school literacy teacher. My perspective is influenced by the stories told by Chavo, his mother, and his teachers and my past research and reading on masculinities and literacy. I have a great interest in boys, literacy, and the influence that Discourses associated with sports have on literacy and schooling, in part, because of my two sons. I have watched as one of my sons quit reading as a high school student and as the other never developed a love or respect for reading. I also remember the boys who hid in the back of my classroom to read paperback books and magazines when I was a reading teacher at an alternative high school. I have long wondered about boys and literacy and have read with great interest theories of masculinities and boys and literacy. I want to understand the complexities of being a boy and doing literacy and the multiple ways social contexts and Discourses of masculinity influence boys' participation in school and school literacy.

What I find so interesting in the stories of Chavo is the power of cultural models to shape beliefs and actions related to literacy and masculinities. Chavo defined masculinity as having to do with strength, courage, sticking up for what you believe, and responsibility as the following transcript depicts:

> Someone who shows like strength and courage, and
> Has the ability to stick up for what they believe.
> And someone who is willing to do whatever it takes . . . like on an everyday basis.
> Like when you're older going to work everyday, that kind of thing.
> Of just going to school everyday and just getting what you have to do and like getting it done.
> My dad (epitomizes masculinity)
> Because . . . he could be getting paid a lot of money [as a doctor in private practice], but instead he is working for people that really can't afford the health insurance and stuff. He's working for those kind of people and manages to find money to provide for his family. Sometimes he worked on weekends, he did what he had to do to support his family. And if we ever have a problem we go to him. . . .

The cultural model of masculinity exemplified by his father's actions played an important role in Chavo's constructions of masculinity and being a student. He learned to incorporate and emulate this model of masculinity into the Discourses he claimed membership. The attributes of masculinity—strength, courage, sticking up for your beliefs, and responsibility—were evident in how he represented himself through language and social practices.

Chavo looked like an athlete. His muscular body, brown skin, and big dark eyes provided him the look of an athlete. He worked out regularly in the school weight room and ran to stay in optimal shape. He pushed himself in the weight room and bragged to his teammates about the number of pounds he could lift. On occasion, I observed him and his teammates measuring their biceps to compare arm sizes and amount of growth. His clothing also helped others recognize him as a certain kind of young man (Harris, 1995). He selected clothes to wear such as tight t-shirts and baggy shorts or athletic wear, which accented his muscular, athletic body. If that did not do it, he wore team garb and his varsity jacket to school with many letters and awards sewn onto it. No one could mistake it, he was an athlete.

Chavo acted the part. In addition to being a good athlete, he was known to be a tough competitor and good leader. He was well liked and respected by his peers, as evidenced by being voted captain of two sports teams—soccer and cross-country. He took responsibility for leading the cross-country teams to a state championship—this required both physical and emotional strength. As he positioned himself as a popular athlete, Chavo earned the respect of his peers and worked to *not* be recognized as a good student. Yet he was. His mother knew he was and was frustrated that his teachers did not challenge him. His humanities teacher did not know him as a good student, but made assumptions based on his status as an honor student. He started hiding his inclination to be a good student in middle school when he stopped reading honors books and stayed quiet about his grades as he learned the practices of the Discourse of popular boy athlete at his school. By his senior year in high school, he was an expert at doing his version of popular male athlete and student. No one would doubt that he was bored and did not like humanities. His whole body told the story, and he never spoke during class discussions. Yet he took responsibility for doing what had to be done to make a good grade. He exemplified the practices of masculinity he revered in both social contexts—school and sports.

Surprisingly, Chavo, the good student, became visible during the last month of school. He won the contest for the best end-of-year humanities project. The project was designed to synthesize and extend what they had learned about humanities. The students selected a modern-day thinker, artist, and activist and made video or computer presentations about a common cultural theme the three shared. Chavo and the two guys he sat next to in humanities focused their presentation on three people associated with sports—Jerry Colangelo (great thinker who brought professional sports to Phoenix), Michael Jordan (great artist), and Chris Berman (a sports anchor and activist)—and demonstrated how they contributed to a culture that treated sports in similar ways as the ancient people did religion. His group worked long hours on the script and video presentation to integrate what they had learned about human thought and culture with modern-day cultural concerns and emphasis on sports. His voice was the narrator on the video, giving rise to Ms. Brown exclaiming after the video showing, "I haven't heard you speak that many words all year." Chavo's group project was deemed "the best" by his classmates and teacher. He was recognized with a monetary prize and the grade of A on the project. One is left to wonder whether this is the kind of challenging curriculum his mother hoped for and what might have happened if Chavo had been asked to do similar kinds of literacy activities before the last month of school.

Although both Chavo's mother and teacher hold a cultural model that gender does not matter, Chavo believed girls participated differently. Gender, or his beliefs about what it meant to be masculine in a literacy classroom, played a role in the decisions Chavo made about literacy participation. This was especially evident in the humanities class, where he reported feeling overpowered by women in the class and did not like the way the girls acted in class. The sheer numbers of female students made him uncomfortable. He believed there were differences in how girls and guys approached literacy courses. He participated in the way that he thought would best represent him as masculine. For example, he felt it was important to stick to his beliefs, although they were different than the teacher's. He did not think the girls did this. For him, the Discourse of popular athlete included being masculine—strong, courageous, responsible, and having strong convictions. He demonstrated these qualities in the class as he resisted his teacher's enthusiasm for humanities and his mother's belief in reading, all the while making good grades and excelling in a class literacy project.

In addition to strong beliefs that gender did not matter, Chavo's mother, teacher, and Chavo held firm notions of what counted as acceptable literacy practices. Even though he pronounced he did not read anymore, he confessed to reading the newspaper daily, particularly the sports pages. This apparently did not count as reading, but was an acceptable literacy within this particular Discourse of popular male athlete.

It is important to note that in my analysis of Chavo there is only a hint about influences of social class and ethnicity. While Chavo's mother is Hispanic, she and her husband share many of the same middle-class values and expectations as Chavo's teacher and myself, the researcher. All of us live in the same neighborhood, go to the same grocery stores, send our kids to the same schools, and share similar hopes and dreams for our children. Chavo's brown skin, dark hair, and Hispanic heritage did not come up in any of the interviews, although I suspect it is always present in his interactions with others. I wish I had asked Chavo's mother how she thought her Hispanic heritage might have influenced the teachers' response to her when she requested more challenging curriculum for Chavo and how she thought it influenced Chavo's beliefs about his own masculinity and literacy practice. I also wish I had found out from Chavo how being Hispanic might have influenced his belief is different cultural models about masculinity and literacy or if it did at all. Further, I wish I knew how it influenced Chavo's past teachers' academic expectations and interactions with him. These unanswered questions are limitations to my analysis, and answers to these questions are needed to fully understand how Chavo learned to be a boy in a literacy classroom and multiple ways of being masculine.

Critical Discourse Analysis involved moving back and forth between the microanalysis of the transcripts to the macroanalysis of social practices and cultural models. Using Gee's tools for analysis made the analytical process systematic and allowed a balance between looking at the form and function of language and the larger social contexts. It highlighted the tensions associated with being male and participating in literacy practices and made visible how the cultural models of Chavo and individuals close to him impacted how he was a boy and how he participated in literacy. It also provided insight into the ways that practices of masculinity and literacy are regulated and learned. Chavo sought to be a certain kind of male student—

one with high status among his peers. He achieved that status, but at what cost? We can only wonder.

RECOMMENDED READINGS

Gee, J. P. (1999). *An introduction to discourse analysis: Theory and practice.* London: Routledge.

Hicks, D. (2002). *Reading lives: Working-class children and literacy learning.* New York: Teachers College Press.

Hinchman, K. A., Payne-Bourcy, L., Thomas, H., & Olcott-Chandler, K. (2002). Representing adolescents' literacies: Case studies of three white males. *Reading Research and Instruction, 41*(3), 229–246.

Newkirk, T. (2002). *Misreading masculinity: Boys, literacy, and popular culture.* Portsmouth, NH: Heinemann.

Smith, M. W., & Wilhelm, J. D. (2002). *"Reading don't fix no Chevy's": Literacy in the lives of young men.* Portsmouth, NH: Heinemann.

Young, J. P. (2000). Boy talk: Critical literacy and masculinities. *Reading Research Quarterly, 35,* 312–337.

REFERENCES

Beaupre, B. (2003, March 9). Boys, not girls, on worse end of education gap. *Chicago Sun-Times.* (Retrieved March 13, 2003, from http://www.suntimes.com.)

Brozo, W. G. (2002). *To be a boy, to be a reader: Engaging teen and preteen boys in active literacy.* Newark, DE: International Reading Association.

Connell, R. W. (1987). *Gender and power: Society, the person and sexual politics.* Stanford, CA: Stanford University Press.

Connell, R. W. (1995). *Masculinities.* Oxford, UK: Polity.

Connell, R. W. (1996). Teaching the boys: New research on masculinity and gender strategies in schools. *Teachers College Record, 98,* 206–235.

Fairclough, N. (1992). *Discourse and social change.* Cambridge, England: Polity.

Fairclough, N. (1995). *Critical discourse analysis.* London: Longman.

Faludi, S. (1999). *Stiffed: The betrayal of the American Man.* New York: William Morrow.

Fonda, D. (2000, December 2). The male minority. *TIME Magazine.* (Retrieved March 13, 2003 from http://www.TIME.com)

Gee, J. P. (1996). *Social linguistics and literacies: Ideology in discourses* (2nd ed.). Bristol, PA: Taylor & Francis.

Gee, J. P. (1999). *An introduction to discourse analysis: Theory and method.* London: Routledge.

Gee, J. P., & Crawford, V. M. (1998). Two kinds of teenagers: Language, identity, and social class. In D. E. Alvermann, K. A. Hinchman, D. W. Moore, S. F. Phelps, & D. Waff (Eds.), *Reconceptualizing the literacies in adolescents' lives* (pp. 247–264). Mahwah, NJ: Lawrence Erlbaum Associates.

Goodman, E. (2002, September 4). What a surprise: College gender gap in deemed in crisis. *Arizona Republic,* p. B9.

Harris, I. M. (1995). *Message men hear: Constructing masculinities.* Bristol, PA: Taylor & Francis.

Hedges, L., & Nowell, A. (1995, July 7). Sex difference in mental test scores, variability, and numbers of high-scoring individuals. *Science, 269,* 41–45.

Hinchman, K. A., Payne-Bourcy, L., Thomas, H., & Olcott-Chandler, K. (2002). Representing adolescents' literacies: Case studies of three white males. *Reading Research and Instruction, 41*(3), 229–246.

Institute of Oral History. (2001, April 14). *Oral history workshop on the Web: Transcribing style guide.* (Retrieved January 31, 2003 from http://www.baylor.edu/Oral_History/Styleguide. html.)

Jackson, D., & Salisbury, J. (1996). Why should secondary schools take working with boys seriously? *Gender and Education, 8,* 103–115.

Kimmel, M. S. (2000). *The gendered society.* New York: Oxford University Press.

Klein, A. M. (2000). Dueling machos: Masculinity and sport in Mexican baseball. In J. McKay, M. Messner, & D. Sabo (Eds.), *Masculinities, gender relations, and sport* (pp. 67–85). Thousand Oaks, CA: Sage.

Lesko, N. (2000). *Masculinities at school.* Thousand Oaks, CA: Sage.

Martino, W. (1999). "Cool boys," "party animals," "squids" and "poofers": Interrogating the dynamics and politics of adolescent masculinities in school. *British Journal of the Sociology of Education, 20,* 239–263.

Martino, W., & Meyenn, B. (Eds.). (2001). *What about the boys? Issues of masculinity in schools.* Philadelphia: Open University Press.

Myers, G. (1999). Functions of reported speech in group discussions. *Applied Linguistics, 20*(3), 376–401.

National Center for Education Statistics. (2000). *Trends in educational equity of girls and women.* Washington, DC: U.S. Department of Education.

Reed, L. R. (1999). Troubling boys and disturbing discourses of masculinity and schooling: A feminist exploration of current debates and interventions concerning boys and schools. *Gender and Education, 11,* 93–110.

Rowen, L., Knoeble, M., Bigum, C., & Lankshear, C. (2002). *Boys, literacies and schooling: The dangerous territories of gender-based literacy reform.* Philadelphia: Open University Press.

Scieszka, J. (2003). *Guys read.* (Retrieved June 24, 2003, from http://www.guysread.com.)

Skelton, C. (1998). *Schooling the boys: Masculinities and primary education.* Philadelphia: Open University Press.

Smith, M. W., & Wilhelm, J. D. (2002). *"Reading don't fix no Chevy's": Literacy in the lives of young men.* Portsmouth, NH: Heinemann.

Sommers, C. H. (2000). *The war against boys: How misguided feminism is harming our young men.* New York: Simon & Schuster.

Strauss, C., & Quinn, N. (1997). *A cognitive theory of cultural meaning.* New York: Cambridge University Press.

Tyack, D., & Hansot, E. (1990). *Learning together: A history of coeducation in American schools.* New Haven, CT: Yale University Press.

Young, J. P. (2000). Boy talk: Critical literacy and masculinities. *Reading Research Quarterly, 35,* 312–337.

Young, J. P., & Brozo, W. (2001). Conversation: Boys will be boys, or will they? Literacy and masculinities. *Reading Research Quarterly, 36,* 316–325.

Young, J. P., Hardenbrook, M., Esch, M., Hansen, K., & Griffith, A. (2003). *What's happening with/to boys in adolescent literacy classrooms?* Manuscript in process.

Chapter **8**

Language, Power, and Participation: Using Critical Discourse Analysis to Make Sense of Public Policy

Haley Woodside-Jiron
University of Vermont

CENTRAL CONCEPTS

Fairclough's Model:

Text—spoken as well as written language

Discourse practice—text production, distribution, and consumption

Social practice—discourse as ideology and power

Bernstein's Model:

Instructional discourse—discourse that creates specialized skills and their relations to each other

Regulative discourse—moral discourse that creates order, relations, and identity and ultimately controls instructional discourse

Pedagogic device—the relationship between *regulative* and *instructional* discourses

Political discourse provides the clearest illustration of the constitutive power of discourse: It reproduces or changes the social world by reproducing or changing people's representations of it and the principles of classification which underlie them. It also clearly shows the inseparability of ideational and interpersonal processes in discourse: it can reproduce or change the social world only in and through reproducing and changing social classes and groups—it works simultaneously on representations and classifications of people. The power of political discourse depends upon its capacity to constitute and mobilize those social forces that are capable of carrying into reality its promises of a new reality, in its very formulation of this new reality. (Fairclough, 1995a, p. 182)

Never has there been a time in our history when reading has captured the attention of state and federal policymakers more than now. Nationwide we have seen a tremendous increase in state legislation around reading and phonics (Paterson, 1998, 2000). This change is not only represented at the state level, but also at the federal level. We experienced the No Child Left Behind (NCLB) Act and Reading First legislation, which increased U.S. federal reading funding from $300 million in FY 2001 to more than $900 million in FY 2002. NCLB links this increased funding to "scientifically proven methods of reading instruction" (NCLB, 2003, p. 2). These changes mark a significant shift taking place not only around reading, but also around the role of elected officials in defining how to teach. Traditionally, issues of pedagogy or how to teach specific content has been left to the educational experts (i.e., teachers, administrators, higher education). These more recent trends in policymaking, however, take a different approach—one that pushes against constitutional rights for local control.

These shifts have not taken place in a vacuum. In newspapers across the country, we hear about all children reading on grade level by Grade 3—that there is a crisis in education, and that scientific research should be the basis for most if not all decision making. Despite the barrage of this agenda and the convincingness of the media and agenda setters, we need to complicate these discourse practices of cultural models and expertise. Instead of assuming that they are correct, we need to reach the text, discourse practices, and social practices behind them (see Coles, 2000; Edmondson, 2000).

By combining the works of Fairclough (1992) and Bernstein (1996), this chapter explores the use of Critical Discourse Analysis (CDA) as a tool in the critical analysis of public policy. Through the close analysis of changes in reading policies in California between 1995 and 1997, this research seeks deeper understandings of how power operates in policy. Specifically, it analyzes the texts, discourses, and social practices that describe, interpret, and explain how reading policies get taken up.

As Fairclough suggested, policies define how we are to act and by what rules we must abide. Through public policy we come to be socialized into what is thinkable and unthinkable (Bernstein, 1996). As such, policy represents the authoritative allocations of values and goals (Ball, 1990). These cultural models (Gee, 1996, 1999) or understandings about the world position people in specific ways. Although it is easy to point to the evidence of power in policymaking and policy documents, it is quite another thing to be able to show *how* that power is generated, the role individuals play in that power structure, and the implications that those lines of power have for policy consumers. Given this complex web, a critical analysis of policy is necessary—one that pushes past questions of efficiency and outcomes to questions of "how power is used to define the parameters of particular questions, to set the rules for particular practices, and to shape particular agendas" (Edmondson, 2002, p. 114).

Prunty (1985) presented policy as an agenda or set of objectives that legitimizes the values, beliefs, and attitudes of its authors. He argued that issues of how problems arise and appear on agendas, how issues are developed, how policy is developed, and how policy is implemented are each important features for critical policy analysis.

Kingdon's (1985) framework for policy analysis speaks to this view of analysis, offering explicit analyses of how policy windows are actually created, the policy professionals who develop shared understandings affecting policy, the role of insider/outsider groups, and the policy tools used to translate policy goals into concrete actions. Although this framework addresses much of what Prunty called for in the critical analysis of policy, it does not engage us in critical social analysis or inquiries into how such political power constructs (and is constructed by) larger social practices. Ultimately, critical analyses of policy, rather than simply accepting the given goals of existing institutions and policies as fact, complicate policy to include inquiry into underlying issues of power and ideology embedded within the definition of the perceived problem and solution. Although more recent analyses of reading policies in the United States make explicit the political nature of policymaking, they do not lead us to examine how political power with respect to dominant voices actually flows throughout (or drives, as the case may be) the policy domain (Woodside-Jiron, 2003). Helpful in thinking about the different layers of inquiry necessary in this sort of policy analysis is Fairclough's (1992) frame for CDA.

CDA, BERNSTEIN, AND POLICY ANALYSIS IN CALIFORNIA

Fairclough and CDA

Fairclough (1992) named discourse as a mode of action—one that is socially constitutive. He identified texts, discourse practices, and social practices and how they each come together to carry constructive effects. In his framework, he adopted a Hallidaian (Halliday, 1978) definition of *text* as spoken as well as written language. Discourse practices involve the processes of text production, distribution, and consumption. Social practices represent discourse as ideology and power.

As Rogers (chap. 11, this volume) points out, local, institutional, and societal levels of interpretation necessarily take place at each of the text, discourse practice, and social levels of analysis in CDA. This makes sense because the local, institutional, and societal levels each contribute to our full understandings of the given phenomena at hand. What I argue here is that placing these in relation to one another as essentially envisioned through the societal level of analysis in CDA is complex and requiring of a more systematic theory and analysis of relationships than is found in Fairclough's frame for CDA (e.g., Chouliarki & Fairclough, 1999; Fairclough, 1992). What is often missing in CDA is the specific analytic procedures—something that Bernstein's framework offers to CDA.

Bernstein and the Pedagogic Device

Bernstein's (1996) work sheds light on this issue by offering a specific theory of relationship among the various levels of discourse under study. Specifically, Bernstein presented the *Pedagogic device* reflecting the relationship between *regulative* and *instructional* discourses. In his framework, Bernstein presented *regulative* discourse as the moral discourse that creates order, relations, and identity and ultimately controls instructional discourse. Instructional discourse is that which creates specialized skills and their relationship to each other. Bernstein suggested that the regulative discourse ultimately controls the instructional discourse. By placing these discourses in detailed relation to one another and examining how the regulative discourse actually shapes the instructional discourse, we begin to understand the pedagogic device or specific power relations between the two. The charge to the researcher combining this frame with Fairclough's CDA is to thoughtfully and systematically identify these discourses (i.e., texts, discourse practices, social practices) as regulative, instructional, and pedagogic so they can be then examined in relationship to one another, offering a more complete understanding of the social analysis present in CDA (see Table 8.1). This again offers a way for the critical policy analyst to explore not only the presence of power structures in social change, but also *how*, specifically, power structures influence social change.

Understanding that the text, discourse practice, and social practice referred to in Fairclough's CDA, and that the instructional discourse, regulative discourse, and pedagogic device (respectively) in Bernstein's work are combined in my use of CDA in critical policy analysis, I (for the ease of discussion) refer to them simply as text, discourse practice, and social practice throughout the rest of this chapter.

Fairclough and Bernstein's Frames in the Context of Critical Policy Analysis

Using the CDA frame in the critical analysis of policy draws attention to particular texts, discourse practices, and social practice issues that are particularly relevant to thinking about the engineering of social change

TABLE 8.1
Combining Lenses to Inform Critical Discourse Analysis

Fairclough/ Chouliaraki	Bernstein	Implications for Research/ Reflexivity
Local context: Interactions or outcomes of the institutional context	Instructional discourse: What is thinkable/unthinkable	Places where things are being redefined for the larger public (language/text). Issues of genre or ways of interacting
Institutional context: Social and political institutions that frame the local context	Regulative discourse: Dominant forces, voices, or decision makers	Governing bodies that name those redefinitions (organization/discourse practice). Issues of discourse or representing
Societal context: Larger governing bodies including policies, mandates, and political climates that influence the local and institutional contexts	Pedagogic device: Relationship between the two. Sociological nature of pedagogic knowledge. What makes this kind of communication/ phenomena possible?	What larger context/ideas make this arrangement of knowledge and decision making possible? (cultural models/norms/member resources/social practice) Issues of style or ways of being

through language and practice. In working to understand how policy and power fit together in creating change, Fairclough (1995a, 1995b) referred to *cruces tension points* as moments of crisis. These are times when things are changing or going wrong. What is significant about these moments in time is that they provide opportunities to deconstruct the various aspects of practices that are oftentimes naturalized and therefore difficult to notice. These moments in time are particularly interesting to watch in terms of the language practices being used. They often shed light on language practices that naturalize relations of power and domination (Rogers, 2003). Here policy documents, documents that serve to redefine current thinking that have high circulation rates, and specific events where particular voices, ideas, or agendas are brought to the front and acted on all become important sites for investigation.

The rest of this chapter is focused on understanding policy changes that took place around reading in California between 1995 and 1997. This inquiry is designed to go beyond describing and interpreting these changes to explaining them through the use of CDA. As such my research questions include: How did such radical changes between 1995 and 1997 in how reading and reading instruction were conceived in California occur? What made such upheaval possible?

Methodology

California was selected as the site for this particular inquiry for several different reasons. First, the state of California has the largest population in the United States, with 5 million elementary and middle school-age students currently being affected by the reading policies recently put into place. Second, California is the second largest textbook adoption state. The textbook market is a fiercely competitive market. Whichever publishers win California adoption typically win a huge chunk of the national textbook market (Manzo, 1997). Therefore, the legislated reading policies being passed in California inevitably find their way into textbooks and thousands of classrooms across the nation. Many students and teachers across the entire country are affected by California's policies by default. Third, California provides an extremely visible account of considerable policy change over a relatively short amount of time facilitating critical conversations around change—questions ignored in the functional analysis of policy. This politically important case sampling strategy (Kuzel, 1992; Patton, 1990) allows a particular advantage in making explicit how policy can be used as a means to create social change with respect to teaching and literacy learning—a method that has perhaps since been used in other states to introduce and mandate "systematic, explicit phonics" and "phonemic awareness instruction." Each of these factors in California combines to influence the way in which reading is to be taught in California, ultimately influencing students' apprenticeships into literacy (Collins, 1995; Egan-Robertson, 1998; Ferdman, 1990; Gee, 1996; Mahiri & Godley, 1998; Mertz, 1996; Vygotsky, 1978).

Data

The data for this study were collected most intensively over a 2-year period of time extending from 1995 to 1997. During this time, formal and informal documents were collected. These *texts* were both written and oral in nature. They included legislated policy documents, official state education agency documents, professional listserve and private correspondence, newspaper articles, and documents from popular media sources with high circulation rates such as *Time* and *Newsweek*. Related *discourse practices* were also included in the data set. Following the political climate of California, historical context data were drawn from significant events that took place in California around this new body of policy. These historical events included electoral events, shifts in the organization of educational decision-making procedures specific to California's governance system, temporal links between various documents, and legislative hearings (videotapes) where consistent and influential voices were present. Combining discourse analysis with ethnographic approaches in this way allows researchers to explore cultural models and how they interact with moments of change. This combined approach allows researchers to examine how educational processes and practices are constructed across time and how discourse processes and practices shape what counts as knowing, doing, and being within and across events (Gee, 1996, 1999; Gee & Green, 1998; Rogers, 2003). While steeped in this collection process, detailed field notes and research journals were maintained to record analytical decisions and explanations of *social practices* over time and to provide researcher reflexivity. Fairclough (1995a) noted that this third level of analysis is the most explanatory and thus requires such a system of accountability.

Analysis of Text

Fairclough (1992) suggested that the analysis of spoken and written texts can be organized under four main headings: vocabulary, grammar, cohesion, and text structure. Particularly interesting in the critical analysis of policy are features of text that speak to the genre (Chouliarki & Fairclough, 1999) of policy. Specifically, the vocabulary used while presenting new rules about the way people are to function and the way in which policies are written so as to produce cohesion are of particular importance. Here authoritative sentence structure in the introducing of new information and the intertextual features of the text work together to create cohesion (which is neither a property of a text nor the interpreter, but rather the intersection of the two).

For this analysis, I have broken the text into information units (Halliday, 1994) and identified *theme* and *rheme* in the sentence structure to interpret their structural role in the introduction of new information. Also it is productive to look at the nonstructural features of text that contribute to particular interpretations of text and social change. Specifically, I look at the use of determiners in establishing authority and facts as well as the consistency of vocabulary in contributing to the cohesion of the overall text. Analyzing these texts is important because of the *intertextual* and *interdiscursivity* nature in establishing a perceived consensus during a time of policy change.

Analysis of Discourse Practice

Interesting in the critical analysis of policy through CDA is how policies are layered on top of one another to create cohesive collections of policy. Through repetition and constantly being pointed to as authority, these texts come to be established as fact or normal when they are simply individual texts packaged together. Also important in studying the production, distribution, and consumptions of these texts is the social and politi-

cal context from which they come. In this study, I point to the opening of
policy windows in California and the way in which new policies and text
are strategically linked to established texts to promote *minimal resistance*.
Further still, I interpret the ways in which people are actually forced to
consume the policy through mandatory and monitored professional development experiences.

Analysis of Social Practice

In my research I have found it necessary to analyze text, discourse practice,
and social practice in the more detailed context of the pedagogic device and
its instructional and regulative discourses. Although I adopt the language of
text, discourse practice, and social practice, my analysis is the blending of
that with Bernstein's pedagogic device linking text with instructional discourse, discourse practice with regulative discourse, and social practice with
the pedagogic device. This extension blends nicely with the more recent
thinking about CDA and local, institutional, and societal analyses (see
Chouliarki & Fairclough, 1999). Again although each of these levels is ultimately a part of thorough analysis in CDA, putting specific text, discourse
practices, and social practices in the context of their local, institutional, and
societal influences makes more clear the social phenomena and constitutional power of the given relationships. Here I pay particular attention to the
way in which consensus is actually *crafted* by influential policy professionals
both in the context of legislative policymaking and the popular media. Here
we are able to explain levels of participation in the construction of new
knowledge and think about how that new knowledge gets presented. In looking at the legislative and public contexts, we can begin to explain how particular individuals and research were strategic in the development of legislative
policy and the preparation of the public for these policies through the popular media. Being able to then turn these understandings back on the prior
analyses of texts and discourse practices in relationship to one another, as
Bernstein's frame allows, strengthens my analysis of social practices and how
people come to be positioned in various ways. Having introduced critical
policy analysis into the frame of CDA, now let us explore one such case
study of policy.

THE LANGUAGE OF POLITICS AND THE POLITICS
OF LANGUAGE IN CALIFORNIA READING POLICY

As I analyze the changes that took place throughout California's reading
policies, it is interesting to watch the ways that a seemingly small assumption grows up to mandated teacher practices and instructional materials. As
I show here, the first of the five policies presented, "the fundamental skills

required" in reading, which would then, throughout subsequent policy, become the stem from which basic instructional materials and current and confirmed research would be named.[1] As each of these policies gained speed individually and collectively, the restrictive nature of the policy increased further narrowing decision-making processes and the definition of reading, teaching, and learning. By engaging in this close analysis of changes that took place over time, I am able to not only describe the changes, but push further to explain how these changes occurred—an important feature of CDA.

Text

Halliday (1978) noted, "there is a systematic correspondence between the semiotic structure of the situation type (field, mode, tenor) and the functional organization of the semantic system" (p. 32). As one analyzes spoken and written texts in CDA, one is at the same time addressing questions of form and meaning.

Texts and Themes in the CDA of California's Reading Policies. In January 1995, A. B. 170, the first of five bills that would later redefine reading in California, was introduced. These bills collectively influenced how reading was to be defined, the instructional materials made available, and mandatory teacher inservice training. These bills were strategically used to focus California's attention on "the fundamental skills" in reading. Although a relatively small policy document, it served as a springboard for those to follow in helping create a perceived consensus around reading, teaching, and learning in California.

Given this surge of California legislation and the tremendous impact it had in creating radical changes in California's state documents, instructional materials, and professional development experiences, it makes sense that these legislative documents would become data in the critical analysis of California policy. These policies (individually and collectively) represent radical changes in how California named reading in K to 3 and also the underlying assumptions about teaching and learning. Again particularly influential in initiating the changes in how California named reading was AB 170—the first policy.[2]

---

[1]We are seeing this at the federal level today too as NCLB legislation links this increased funding to "scientifically proven methods of reading instruction" (NCLB, 2003, p. 2).

[2]Although the larger analysis (Woodside-Jiron, 2002) studied California State Frameworks, Every Child a Reader, and so on, here we look at the first piece of reading legislation that was passed because it represents cruces or a moment of change that would have interdiscursive and intertextual implications and effects throughout the other policies and the larger public discourse.

Making the Unfamiliar Familiar Through Text Structure. Throughout the bills in California, there was an underlying assumption or assertion (no small difference there) that there were some predetermined "fundamental skills required)" in reading. This language was first introduced (and mandated) through Assembly Bill 170 (1995a), Instructional Materials.

Fairclough (1992) highlighted that, "it is always worth attending to what is placed initially in clauses and sentences, because that can give insight into assumptions and strategies which may at no point be made explicit" (p. 184). In the analysis of the semantic relationship between information structure and thematic structure, Halliday (1994) noted that generally a speaker will "choose the Theme from within what is Given and locate the focus, the climax of the New, somewhere within the Rheme" (p. 299). *Theme* can most easily be defined as the initial part of a clause, whereas *rheme* is the later. This particular type of writing—where new information is linked with given, more familiar information in legislation—is important because it provides a set of conditions that exploit the potential of the new information being presented. *New* information here does not necessarily mean brand-new methods of instruction or definitions of reading. To be sure, California has experienced several cycles of more and less phonics-based methods of reading and instruction throughout its educational history. Rather new here in this analysis means new with respect to its presence in the given conversation. For example, in 1987, "these details [phonics, word attack skills, vocabulary, and the conventions of language], when taught, should be in context and not in isolation" (Honig, 1991, p. 110). In the 1999 framework, however, "students first learn to apply and practice decoding and word-attack skills in carefully controlled, decodable texts" (California Department of Education, 1999, p. 4). A significant shift has taken place here with respect to how reading, teaching, and learning were being presented in California's framework. The phonics and word recognition approach is considered new because it provides such a contrast to the previous framework, which emphasized meaning. Let us now look at the language of the first bill (A. B. 170, 1995a) with a critical eye for how new and given information were actually positioned within the text to ensure particular interpretations.[3]

1. 600200.4. (a) The State Board of Education shall ensure that the basic instructional materials that it adopts for mathematics and reading in Grades 1 to 8, inclusive, are based on the fundamental skills re-

---

[3]Note that these have been broken into information units (Halliday, 1994) and the theme is left as is, whereas the rheme is underlined.

quired by these subjects, including, but not limited to, systematic, explicit phonics, spelling, and basic computational skills.

2. (b) It is the intent of the Legislature that the fundamental skills of all subject areas, including systematic, explicit phonics, spelling, and basic computational skills, be included in the adopted curriculum frameworks and that these skills and related tasks increase in depth and complexity from year to year.

3. It is the intent of the Legislature that the instructional materials adopted by the State Board of Education meet the provisions of this section.

We can see specific patterns in how tensions between language and language structure present opportunities to make the unfamiliar familiar. These ultimately represent struggles over meaning and truth. The first information unit begins with a theme possessing a given:

1. "The State Board of Education shall ensure that the basic instructional materials that it adopts for mathematics and reading in grades 1 to 8, inclusive . . ."

California has long been a textbook adoption state (Honig, 1991; Manzo, 1997). The State Board of Education is the governing force in this process. Therefore, the given information in the initial positioning of this sentence refers to this long-standing policy of textbook adoption. The new information is then presented in the final position of the sentence:

1. are based on the fundamental skills required by these subjects, including, but not limited to, systematic, explicit phonics, spelling, and basic computational skills.

The way in which this new information follows an already established fact relays to the reader a sense of order and logic. Here new ideas are attached to more familiar ideas, thus naturalizing the new concept at hand (Fairclough, 1992, 1995b). In the next sentence, this new information is picked up and placed in the initial position, thus relaying that it is now *given* information and used to introduce additional new information:

2. (b) It is the intent of the Legislature that the fundamental skills of all subject areas, including systematic, explicit phonics, spelling, and basic computational skills, be included in the adopted curriculum

frameworks and that these skills and related tasks increase in depth and complexity from year to year.

Here policymakers strategically link yet another established policy (curriculum frameworks) with the newly introduced "systematic, explicit phonics." However, specific attention was also being given to the order and sequence of skills to be taught ("increase in depth and complexity"), which again marks a change from previous legislative authority. These maneuvers typically feel obvious and natural to the reader given their flow and reference to already established policies. They have come to be naturalized. In essence, however, they represent the privileging of particular ideologies and paradigmatic commitments.

Finally, the authors of A. B. 170 use the last information unit in this sample to reiterate the purpose of the document:

3. It is the intent of the Legislature that the instructional materials adopted by the State Board of Education meet the provisions of this section.

In summarizing new information in this way, the authors make what was initially unfamiliar familiar. The information that sounded new at the outset of this policy ("the fundamental skills required," "systematic, explicit phonics," sequential "depth and complexity") is now established as fact ("*the* provisions of *this* section"; italics added). Although here in A. B. 170 views about reading, teaching, and learning are manipulated via theme and rheme, later in the 1999 framework these same principles of order and complexity attain the status of fact claiming "the reality that standards in the earlier grades are building blocks for proficiency in the later grades" (California Department of Education, 1999, p. viii)—a significant shift.

Here, in part through the structuring of the text, the elected officials have come to naturalize new information that was not present in California's reading policies immediately prior to that time, thus knowingly changing the language being used in conversations around reading and reading instruction. In essence, they are claiming a moral high ground of sorts from which they are able to establish moral order as a given. This particular method of structuring policy text (genre) is important.

Whereas the analysis of theme/rheme and the structuring of given/new information inform our understanding of how meaning is organized at the elemental level, the analysis of *lexical cohesion* offers an understanding of the ways in which continuity is established in text via the use of key words, their repetition, and other words that are used as synonyms. Analyses of these nonstructural features are important in that they also can give any passage of text the status of fact—an important tool in influencing the readers' construction of text.

Lexical Cohesion: Fact or Foe.   One discourse practice often present during times of change in educational policy is the use of specific new terms to name what is important or of value in the given policy (Fairclough, 1995a). These terms are often difficult to identify because they are presented with such authority and *ofcourseness* that we tend to pass over them. For example, "systematic explicit phonics instruction" is repeated time and time again throughout California's reading policies between 1995 and 1997. This phrase is repeated in documents from State Education agencies as well as the popular media. These terms are used as places where particular views of reading, teaching, and learning are systematically mandated.

In the first information unit described earlier, *the fundamental skills required* for reading were introduced. This new information is then repeated in each of the subsequent information units[4] that follow and warrants our attention in terms of how it is used to mandate new definitions of reading and instructional materials.

Significant in the phrase "*the* fundamental skills required" (italics added) is the presence of the word *the*. In this case, *the* is a *determiner* (Gee, 1999), which serves as a cohesive devise communicating that there is some finite and stable set of skills that have been identified that correlate with reading achievement. Although *the* is a seemingly tiny word, it carries with it a tremendous amount of power. It serves in this context to signal some universal agreement on how reading is acquired. It assigns the status of fact to phonics as the fundamental or primary skill required in learning to read. In keeping with the previous analysis of text, such specific skills would typically be introduced earlier in the document, and then the determiner *the* would link back to them. This would indicate that that information was assumed to be predictable or known on the basis of the preceding sentences. Here, however, *the fundamental skills* is only defined later by the newly introduced *systematic, explicit phonics* with respect to reading, thus marking the introduction of new and favored information. It is as if *the fundamental skills* is used to initially arrange a general commonsense agreement among the audience members and is then returned to later and used interchangeably with *systematic, explicit phonics*. It is a discourse practice that has a quiet way of nursing the audience along in your way of thinking.

The intertextual nature of such structuring of change through various influential policy documents (formal and informal) necessitate the close analy-

---

[4]Here *the provisions of this section* refer to *the fundamental skill* further defined as "systematic, explicit phonics, spelling, and basic computational skills."

sis of text in understanding how new information comes to be established as fact. Particularly important in the intertextual chains throughout California's policy changes is the genre of policy. Specifically, the use of grammar and vocabulary in claiming authority while reducing resistance was significant. Together the use of grammar and vocabulary contributed to cohesion through consistency as new information became fact in these policies.

Differences in Discourse.   Toll (2002) suggested that simply investigating our words in discourse will not create change. She suggested that instead we need to open up the conversations about the differences in discourse. The use of CDA in critical policy analysis is one way to open up such conversation. Toll stated, "A key consideration in shaping the success of meta-discourses about school change is how educators deal with difference" (p. 152). This has implications for our classrooms both at the elementary/secondary and higher education levels. However, changing how educators deal with difference is a complex process to say the least. We know this from the research on teacher change. This is made even more complicated in the current educational policy context because there are restrictive measures being placed on how educators are, in fact, able to respond to the given change.

As we see as we begin to engage in the interpretive analysis of discourse practice in the changes taking place, California policy in mandating systematic, explicit phonics placed restrictive measures on teachers' professional development and knowledge. California legislation went so far as to mandate that "systematic explicit phonics instruction *does not mean* 'embedded phonics instruction' which is *ad hoc* instruction in phonics based on a random selection of sound and word elements" (A. B. 1086, 1997, p. 5; italics added). This means that the professional development that embraced or even entertained such a perspective would not (and did not) receive state funding, which is a huge regulative and restrictive exercise in power affecting how people are positioned. In this case, the opportunities to actually explore differences in discourse and how educators deal with difference are minimized, leaving Toll's advice for a metadiscourse about change defunct.

Discourse Practice

The analysis of discourse practice necessarily involves processes of text production, distribution, and consumption. By investigating these processes, we come to see how various member resources (Fairclough, 1992) are drawn on and how. Fairclough suggested,

> Pin-pointing the context of situation in terms of this mental map provides two bodies of information relevant to determining how context affects the interpretation of text in any particular case: a reading of the situation which foregrounds certain elements, backgrounds others, and relates elements to each other in certain ways; and a specification of which discursive types are likely to be relevant. (Fairclough, 1992, p. 83)

In other words, understanding how texts are produced, distributed, and consumed informs our understanding of how authors work to ensure particular interpretations of text and how this engages our various member resources.

Discourse Practices and Themes in the CDA of California's Reading Policies. During this period of change in California's legislative and state policies, larger political changes were also taking place. In November 1994, California Republicans gained control of the State Assembly, the majority of the nation's governors were Republican for the first time in decades, and bipartisan agreement over issues of education began (Carlos & Kirst, 1997).

At the same time that California's new reading policies were being mandated, California's system of educational decision making was also changing through the reorganization of power. Traditionally in California the State Department of Education (CDE) had been charged with turning legislative policy into more local policy (e.g., English/Language Arts frameworks designed to "share with teachers the state's educational philosophy, theory, current research, and best practices teachers are to follow" (Chrispeels, 1997, p. 459). The State Superintendent, Bill Honig, was significant in his role in overseeing this process. However, dismal test scores, fiscal improprieties, and bipartisan agreement with a back-to-basics agenda presented a unique policy window, and as the State Superintendent resigned, power shifted from the CDE to the State Board of Education (SBE). Important in California's educational governance system is the fact that members of the SBE are appointed by the governor who is the head of the Executive Branch at the state level. This meant that with the shift in control from the CDE to the SBE came more top–down power and political influence from elected officials via the governor's influence over the SBE. Instead of CDE members turning policies into action, now members of the SBE, handpicked by the governor, held this power. Also important is that this change took place in the context of fear and disbelief among the larger public in California. Again this represents another narrowing of decision making among a governing body that is responsible for much of the translating of legislation into local-level policy and instruction ultimately affecting California's teachers and students.

Assigning "Current and Confirmed Research."   One month after A. B. 170 or the Instructional Materials bill (1995a) was introduced in California, the second ABC bill, A. B. 1504 (1995b—Instructional Materials: Spelling), was introduced. This bill was introduced by the same legislators (Burton, Alpert, and Conroy) and was designed with the legislative intent of ensuring the adoption of "basic instructional materials."

In this second ABC bill, legislators specified the criteria for the adoption of instructional materials mandating that:

(1) The submitted basic instructional materials are consistent with the criteria and the standards of quality prescribed in the state board's adopted curriculum *framework*. In making this determination, the state board shall consider both the framework and the submitted instructional materials as a whole.

. . .

(3) The submitted instructional materials are factually accurate and incorporate principals of instruction reflective of *current and confirmed research*. (A. B. 1504, 1995b, p. 2)

There are two different features of this policy text that warrant our attention with respect to the institutional shaping of discourse. First, in this policy, legislators have made an explicit link between the frameworks that were, at that time, under revision and the textbooks that the SBE could approve. Aligning instructional materials in this way with "the state's educational philosophy, theory, current research, and best practices teachers are to follow" (Chrispeels, 1997, p. 459) is a pedagogic maneuver influencing both how reading is defined and how it is to be taught. Such legislated policies serve to place power over many among a small number of elected and appointed officials. It also reduces access to the naming of reading and reading instruction because fewer people are making decisions. Because of this decision-making structure or pedagogic device, there is little room for debate or conflict. Decision-making information is not provided, and public voice is not welcomed. The legislators mandating this link with a curriculum framework, which is ultimately, although implicitly, subjective and ideological, creates an understanding of and a compliance with a social order that, in this case, positions elected and appointed officials as authority.

The second feature of this policy sample is that "principals of instruction reflective of current and confirmed research" are introduced and named as criteria for selecting textbooks. Here "principals of instruction reflective of current and confirmed research" represent an intrinsic logic and favored agenda. Remember that this bill was making its way through the legislature at the same time dismal scores from the National Assessment of Educational Progress (NAEP) and California Learning Assessment System

(CLAS) were being reported and local and national newspapers were riddled with conversations about America falling behind, "scientific research," America Reads, and reading on grade level by third grade. Gee (1999) suggested that such understandings are simplifications about the world that leave out many complexities. Problematic is that cultural models like this can do harm by "implanting in thought and action unfair, dismissive, or derogatory assumptions" (p. 59).

As systematic, explicit phonics, spelling, and basic computational skills were boldly named among *the* fundamental skills in mathematics and reading in the first ABC bill (A. B. 170, 1995a) without explicit and grounded logic, so we see instruction being linked with current and confirmed research here in this policy. Although legislators go no further than to define the research that instruction is to be based on as "current and confirmed" in this particular policy, later this principal was extended and transformed considerably. Two years later in A. B. 1086: Reading Instruction (1997), *current and confirmed research* would be further defined as:

> (j) . . . "Current" research is research that has been conducted and is reported in a manner consistent with *contemporary standards of scientific investigation.* "Confirmed" research is research that has been *replicated* and the results duplicated. "Replicable" research is research with a structure and design that can be *reproduced.* "Generalizable" research is research in which samples have been used so that the results can be said to be true for the *population* from which the sample was drawn. (A. B. 1086, 1997; italics added)[5]

Control over such discourse defining reading and how it is to be taught (Bernstein's regulative and instructional discourse) ultimately creates the rules of social order in educational decision making. This process of top–down decision making by elected officials in deciding what is important in education and how to best implement related content and practices is significant. This is a process of *recontextualzation*—of redefining knowledge with respect to reading, teaching, and learning. It is the process of regulations being placed on the formation of a specific pedagogic discourse. This legislation serves to eliminate entire bodies of quality research, including qualitative research that report by means different from the replicable, generalizable "contemporary standards of investigation." Such a maneuver is a significant tool in naming what is thinkable and unthinkable in California's teaching of reading. As Bernstein (1996) suggested, it attempts to regulate those who have access to this site and in this way control alternative possibilities. We see this being done in the naming of instructional princi-

---

[5]It is interesting that these terms are all present in G. Reid Lyon's testimony before the Assembly Education Committee Hearing on Reading on May 8, 1996.

ples based on current, confirmed research complying with contemporary standards of scientific investigation in California's reading policies.[6]

Eliminating Resistance: A. B. 3482 and A. B. 1086—California's Teacher Training Bills. Up to this point, we have been talking about policy documents as if there is a direct relationship between policy and practice. Of course, this is not necessarily true, and policymakers know this. To ensure the success of policy, one must engage in discourse practices that eliminate as much resistance as possible. This can take many forms. In California it took the form of mandatory and heavily screened professional development for teachers.

Less than a year after both Instructional Materials or ABC bills had been passed (A. B. 170, 1995a; A. B. 1504, 1995b), Education: Teacher Reading Instruction (A. B. 3482, 1996) was introduced. This was the first of two bills dedicated entirely to influencing teacher inservice training. It mandated that:

> 44756. To be eligible for funds pursuant to this chapter, a school district shall certify to the State Department of Education that not less than 90 percent of its certificated employees who provide direct instructional services to pupils enrolled in Kindergarten or any of grades 1 to 3, inclusive, have received the type of inservice training described in [the policy].

Whereas the prior ABC bills had targeted instructional materials primarily, this legislation mandated that the vast majority of California's K to 3 teachers receive specified inservice training in how to teach reading. A. B. 1086 specified that teachers must abide by *developmental progressions* and that their instruction must be direct, systematic, and explicit. *Embedded phonics instruction* was not to be taught in these service training sessions because it was deemed by policymakers to be "ad hoc instruction in phonics based on a random selection of sound and word elements."

This policy was then followed by the last of the policies in California's surge in reading policies: Reading Instruction (A. B. 1086, 1997). This bill provided explicit details about the specific criteria for the teacher inservice training sessions mandated in A. B. 3482 (1996), again reinforcing Bernstein's ideas about the power in the pedagogic device used to regulate pedagogic communication and meaning potential with respect to reading, teaching, and learning via policy.

---

[6]At the national level, we see this being done through the Congressionally mandated review of research by the National Reading Panel. Their review included a restrictive screening process by which whole bodies of research were systematically eliminated.

One year later, the subsequent advisory report *Teaching Reading: A Balanced, Comprehensive Approach to Teaching Reading in Prekindergarten Through Grade 3* (Reading Program Advisory, 1996) was published. Principal authors of this 34-page advisory were the State Superintendent of Public Instruction, the SBE, and the California Commission on Teacher Credentialing. It was designed with the specific intent to "provide the policy direction and instructional guidance needed to support the improvement of reading achievement in California" (p. v).[7] Recognized as being influential in the content provided were 10 of the 27 authors of the earlier Task Force report issued the year before. Tracing the authors in this way is an important part of critical policy analysis because it enables us to further explore which voices are influential and which power sources dominate. For instance, the State Superintendency is an elected position in California, as is the office of governor. The SBE and this taskforce, however, were appointed positions controlled by Governor Wilson and State Superintendent Eastin at that time. Making explicit the pedagogic device, who controls knowledge, and how control over time, text, and space come to exist (Bernstein, 1996) is essential in the critical analysis of policy. Given that these reports were intended to inform policy and resulted in more prescriptive policies, we see how increased control over issues of educational content and instruction are situated among a relatively small number of elected and appointed officials. Again these connections represent the naming and distribution of influential ideas and ideologies about reading and reading instruction in California.

Teaching Reading is in direct response to the recommendations outlined in the report of the Superintendent's Reading Task Force, *Every Child a Reader* (September 1995). It is also designed to support two new statutes known as the ABC bills (Assembly Bill 170, Chapter 765, Statutes of 1995, and Assembly Bill 15, Chapter 764, Statutes of 1995), which require, in part, that the SBE adopt materials in Grades 1 through 8 that include "systematic, explicit phonics, spelling, and basic computational skills." The advisory amplifies both the recommendations of the Reading Task Force report as well as the new requirements in law, and it is offered as a policy statement rather than a "how-to manual" (Reading Program Advisory, 1996). Particularly interesting in our inquiry here are (a) the intertextual link and "support" for the previous ABC bill, and (b) the statement that *Teaching Reading* was not intended to be a "how-to manual."

The fact that this is a Reading Program Advisory means that it will be distributed to all of the schools in the state. As such the intertextual link with

---

[7]Baldwin referenced this report as if looking forward to it in a policy decision making in the May 1996 hearing.

the ABC bills and its support for such policy, *Teaching Reading* serves to add
to the cohesiveness of this movement in reading ideology toward systematic, explicit phonics instruction and current and confirmed research.

The second feature—the statement that *Teaching Reading* was not intended to be a how-to manual—is important in that it extends beyond
intertextual to intratextual relations.

Bernstein (1996) noted:

> In the case of texts in the field of the production of discourse the inter-
> textuality of the discourse is transformed into intra-textuality. A text in this
> field is expected to be original to have the highest renown. Ideally, it should
> be the first text of its kind and be the product of a single mind or a single
> dominating mind or joint minds. This text endeavors to proclaim its unique-
> ness and may contain strategies which mask, blur or differently position its an-
> tecedents. In this way inter-textuality is transformed into intra-textuality in the
> process of constructing unique authorship. (p. 53)

Although its authors express that *Teaching Reading* was not intended to
be a how-to manual, we find, in the same text, the contradictory intent
that it will "provide the policy direction and instructional guidance
needed to support the improvement of reading achievement in California" (Reading Program Advisory, 1996, p. v). These two intentions are in
conflict with one another. Although the Task Force states that it is not intended to be a how-to manual, they did state their intent that it provide
"policy direction and instructional guidance." The recommendations
from this document would later be found in the subsequent legislative
policy (A. B. 1086, 1997). Here we see a discourse practice being used that
leads readers to believe that this report is something that it is not creating
dissonance between what is being articulated and what is actually being
carried out. Bernstein (1996) referred to this as the carrier versus what is
carried. This makes manifest the institutional power that elected and appointed officials have in producing new information and ideas via such influential documents and legislation.

Institutional Arrangement and Power.   Throughout the development and
implementation of these policies, we witness Bernstein's (1996) regulative
discourse. As particular concepts such as *current and confirmed research* come
to be privileged and defined with more and more detail, we can see a narrowing of those doing the defining. Understanding this shifting of power
and the ways in which it changes the larger discourse is key in moving beyond recognizing the presence of power to understanding how such political power constructs and is constructed by larger social practices.

Social Practice

While understanding how texts are produced, distributed, and consumed informs our understanding of how authors work to ensure particular interpretations of text, the analysis of social practices makes explicit the connections between the discourse practices and the social practices of which they are a part (Fairclough, 1992). Discourse as a political practice is not only a *site* of power struggle, but also a *stake* in power struggle: Discursive practice draws on conventions that naturalize particular power relations and ideologies, and these conventions and the ways in which they are articulated are a focus of struggle (Fairclough, 1992).

The Role of the Expert in Influencing the Policymaking Forum and Building Consensus. Immediately following the first of the [teacher bills] (A. B. 3482, 1996), a special Hearing on Reading of the Education Committee of the California State Assembly was held on May 8, 1996 (Honig, 1996). During this hearing, former State Superintendent Bill Honig was called on to provide expert testimony. Throughout Honig's testimony, one of his main messages was that of a need for *consensus*:

> . . . this research that you are about to hear [NICHD research]. It's very powerful stuff. I think it *backs up* this consensus position. It shouldn't be a right, or left, or moderate, or at all. It really is what works with youngsters and if enough of us *get behind it* I think we're going to make a difference in California. (italics added)

During his testimony, Honig made several references to the "convergence of research and best practice," "the secret to getting a consensus position," "fashioning a message," "singing the same tune on this position," and the need for major players such as the State Board, Department of Education, legislators, governor, and educators to "get behind" this consensus message. His message was clear to the Assembly Education Committee: Together, they were *crafting* a consensus (Allington, 1999) for the educational institution and larger public to consume. This is an important point because:

> Particular interpretative principles come to be associated in a naturalized way with particular discourse types, and such linkages are worth investigating for the light they shed on the important *ideological functions of coherence in interpellating subjects*. That is, texts set up positions for interpreting subjects that are "capable" of making sense of them, and "capable" of making the connections and inferences, in accordance with relevant interpretative principles, neces-

sary to generate coherent readings. These connections and inferences may
rest upon assumptions of an ideological sort. (Fairclough, 1992, p. 84; italics
added)

Also during this hearing, G. Reid Lyon of the National Institute of Health
(NIH), then acting chief of the division of Child Health and Development,
among others, was invited to provide expert testimony with respect to reading research. During his testimony, Lyon made clear that phonemic awareness, phonics, and high-interest, decodable texts are necessary to ensure
the "fast, accurate decoding of words." Lyon manipulated his testimony to
best persuade his audience with respect to what is rational and what is not
in terms of reading and reading instruction (*thinkable* and *unthinkable* in
Bernstein's terms). Via his title, and supported by the cultural assumptions
about "science and research" that he brings and appeal to the Assembly's
common sense, he painted a simple picture of what reading is and how best
to go about teaching it.

The Education Committee assembled was chaired by Assemblyman
Steve Baldwin with Committee Vice Chairwoman Mazzoni. Nine months
later, they would become first and second authors of California's most restrictive professional development bill yet, A. B. 1086. During this special
hearing, Assemblyman Baldwin introduced Lyon to the rest of the Assembly
as clearly being *the* authority figure on reading.

Baldwin: How many years, Dr. Lyon, have you been involved in researching
           the reading issue?

Lyon: Since 1974

Baldwin: Since 1974? That has been your full time job?

Lyon: Well, for many years I was what you would consider a line re-
           searcher, that is, I was doing a good deal of the research myself.
           Because I am cross trained, I'm a neurobiologist neophysiologist
           as well as someone who has expertise in language and reading, I
           was recruited by the NIH which is the federal biomedical research
           arm to develop a research program in this area so that we could
           understand issues about child development and how they learn as
           well as the genetics and neurobiology.

Baldwin: Would it be accurate to say that you are probably the lead person
           within the federal government when it comes to research on read-
           ing issues?

Lyon: By way of the time I spend in it maybe more than my knowledge
           but yes.

Baldwin: Great, great. Please proceed with your presentation. (Lyon, 1996)

Through this introduction, Baldwin set the stage for the Assembly by presenting Lyon as *the* authority on "the reading issue." Lyon then proceeded in

his own testimony to further establish his credibility to the Assembly member quorum. He first linked himself with *real* science (e.g., neurobiologist neophysiologist, biomedical research, genetics). He then emphasized that he was "recruited" by the federal government to develop the research he was about to share. This discourse practice is effective in appealing to the Assembly members present and positioning himself as expert. Further, he emphasized that the NIH oversees 12 research sites around the country that are studying "the reading issue" to which Baldwin referred. He offered that the annual budget for NIH reading research is $14 million, and "since 1983 the cumulative budget looking at these issues that I'll talk with you about today is about $104 million dollars." Coupled with his prestigious introduction, this information serves to help secure his expanding authority among Assembly members. Not only was he recruited by the NIH based on his "expertise," but he also has serious federal money backing "my institute, the Child Health Institute" and the research that he shares throughout his testimony. Despite his deep investment in this particular collection of research, however, he strategically positioned himself as being "unbiased"—another important discourse practice in establishing credibility.

> Lyon: You wont hear me endorse any reading approach today or any reading method. That's not the job of the NIH. The job of the NIH is to distill the information so we understand "what does a human being have to do to be able to read?"

To be sure, Lyon has a vested interest in maintaining the health of the NIH research budget—his own paycheck depends on it. Yet he claimed to remove himself politically and ideologically from the testimony he was about to give—he was only there to provide the *distilled information* and *inform policy*. This image of distilled information relayed a message to the audience that they were about to receive "facts" about the "reading issue" in their most pure and unbiased form. This, of course, is misleading because as with any kind of inquiry come choices about which information is valued and which is dismissed. One of the more recent and visible examples of this is the Congressionally commissioned National Reading Panel and their *distillation* process. That panel, in attempts to "build on the recently announced findings presented by the National Research Council's Committee on the Prevention of Reading Difficulties in Young Children," limited the research that they reviewed and that would be used to "identify gaps in the knowledge base for reading instruction and the best ways to close these gaps" (National Research Council's Committee on the Prevention of Reading Difficulties in Young Children, 1998). Certainly this can be considered distilled information, but the remaining information is dependent entirely on the original solution or, in this case, research. Lyon knew that this was an issue in terms of validity and attempted to smooth over this conflict in his testimony:

> Lyon: An issue that stands in the middle of these discussions as you're having today consistently is, well, can't research show anything you want it to show? Why should one believe, for example, the research that Mr. Honig was talking about or I may present? And that's a very clear question that one needs to address. (Lyon, 1996)

This point from Lyon stemmed partly from previous attacks on NICHD research as being primarily based on narrow learning disabled student populations (see Allington & Woodside-Jiron, 1999), yet being used to inform large-scale instruction. In his testimony, he appealed to the Assembly's "common sense" and stressed that the NICHD research *replicates* this common sense. This tactic of naturalizing particular concepts is powerful. It serves to foster feelings among the Assembly members that these facts or ideas are so common sense that they are not worth debating and fit within their own frames of understanding. Lyon blended scientific language pertaining to the sampling techniques used in the research (e.g., "children in the main," "entire populations," "over time," "unbiased"). Of interest, however, is that his main defense against the prevailing argument—"Can't research show anything you want it to show?"—is to discuss simple sampling techniques, again perhaps a knee-jerk reaction to the public debate about the nature of the NICHD research being centered around the small population of children who were learning disabled, but also in response to the growing definition of *current and confirmed research.* This is telling nonetheless. Later in his testimony, when responding to a question from Assemblyman Baldwin about how researchers are actually able to "track a child's neurology as they go through different reading processes," he revealed the more complicated nature of inquiry research. As he explained the "expensive equipment" (Lyon, 1996) and the activities that children are doing while being tested, he said,

> It's easy to do, *it's extremely complex to figure out how to design the work and so forth* but we have nice replication on the fact that lousy readers, these slow, labored readers who are having difficulties getting the print off the page because not understanding that the sounds exist in words show us a different neurophysiological signature in brain and it's highly replicable. I would like to also say to Assembly Woman Kuhn . . . that lousy singers show us different signatures as well. [laughter]. (Lyon, 1996; italics added)

Here he briefly touched on the heart of the existing debate about much of the scientific research on reading (possibly by mistake), but then quickly redirected the Assembly's attention by first belittling it ("it's extremely complex to figure out how to design the work and so forth"). He then grounded himself comfortably in the language of replication. Understanding his audience and to hold their attention and interest, he again attempted to make personal connections with Assembly members through humor and appeal to common sense: "I would like to also say to Assembly Woman Kuhn . . . that lousy singers show us different signatures as well" [laughter] (Lyon, 1996). This reeled his Assembly audience in and he was rewarded with laughter, again reducing potential resistance and developing the feeling of common ground and familiarity among the audience present.

Lyon also appealed to the Assembly members present with the agenda of improving reading education by claiming what he believed to be an irrefutable truth: "If you don't learn to read, you simply don't make it in life." Such a declarative moral and causal statement fanned the flames of existing fears and tuned the ear of his captive Assembly member audience. After all, the Assembly members' job is to serve the people and preserve the peace. Surely finding a way to ensure that we "make it in life" qualifies as an agenda for immediate action. It primed the Assembly and positioned them as recipients for the distilled information and research provided in Lyon's testimony. He linked illiteracy with those who do not finish school, end up in prison, and become unwed mothers. Such presuppositions are effective ways to manipulate people because they are so difficult to challenge (Fairclough, 1992). Here they are presented as fact and in causal relationship. There is little room in Lyon's discourse practice here to challenge these assumptions because he distilled the information, insisting that he does not want to "belabor or bore" the Assembly with the "technical issues." Ultimately, this means they are not able to evaluate the information firsthand, but rather are forced to go on his own expert interpretation. There is little room for debate because of the moral high ground laced throughout his argument. As such, anyone who would get in the way of policy intended to "help children learn to read" would be seen as ultimately getting in the way of children and success. This is a moral battleground that few are willing to enter—especially those who are publicly elected and rely on people's votes. Here Lyon claimed the moral highground and positioned himself as a *good guy* in the battle for children's success.

Despite Lyon's admission that he is the lead person within the federal government by way of the *time* he spends in it versus his *knowledge*, he offered and claimed the authority to name reading as "fast, rapid, automatic decoding and recognizing of words" and "fast, accurate decoding of single words." He then identified phonological or phonemic awareness as the solution, which in just 9 short months would be found in the final policy and criteria for mandated inservice providers, effecting at least 90% of all California's primary teachers and their students.

The Role of the Expert in Influencing the Larger Public and Building Consensus. This consensus was also portrayed throughout the popular media during California's changes in reading and instruction policies. October 27, 1997, was a particularly interesting day in popular print media with respect to education and, more specifically, reading education. On this day, *both Time* and *Newsweek,* two of the most widely circulated and accessible print media sources, ran feature articles specific to how children learn to read. It was no small coincidence that these feature articles were distributed the week prior to when the Reading Excellence Act (1998) was to pass through Congress, reinforcing the consensus position that Honig referred to earlier (see Coles, 2000; Taylor, 1998).

The *Newsweek* (Wingert & Kantrowitz, 1997) reporter reported that:

> Researchers have identified *four* distinct steps in learning to read; breakdowns anywhere in this process can explain severe reading problems. G. Reid Lyon, acting *chief* of the child-development and behavior branch of the National Institutes of Child and Human Development, says that reading for all children begins with phonological awareness. (p. 60; italics added)

Note that it is the reporter and not G. Reid Lyon speaking himself—an interesting reporting style because it removes the reader from the original source of information. We saw the same authorial move by Lyon in his testimony when he said things like, "I don't want to belabor or bore you" with the technical details (p. 7). We also experienced this in Honig's testimony when he made broad claims about the NICHD research as being "powerful stuff." We also hear this in many, many different arenas as people claim "the research shows" yet do not provide the original research so that the intended audience can decide for themselves.

This *Newsweek* quote goes on to complete the list of four steps that include linking sounds with specific letters, becoming fast readers, and finally concentrating on the meaning of the words. This information is the same that Lyon presented in his testimony before the Assembly.

It is interesting to note that, in this article, Lyon's *voice* consumes more space than any of the other experts or researchers referenced throughout the article. Also Lyon is introduced with the long and authoritative title of "acting chief of the child-development and behavior branch of the National Institutes of Child and Human Development" attached to his name. This use of status, as in the prior legislative hearing, lends him credibility as an expert throughout this article.

In the *Time* (Collins, 1997) article, Lyon is again referenced directly—this time on the heels of two other well-known researchers. The reporter in this article foregrounded similar steps to learning to read via these researchers and then went on to say:

As the 1990s progressed, more verification of the importance of phonemic awareness came from studies conducted by the National Institute of Child Health and Human Development at the National Institutes of Health. Under the direction of Reid Lyon, *researchers have found* that problems with phonemic awareness correlate extremely closely with reading failure. Other NICHD studies have reaffirmed the conclusions reached by Chall and Adams—that programs with some systematic phonics instruction lead to better outcomes. (p. 80; italics added)

There are a number of important features in each of these reports that deserve our analytical attention as we seek to better understand the ways in which change is engineered via discourse. In essence, it is the active construction or manufacturing of a perceived consensus both in terms of the problem at hand and the solution. The first is the authority given to research. Throughout the prior texts, research *identifies, verifies, finds,* and *reaffirms conclusions.* These are powerful and uncontested actions in this context. From these claims specific assumptions about reading, teaching, and learning are advanced. As we saw in the legislative changes discussed earlier in this chapter, such claims have significant impacts on how children come to experience reading and reading instruction in the classroom. In keeping with Bourdieu's (1991) theory that "the power of suggestion . . . is the condition for the effectiveness of all kinds of symbolic power that will subsequently be able to operate on a habitus predisposed to respond to them" (p. 52), understanding the specific ways by which policymakers and scientific research are placed in positions of authority and how they relay certain understandings about knowledge and our role in the production and consumption of knowledge is essential because it is *constitutive.*

What we see through these discourse practices is the fashioning and naturalization of the message that both Honig and Lyon were speaking of in their expert testimony before the Education Committee of the California State Assembly. In naming reading as a series of set steps and in explicitly focusing on a narrow body of research, reading in California was redefined and recontextualized. These ideologies and agendas that I have been making explicit in this analysis were then effectively distributed through what would be the last of California's reading bills to date. These points are important because they push our thinking about the intersection between the text and the reader. Understanding this relationship makes more explicit and offers us the opportunity to explain the ways in which learning takes place throughout the many facets of policymaking (e.g., participation in policymaking, the way in which participation—limited or not—positions people, and the structural power that that contributes to in the policymaking process and, in this case, the power of few over many).

Benveniste (1977) suggested that, through such political use of expertise, policy advocates consolidate a monopolistic position by promoting the appearance of an external professional consensus on a policy issue. Lyon and Honig's testimony points to the inevitable presence of power and politics in decision making. Gee suggested that we do not have a reading crisis in our schools. Rather, we have an *affiliation crisis*. To affiliate with particular people, practices, institutions, methods, and so on is to "participate fully in the attitudes, values, and norms the practice requires" (Gee, 2001, p. xviii). This is not realistic for many students coming in contact with legislated and one-size-fits-all policy, curricula, and assessments. We need to find ways to engage in larger dialogue and systematic research about how the ways in which literacy-related social practices do and do not recruit children's affiliation (Gee, 2001).

DISCUSSION

Extending critical analyses of policy to include explanations of how political power constructs and is constructed by larger social practices is an important process because policy is constitutive. It serves not only to distribute, but *mandate* such ideals across a much larger forum—the educational institution and its members. As we have seen here, the close analysis of text, discourse practice, and social practice through CDA extended by Bernstein's theory of relationships makes explicit the ways in which text, discourse practice, and social practice come together to foster social change. Across all three of these dimensions was the drive to created consensus and restrict potential resistance.

Typical to information structures, we saw in California's policies the ways in which text was structured to ensure particular interpretations. In the close analysis of text, we saw how informational units were structured so that given information preceded the new. Structuring text in this way contributes to what is known as the "good reason" principle (Halliday, 1994, p. 308; see also Habermas, 1996, for a more thorough discussion) and ultimately constitutes the internal resources for structuring the clause as a logical, grounded message. This contributes to the process of *naturalization* (Fairclough, 1992).

Analyzing this process of naturalization in the structural analysis of text, we come to understand they ways in which ideologies are embedded in discursive practices and made more effective by becoming naturalized. When this happens, the ideologies and discourse practices attain the status of common sense and become difficult to recognize or push against.

Naturalization takes place not only in the structural elements of text, but also in the nonstructural elements. Lexical cohesion through consistent vocabulary or reference to "current and confirmed research" also builds cohesion and helps naturalize a text. Regardless of whether there is intrinsic logic to "current and confirmed research," the ways in which it is promoted and imposed on the educational institution are what Bernstein (1996) called *social facts*. In transmitting this particular idea about how things are and should be, policymakers are positioning themselves in a rather dictatorial way, which means that others must be more passive and receptive. At the core of this naming of what counts and what does not is a power relation between dominant and passive participants, thus influencing principles of selection.

As elected and appointed officials force changes in the terms that we use, the focus of our attention changes theoretically, creating similar conversations among larger populations and thus altering what is perceived as normal or right. By doing this, resistant readings of the policy are reduced by way of anchoring new and often vague terms against specific bodies of research, proclaimed experts, and instructional materials. In changing which instructional resources are to be made available and prohibited, we not only further influence what practices and conversations are likely to take place, but also the potential content and pedagogical knowledge made available to teachers. The implications of such positioning are major in that such discourse methods actually gather steam from the people being systematically eliminated from them in the first place. Also important is that the readers contribute to this unknowingly because the text is structured to be seamless and naturalized.

Understanding the shift in California's system of educational decision making in power (CDE to SBE), we must also look at *how* the ideologies and agendas represented by influential players were advanced both within the policymaking forum and among the larger public. Studying the relationship between power and ideology in this way extends Fairclough's attention to text and context via CDA. "Particular interpretive principles come to be associated in a naturalized way with particular discourse types, and such linkages are worth investigating for the light they shed on the important ideological functions of coherence in interpellating subjects" (Fairclough, 1992, p. 84).

The presence of the NICHD research in these policy development forums, as well as the ways in which it is naturalized and effectively distributed, cannot be ignored. It represents a body of research that has been hand picked by the federal government and policymakers, which many have been passively selected as *the* authoritative source on reading and reading instruction. Influential reviews (sometimes including second- and third-generation published research) as well as the physical presence of NICHD researchers and staff members in legislative sessions have influenced how reading has come to be defined and taught via legislation in California.

As reflexive and critical discourse analysts, we must make decisions about how to interpret, describe, and explain texts, discourse practices, and social practices. Bringing Bernstein's pedagogic device to CDA offers us the opportunity to understand how text, discourse practice, and social practice represent the elements of social analyses that Fairclough highlighted (i.e., social matrix, orders of discourse, and the ideological and political effects of discourse). In placing text and discourse practice in relation to one another in this way, we come to see not only the function of language in change, but also the social network that underlies the degree of success or failure to impact change that language and discourse practices can have.

CONCLUDING THOUGHTS

"Like other features of classroom life, the literary culture of a classroom is created through social codes and practices that authorize particular worldviews" (Lewis, 2001, p. 174). As we have seen here, educational policy has a strong hand in shaping these social codes and practices. The critical analysis of policy using CDA offers an exciting way into analyzing how power is used in producing and effectively distributing various ideologies, discourse practices, and texts in society and schools. In understanding how power works, we are more sensitive to the ways in which it often works to produce or reproduce power structures representative of and beneficial to the status quo (Giroux, 1997).

Fundamental to this mode of critical policy analysis is the explicit analysis of the process of naturalization in policy development, policy communication, and policy implementation. This is especially important because the procedures and practices may be politically and ideologically invested and because these procedures and practices position people in specific ways. In this *naturalization* processes or shaping of cultural models, some norms are brought to the center and others are pushed to the margin. In the case of policymaking around reading in education, select policy players and policy informants took center stage while parents, teachers, administrators, taxpayers, and students were pushed to the margin. How people participate in the language and power of policy has effects on their surrounding social structures, social relations, and agendas. Often this is an invisible process that strengthens the language, power, and participation processes. This is particularly problematic when participating in this way continues to push select populations to the margin and silence them from the conversation. Such hegemonic processes must be not only brought to light, but aggressively pushed against and restructured.

As researchers and leaders in education, it is essential that we become better at communicating such practices to the larger public being supplied with these crafted consensuses around such constructs as *scientific research,* *reading crisis,* and one-size-fits-all solutions like *systematic, explicit instruction.* Such balances of power and orders of discourse have serious implications. Such manipulative (discursive) practices shape our children and their literacy learning experiences. CDA as a framework for analyzing power and cultural models offers a promising means to better understand the links between policy and those who experience policy firsthand and offers a social lens for change.

Reflection and Action

1. Visit the U.S. Department of Education Web site (http://www.ed. gov/nclb/methods/reading/edpicks.jhtml?src=rt) and explore the ways in which reading is defined through the No Child Left Behind Act. What specific language is used with respect to reading? [Text]

2. What are the ways in which "scientifically based research" is currently being packaged? What is the intertextual nature of the research being promoted? Consider the impact factor of the Web site and the capacity it has for the distribution of information. [Discourse Practice]

3. What effects might the way that reading is being defined have on how children come to experience learning to read? Are there alternative viewpoints? Do those alternative viewpoints represent marginalized populations? How might this ultimately affect teaching and learning? [Social Practice]

RECOMMENDED READINGS

Atkinson, T. S. (2002). "We're not just whistling Dixie": Policymakers' perspectives on state education reform. *Reading Research and Instruction, 41*(4), 289–308.
Fairclough, N. (1995). *Media discourse.* New York: Oxford University Press.
Hastings, A. (1998). Connecting linguistic structures and social practices: A discursive approach to social policy analysis. *Journal of Social Policy, 2,* 191–211.
Marshall, C. (2000). Policy discourse analysis: Negotiating gender equity. *Journal of Educational Policy, 15*(2), 125–156.
Ravitch, D. (2003). *The language police: How pressure groups restrict what students learn.* New York: Alfred A. Knopf.
Stevens, L. P. (2003). Reading first: A critical policy analysis. *Reading Teacher, 56*(7), 662–668.

REFERENCES

Allington, R. L. (1999). Crafting state educational policy: The slippery role of educational research and researchers. *Journal of Literacy Research, 31,* 457–482.
Allington, R. L., & Woodside-Jiron, H. (1999). The politics of literacy teaching: How "research" shaped educational policy. *Educational Researcher, 28*(8), 4–13.
Assembly Bill 170, Instructional materials, Chapter 765 (1995a).

Assembly Bill 1504, Instructional materials: Spelling, Chapter 764 (1995b).
Assembly Bill 3482, Education: Teacher reading instruction, Chapter 196 (1996).
Assembly Bill 1086, Reading instruction, Chapter 286 (1997).
Ball, D. L. (1990). Reflections and deflections of policy: The case of Carol Turner. *Educational Evaluation and Policy Analysis, 12*(3), 247–259.
Benveniste, G. (1977). *The politics of expertise.* San Francisco, CA: Boyd & Fraser.
Bernstein, B. (1996). *Pedagogy symbolic control and identity: Theory, research, critique.* Bristol, PA: Taylor & Francis.
Bourdieu, P. (1991). *Language and symbolic power.* Cambridge, MA: Harvard University Press.
California Department of Education. (1999). *Reading/language arts framework for California public schools.* Sacramento: Author.
Carlos, L., & Kirst, M. (1997). *California curriculum policy in the 1990's: "We don't have to be in front to lead."* Paper presented at the annual meeting of the American Educational Research Association, Chicago, IL.
Chouliaraki, L., & Fairclough, N. (1999). *Discourse in late modernity: Rethinking critical discourse analysis.* Edinburgh: Edinburgh University Press.
Chrispeels, J. H. (1997). Educational policy implementation in a shifting political climate: The California experience. *American Educational Research Journal, 34*(3), 453–481.
Coles, G. (2000). *Misreading reading: The bad science that hurts children.* Portsmouth, NH: Heinemann.
Collins, J. (1995). Literacy and literacies. *Annual Review of Anthropology, 24,* 75–93.
Collins, J. (1997, October 27). How Johnny should read. *Time,* pp. 78–81.
Edmondson, J. (2000). *America Reads: A critical policy analysis.* Newark, DE: International Reading Association.
Egan-Robertson, A. (1998). Learning about culture, language, and power: Understanding relationships among personhood, literacy practices, and intertextuality. *Journal of Literacy Research, 30*(4), 449–487.
Fairclough, N. (1992). *Discourse and social change.* Cambridge: Polity.
Fairclough, N. (1995a). *Media discourse.* London: Arnold.
Fairclough, N. (1995b). *Critical discourse analysis: The critical study of language.* New York: Longman.
Ferdman, B. M. (1990). Literacy and cultural identity. *Harvard Educational Review, 60,* 181–203.
Gee, J. P. (1996). *Social linguistics and literacies: Ideology in discourses* (2nd ed.). Bristol, PA: Falmer.
Gee, J. P. (1999). *An introduction to discourse analysis theory and method.* New York: Routledge.
Gee, J. P. (2001). Forward. In C. Lewis (Ed.), *Literacy practices as social acts: Power, status, and cultural norms in the classroom* (pp. xv–xix). Mahwah, NJ: Lawrence Erlbaum Associates.
Gee, J. P., & Green, J. L. (1998). Discourse analysis, learning, and social practice: A methodological study. In P. D. Pearson & A. Iran-Nejad (Eds.), *Review of research in education.* Washington, DC: American Educational Research Association.
Giroux, H. (1997). *Pedagogy and the politics of hope: Theory, culture, and schooling.* Boulder, CO: Westview.
Habermas, J. (1996). *Between facts and norms: Contributions to a discourse theory of law and Democracy* (W. Rehg, Trans.). Cambridge, MA: MIT Press.
Halliday, M. A. K. (1978). *Language as a social semiotic: The social interpretation of language and meaning.* London: Arnold.
Halliday, M. A. K. (1994). *An introduction to functional grammar* (2nd ed.). London: Arnold.
Honig, B. (1991). California's experience with textbook improvement. In P. G. Altbach, G. P. Kelly, H. G. Petrie, & L. Weis (Eds.), *Textbooks in American society: Politics, policy and pedagogy* (pp. 105–116). New York: State University of New York Press.
Honig, B. (1996, May 8). Hearing on reading. Testimony before the Education Committee of the California State Assembly.

Kingdon, J. W. (1995). *Agendas, alternatives, and public policies* (2nd ed.). New York: Longman.

Kuzel, A. J. (1992). Sampling in qualitative inquiry. In B. Crabtree & W. L. Miller (Eds.), *Doing qualitative research* (pp. 31–44) (Research Methods for Primary Care Series, Vol. 3). Newbury Park, CA: Sage.

Lewis, C. (2001). *Literacy practices as social acts: Power, status, and cultural norms in the classroom.* Mahwah, NJ: Lawrence Erlbaum Associates.

Lyon, G. R. (1996, May 8). Hearing on reading. Testimony before the Education Committee of the California State Assembly.

Mahiri, J., & Godley, A. J. (1998). Rewriting identity: Social meanings of literacy and "revisions" of self. *Reading Research Quarterly, 33*(4), 416–433.

Manzo, K. (1997, January 15). California text adoption puts emphasis on phonics. *Education Week*, p. 12.

Mertz, E. (1996). Recontextualization as socialization: Text and pragmatics in the law school classroom. In M. Silverstein & G. Urban (Eds.), *Natural histories of discourse* (pp. 229–249). Chicago: The University of Chicago Press.

National Research Council's Committee on the Prevention of Reading Difficulties in Young Children (NIH News Release March 27, 1998).

NCLB Act of 2001: Reauthorization of the Elementary and Secondary Education Act Legislation and Policies Website. (January 17, 2003). (www.ed.gov/offices/OESE/esea/factsheet. html.)

Paterson, F. (1998). Mandating methodology: Promoting the use of phonics through stat statute. In K. S. Goodman (Ed.), *In defense of good teaching: What teachers need to know about the "Reading Wars"* (pp. 107–125). York, ME: Stenhouse.

Paterson, F. (2000). The politics of phonics. *Journal of Curriculum and Supervision, 15*(3), 179–211.

Patton, M. Q. (1990). *Qualitative evaluation and research methods.* Beverly Hills, CA: Sage.

Prunty, J. J. (1985). Signposts for a critical educational policy analysis. *Australian Journal of Education, 29*(2), 133–140.

Reading Excellence Act, 20 U. S. C.§ 6601. et. seq. (1998).

Reading Program Advisory. (1996). *Teaching reading: A balanced, comprehensive approach to teaching reading in prekindergarten through grade three.* Sacramento, CA: California Department of Education.

Rogers, R. (2003). *A critical discourse analysis of family literacy practices: Power in and out of print.* Mahwah, NJ: Lawrence Erlbaum Associates.

Taylor, D. (1998). *Beginning to read and the spin doctors of science: The political campaign to change America's mind about how children learn to read.* Urbana, IL: National Council of Teachers of English.

Toll, C. A. (2002). Can teachers and policy makers learn to talk to one another? In R. L. Allington (Ed.), *Big Brother and the national reading curriculum: How ideology trumped evidence* (pp. 137–154). Portsmouth, NH: Heinemann.

Vygotsky, L. S. (1978). *Mind in society: The development of higher psychological processes* (M. Cole, V. John-Steiner, S. Scribner, & E. Souberman, Eds.). Cambridge, MA: Harvard University Press.

Wingert, P., & Kantrowitz, B. (1997, October, 27). Why Andy couldn't read. *Newsweek*, pp. 56–64.

Woodside-Jiron, H. (2002). *The language of politics and the politics of language: A critical discourse analysis of California reading policy.* Unpublished doctoral dissertation, University of Albany–SUNY, New York.

Woodside-Jiron, H. (2003). Critical policy analysis: Researching the roles of cultural models, power, and expertise in reading policy. *Reading Research Quarterly, 38*(4).

Chapter 9

Locating the Role of the Critical Discourse Analyst

Lisa Patel Stevens
University of Queensland

CENTRAL CONCEPTS

Critical Discourse Analysis—A theory and method that draws on the dialogic relationship between texts and social practices.

Learning—A conscious activity that involves explicit instruction.

Acquisition—A preconscious activity that involves being immersed in discourses.

Reflexivity—Attention to examine the social, cultural, political, and interpersonal fields of discourse analysis and how the researcher is implicated into such relationships.

Public intellectual—Educators who are consciously working to critique sociopolitical relationships.

This chapter explores various complexities of the critical discourse analyst's role in settings where the analyst is in close contact with the participant(s)—akin to an ethnographic context. In particular, the chapter navigates the terrain of reflexivity and problematizes the role of the critical discourse analyst in relation to research participants in educational settings. This chapter draws on a definition of *Critical Discourse Analysis* (CDA) that underscores the dialogic relationship between texts (primarily oral in this study) and social practices (Fairclough, chap. 10, this volume; Gee, chap. 2, this volume). The data were drawn from a longitudinal study of a 6th-grade science teacher's literacy instruction and talk about the instruction. In this study, I visited the teacher's classroom on a weekly basis, noted the discourse she used in employing literacy in her classroom, and conducted follow-up formal and informal interviews to discuss her practices and views of content area literacy instruction. These interviews and discussions about my analysis of the teacher's literacy practices afforded opportunities to consider the role of the critical discourse analyst in educational settings, with particular attention to *reflexivity*, or an ability to regard with refraction the social, cultural, political, and interpersonal fields of discourse analysis. In this sense, how does the public intellectual, who holds the explicit role of analysis and exploration of ideologies, work in settings where the researcher and participant work together closely? How does this role of the public intellectual interface with relationships that feel more private than personal? In these types of settings, what promise is held by CDA as both an exploration of discourses and social relations and as potentially transformative of those dialectics? To what extents can CDA be turned on itself as a reflexive analytic tool for the interactions between researcher and participant, the dialectic between subjectivity and objectivity, between knowledge and power? As CDA is brought into an educational setting and shared with a classroom teacher, how might this lend itself to learning of a set of social practices and discourses? To what extent does the immersion in a new order of discourse (Fairclough, chap. 10, this volume) mediate the relationship between learning and acquisition? In exploring these questions about learning and acquisition, I draw on Gee's (chap. 2, this volume) delineation between those discourses that we acquire through immersion (acquisition) and those that we acquire through more overt modeling and mimicry of perceived patterns (learning).

The chapter shows that the orders of discourse used in discussing my Critical Discourse Analysis afforded unique opportunities for learning about educational-related ideologies, for both myself and the research participant. Using CDA with participants in educational settings requires high levels of trust and a willingness of both parties to engage in learning and acquiring a metalanguage to explore various plausible descriptions, analyses, and interpretations of discourse.

When I was a literacy specialist working at a middle school, I worked primarily with content area teachers, modeling effective literacy strategies and lessons in their classrooms and mentoring their use of the literacy practices. In that context, my interactions with Dawn Scolari (pseudonym), an experienced sixth-grade life science teacher, typically went something like this:

Dawn: Hey, Lisa, that vocab strategy worked really well the rest of the day.
The kids seemed to like it a lot.

Lisa: Great.
         They should be used to adding the pictures and sentences,
         since we already practiced that with the vocab cards.
Dawn: Mmhmm.
         I'll save some samples so you can see their work.
Lisa: OK, cool.
         Hey, I've got another strategy that has the kids do the same
         thing, except they take more of the lead in picking words they
         don't know well.
Dawn: Yeah?
Lisa: Yeah. I'll drop a copy in your box.
         And maybe I can come back in to demo it.
Dawn: Sounds good. See you later.

What is superficially a simple exchange about both past and present interactions contains nuances of our different educational roles. From a discourse analysis view (Gee, 1996) of this exchange, there are clearly defined
differentiations in our roles, although we share a few key identity kit aspects
being female and teachers at the same middle school. Another view of the
interaction, with some discourse analysis notations, shows more clearly the
shades of distinction between our roles:

Dawn: Hey, Lisa, that vocab strategy worked really well the rest of the
         day.
         The kids seemed to like it a lot. *Report of last interaction and refer-
         ence to student response as indicator of success.*
Lisa: Great.
         They should be used to adding the pictures and sentences,
         since we already practiced that with the vocab cards. *Confirma-
         tion of report.*
Dawn: Mmhmm.
         I'll save some samples so you can see their work. *Offer of support for
         claim of the report. Reference to student work as another source of support.*
Lisa: OK, cool.
         Hey, I've got another strategy that has the kids do the same thing,
         except they take more of the lead in picking words they don't
         know well. *Offer of similar activity follow-up, with slight modification.*
Dawn: Yeah? *Expression of interest.*
Lisa: Yeah. I'll drop a copy in your box.
         And maybe I can come back in to demo it. *Reiteration of follow-up
         and offer for assistance.*
Dawn: Sounds good. See you later.

Within our interaction, Dawn assumed the role of reporting back to me, and I used modalities such as *maybe* to offer support for her report and for offering an additional team teaching situation while resisting directives and other strongly worded viewpoints. As the literacy specialist for the school, I was still a teacher on the same professional level as Dawn, but also responsible for mentoring and coaching teachers in their literacy practices. In that sense, Dawn and I maintained a professional relationship in which our discussions were located around explorations of what worked and what lessons we might try next with her students. These patterns also noted my appropriation of Dawn's pragmatic view of teaching and learning, in a way to establish intersubjectivity and shared understandings. Subtext to this discussion was the fluctuating hegemonic relationships we maintained as mentor and learner, more experienced and less experienced teacher, and department chair and literacy specialist. These dimensions were deepened when Dawn participated in a year-long professional development project centered on content area literacy, which I facilitated. The dimensions were further deepened and transformed when I returned to Dawn's classroom as a researcher using ethnographic and discourse analysis to study Dawn's beliefs and practices about literacy.

As a literacy researcher, and one using CDA (Fairclough, 1989, 1992) as a framework and methodology, I navigated different territory with Dawn. Visiting her classroom on a weekly basis for 1 year, I found the role of the critical discourse analyst in an educational setting to be much more complex, tentative, rewarding, revealing, and fraught with confrontation than that of a literacy specialist. As I used CDA as a method of research into the relationship between knowledge and power, I also began to share my findings and perspectives with Dawn. In this sense, CDA became a tool for discussions about her classroom, the school context, and society. Dawn and I shared interactions that touched on much deeper issues than we had previously, including our differing positions and epistemologies as educators. These conversations, in which we used a metalanguage to talk about the discursive choices made both by Dawn and myself, also brought forth an opportunity to explore the potentially transformative nature of CDA. Although the precise use of the term *critical* in this setting evokes, for me, the dialectical relationship between language processes and social worlds, it also holds in a Freirian sense the possibility of analyzing and exploring discourse as a mediational tactic to understanding and transforming these social relations.

As Dawn and I discussed my CDA, I found that our interactions marked a different sort of dialogic process around the ideologies of education, literacy, and young people. In other words, it was only through sharing the CDA and immersing ourselves in the metalanguage of this analysis that we were able to see the patterns in our talk and interactions.

The Research Methodologies

For the discourse analysis, I used Gee's (1996) explication of social linguistics and discourses, as well as Fairclough's (1989) CDA as both frameworks and methodologies.[1] From the perspective of these frameworks, language works to construct us as much as we use language to construct possible worlds (Foucault, 1999). Language both embodies and constructs ideologies, although not alone (Fairclough, chap. 10, this volume).

However, for a study examining literacy practices and beliefs in a largely textually mediated setting, CDA provided an appropriate perspective and methodology. Further, my desire to address close dialectic between language and social relations necessitated the critical perspective that Fairclough's (1989) work lent. Working with these frameworks, I positioned the form and function of language in relation to Dawn's[2] literacy practices. Using Fairclough's orders of discourse (Fairclough, chap. 10, this volume; Rogers, chap. 3, chap. 11, this volume), I analyzed Dawn's words during class and interviews for the genres, discourses, and styles used to create and constrict literate possibilities for her students. I described, analyzed, and interpreted Dawn's school-sanctioned talk about literacy as reflective and refractive of particular and concurrent historical, cultural, and political contexts: local, institutional, and societal. I used these analyses to draw conclusions about the various societal discourses (Gee, 1996) about adolescents and literacy that were supported and perpetuated in Dawn's discourse. The overall purpose of these approaches was to provide a continual mediation between local uses of language and further-reaching social relations. By capturing and using Dawn's discourse as a point of articulation in analysis, I commenced with CDA at the local level, with heavy leanings toward the interpretation aspect, as explained by Fairclough. These interpretations were then juxtaposed and connected to the social realms of education and literacies.

During the weekly classroom visits, participant observation techniques (Merriam, 1998) were used to document the literacy activities in the classroom. I sat in the back portion of the room and recorded field notes on a computer, noting the classroom environs, activities, physical factors, and particularly the discourses during the class sessions. After the field notes were collected, I immediately transcribed them all into detailed descriptions. Additionally, class sessions were audiotaped, occasionally videotaped, and later transcribed for detailed discourse analysis. Each week I created a

---

[1]See Rogers (chap. 11, this volume) for a full discussion of the various assumptions and similarities between Gee and Fairclough's work on CDA.

[2]Dawn was one of two teachers whose discourse was analyzed. Because Dawn and I spent significant amounts of time discussing discourse analysis and her discourse, the interaction with her is the focus of this particular chapter.

one-page summary of my observations and sent it to Dawn. These one-page summaries were first developed to gain feedback from Dawn and ultimately became one of the key tools used to mediate our discussions about her beliefs and practices and my discourse analysis (see Fig. 9.1 for an example of a one-page summary). These one-page summaries became pivotal because they served as the initial launch pads for the conversations that Dawn and I had about my analyses of her literacy practices.

Interviews—both structured and unstructured—were conducted to inquire about specific literacy practices, general notions of literacy in the content classroom, and perceptions of the staff development project and its components. Unstructured interviews, which occurred primarily directly before and after each classroom observation, were noted using field notes and followed the same transcription process as the observation field notes.

The one-page summaries and informal interviews served as the launch pad for the conversations that Dawn and I had about my analyses of her literacy practices and beliefs. At first, I shared the one-page summaries out of advice from another qualitative researcher and because I felt uncomfortable with a system of reporting back to a teacher with whom I had shared a fairly open professional relationship and ongoing dialogue. However, I was trepidatious about what Dawn might think of my analyses. Although I knew

---

Summary of Field Notes
Dawn's class 3/28/2000

Topic of Lesson
Clustering about nonvascular plants

Literacy Events
Clustering (Led by D)
Use of textbook as resource (find facts, see examples, etc.)
Direct Q & A between teacher and students

Link to STAR
Clustering as a notetaking strategy
Strong modeling aspect (first time with this strategy?)
Use of the book in class as something other than traditional, independent reading
Lots of questions about the reading (mostly text-explicit)

Questions
Was this the first attempt at the clustering strategy with this class?
How long have you been using it?
What about this lesson came from STAR [professional development project]?
Why the strong teacher-centered focus with this strategy?
Why so few turn-taking opportunities for students?
Future uses and modifications?

FIG. 9.1.   Sample observation summary.

Dawn would not restrict me from making my own analyses, I was also relatively certain that I would not gain validation in the form of a member check, as is sometimes sought from participants in ethnographic studies. However, I was interested in a method that would help me to be explicit about my subjectivities in Dawn's classroom, and I hoped that sharing my research would help me move fluidly between the reflection and realism for which reflexivity calls (Luttrell, 2000).

Sharing the analyses and findings with Dawn proved complex: Discussions of her discourse and how it often supported what literacy researchers would deem less than desirable ideologies about teaching and learning were difficult topics for discussion. Using discourse analysis revealed much about Dawn's literacy practices and ideologies, but it also raised questions of ethical and moral questions of sharing empirical research findings. A few of these questions are:

- What role should the critical discourse analyst adopt?
- To what extent should the process and results of the discourse analysis be shared with the participant and used in a teaching/learning context?
- How do dialogic processes exploring knowledge and power augment the researcher's reflexivity?
- What theory of learning can assist us in understanding interactions between critical discourse analysts and research participants?

Shifting Roles

Contrasted with the pragmatic and functionalist identities that I enacted with Dawn as an onsite literacy specialist, my purpose as a critical discourse analyst marked an indelible departure from the seemingly apolitical relationship we had previously cultivated. Although many ethnographic and qualitative researchers (e.g., Merriam, 1998; Spradley, 1980) have documented the challenge of working with research participants in qualitative inquiries, the prospect of entering Dawn's classroom to explicitly investigate local, institutional, and societal enactments of ideology in language required more than just gaining access to her physical classroom. Beyond access to her room, I also needed access to her beliefs and practices, and although analyzing her classroom discourse revealed much about her beliefs, I found it necessary to debrief with Dawn after each classroom observation. These discussions marked the first turn we took toward discourse analyst and participant. After one classroom visit, I was talking with Dawn about the schoolwide emphasis on organization. All students were expected to keep a three-ring binder, with one section for each class. In many classes, teachers did spot checks of the binders, including Dawn. She directed her students to number the pages in their binders as a way to make sure that the students all had the same notes, handouts, and worksheets in their science binders. After a classroom observation in November 2000, Dawn and I were discussing this highly structured use of notebooks with her sixth graders:

Lisa: I wonder if this schoolwide emphasis on organization can even be somewhat stifling for the students who don't, um, value that way of learning.

Dawn: Maybe, but that's what they need to get through the system and be successful, don't you think?

Lisa: Without a doubt. I think what I'd like to question, though, is how the system might be too narrow in how it defines success for all students.

Dawn: Yeah, maybe.

Dawn: (after a pause) But that **is** the system we're working in, and that is what these kids need for college, isn't it?

Lisa: Yeah, to certain extent, but also to a certain extent not, 'cause I'm not sure this is the one and best way of getting there. Does that make sense?

Dawn: Um, not really. Until they develop their own systems of organizing their stuff, they need to be shown how to do it.

In this conversation, we can see, on my part, a judicious use of modalities (Halliday, 1985)—words and phrases like *wonder, I'd like to, might, if, I'm not sure,* and *does that make sense.* These are all modalities used to soften my stance that the monochromatic practice of organizing information prioritized certain types and orders of knowledge. What is interesting here is to contrast this pattern of discourse with the example given at the start of the chapter, where I used far fewer modalities. Although the orders of genre and discourse enacted are quite similar, the style or way of being has shifted. The use of modalities is used to tenderize my view, but is also done in the hopes of opening up the conversation to Dawn's viewpoint. This marks the role of the linguistic researcher that is at once analytical of the discourse while also opening possibilities for conversation around differing and alternative views. Looking back, I used these modalities out of my own hesitations at taking up considerable representational power and not yet fully grasping how to name and claim my own subjectivities within the study. It is actually with the refractive view that CDA provides of this interaction that I was able to discern an increase in modalities on my part. I might have suspected that, due to the long-range nature of my relationship with Dawn, I would be more forthright and less guarded about my viewpoints, but the analysis done with CDA shows just the opposite. Although other grounded theories and discourse analyses might offer insights into the conversational pattern, CDA helps provide the particular local, institutional, and societal contexts that make this a compelling example of the delicate hegemony at play.

What is also quite interesting here is to note Dawn's ease and willingness to disagree with me. It may seem probable that the professional relationship we maintained, as specialist (or grant facilitator, or researcher) and classroom teacher, would reflect the hegemony in which the specialist (now researcher) maintains a dominant position in education-related conversations. This does not seem to be the case in the example, however. Rather, the hegemonic stances are both taken up and negotiated by Dawn and myself and shift over time and conversations. For example, although Dawn occupies what could be viewed as a lower status position of being a teacher in juxtaposition to a university-affiliated researcher, she uses phrases like *don't you think so* and *isn't it* as openings and markers for me to take up part or all of what she has just said, exerting her own position and authority as a practicing teacher—one who is in the trenches and fully capable of interacting with theories and research from a practical level.

Pursuant to this more fluid and fluctuating power footing is Dawn's strongly established identity as an experienced and successful teacher of 22 years, her position as department chairperson in the school, and our previous relationship in which she chose what she found useful from what I had to offer as a literacy specialist. Also relevant to these types of exchanges was the relationship we had formed over several years of working together. Dawn and I enjoyed a high level of trust in each other as colleagues. This trust was not borne out of identical ideologies, but instead came out of multiple successful partnerships as teachers, working alongside each other with both her sixth graders and the rest of the science faculty. This trust carried over into my presence in her classroom as a critical discourse analyst, but not without some explicit references to the shifts, as is demonstrated in the following excerpt.

While Dawn and I were debriefing a typical one-page summary in which I posed some questions about school-sanctioned literacies versus other types of literacies, she and I had the following exchange:

Dawn: What did you mean here by "dichotomy between in-school literacies vs. out-of-school literacies"?

Lisa: Well, what I was getting at was that in all of the stuff that I'm listening to, it's just about the kinds of reading, writing, listening, and speaking that's found in schools. And not so much all of the things that we might do well outside of school, like digital literacies, you know, like the Internet, visual literacies. That kind of stuff.

Dawn: (slight laugh). I must be missing the point here. Aren't we supposed to teach them the stuff they need for school?

Lisa: Well, yes and no. It's kind of like the question that kids ask: when
am I ever going to use the stuff that you're teaching today? Um, I
guess what I'm saying is that seems to be a pretty valid question
in today's world. And I'm, uh, wondering about all the literacies
our kids have, maybe even some of our struggling kids, that
don't ever get acknowledged. Ya know?

Dawn: Hmmm. I guess you have more time to think about that kind of
stuff now, huh?

Lisa: Yeah, that's definitely true. But I was thinking about some of this
stuff when I was still here.

In this exchange, we find the same types of modalities used by me and the
same types of attempts for shared understandings from Dawn. Yet what is
perhaps most compelling is Dawn's marker of my shift to a researcher with
far more flexibility over time than the typical teacher enjoys. Dawn's message
is spot on. From a classroom teacher's perspective, researchers and discourse
analysts obviously enjoy great luxuries of time to review myriad nuances of
classrooms, including language, the use of which seems as automatic as the
intake of oxygen. Therefore, the development and use of a metalanguage for
the analysis of something so automatic and pervasive must seem frivolous
and indulgent. It was out of this perception of discourse analysis as something for academics, Dawn's curiosity, and the promise of Critical Discourse
Analysis as transformative (Fairclough, 1989) that I began to share more of
my discourse analysis with her. What is most compelling to me here is Dawn's
gradual uptake of the metalanguage used in my analysis. Antithetically, although Dawn quite cogently levels an implicit critique of the luxury of discourse analysis, she is able to do so from the vantage of acquiring and learning some of those very skills and processes. In other words, Dawn engages in
a conversation about the types of literacies that are sanctioned by school, a
conversation spun into motion from the presence of a researcher, and then
is able to critique the conversation for its dabbling into less pressing matters,
like curriculum and standardized testing.

This instance gives us a point of reflection for the role of learning in
these interactions. First, drawing from Gee's (1996) work, we must first try
to distinguish between learning and acquisition in this situation. I spoke explicitly to Dawn about the methodologies I was using, but we also began to
use terms like, *literacies, metalanguage, sanction,* and *power* in our conversations. In this way, we can see nuances of both acquisitions (through use)
and learning (through explicit explanation) of this metalanguage. As we
gradually began to share a metalanguage, Dawn and I were able to discuss
the connections that I was making between some of her discourses and the

social relations in her classroom and in broader contexts, as seen in the following example about Dawn's discourse about young people.

A large and pervasive societal discourse of youth characterizes them as bundles of raging hormones, virtually devoid of rational thought, as they are at the will of their changing physiologies. This discourse is present not only as a commonly held notion, but also goes largely unchallenged in educational settings (Finders, 1998). Ascribing to this notion that adolescence is a life stage that amounts to little more than a hormonally induced confusion contains common sense, almost teleological, implications for instruction, including positioning the teacher as agent of control in the classroom, choosing activities that allow for minimal student interaction, and using unidirectional, didactic instructional strategies.

This discourse was readily apparent in Dawn's instruction. Using the discourse analysis to note turn-taking patterns, the overwhelming predominance of Dawn's turn taking (Fairclough, 1989) and the series of unidirectional directives underscores Dawn's consistent role as decision maker in her classroom. The discourse is also apparent in the highly structured routine and formatting that her students followed. There was little to no room for students' individual identities to have voice in her classroom, the implication perhaps being that as bundles of raging hormones the adolescents had little sense of identity to offer.

In conversations about teaching sixth graders, Dawn often referred to her duty to *train* them, including showing them how to organize their notebooks according to her system and teaching them how to behave in middle and high school classrooms. Expected behaviors included only speaking during the course of a lesson and only after raising their hands, asking the teacher only those questions deemed by the teacher pertinent to the daily lessons, and following teacher-given directions (Field notes, 3/26/00, 4/15/00, 8/28/00, and 10/12/00). During an interview in March 2000, Dawn also used several discourse metaphors (Fairclough, 1989) of adolescents as animals to describe the characteristics of her sixth graders:

Dawn: It takes me a good month or two to just rein them in.

Lisa: Um, can you tell me a little more of what you mean by that?

Dawn: Well, you know, they come not knowing anything, not how to organize their backpacks, what forms to use, where the bathroom is (laughter), anything!

Lisa: So, they have to be reined in to learn those things?

Dawn: Exactly. I get them under control, herded up, and then we get onto the business of learning, reading and writing.

In my summaries of observations and interviews such as these, I included comments about the pervasive discourse regarding young people. For these analyses, I paid particular attention to the content in Dawn's talk, such as the need for organization, the imperative to discipline, and an ethos of business. These observations of the content of her discourse, along with a rising awareness of the role of language in enacting ideology, prompted Dawn to ask for more explanation and examples of the discourse analysis. She was alternately bothered by and defensive of her characterization of young people as overly hormone-driven. When she and I sat down to review the information and discourse sample provided earlier, we had the following conversation:

Dawn: Geez. That seems kind of bad, doesn't it?

Lisa: What do you think? Is it bad to talk about kids that way?

Dawn: Well, it seems harmless enough and pretty accurate, if you watch them for a while, but what's bugging me is that you think that there's a link between how I teach and how I view them.

Lisa: Yeah, I think so.

Dawn: So, what's the alternative?

Lisa: Well, if you were teaching a group of adults, would you do things in the same way?

Dawn: No, but I wouldn't have to.

Lisa: Right. So. There seems to kind of a link between seeing adolescents as kind of out of control and how you teach them. Does that make sense?

Dawn: It does, but the more I think about it, the more I'm sure that if I didn't do it this way, it would be chaos. Just look at Brian [a seventh-grade earth science teacher down the hall from Dawn]. His kids are totally out of control.

Lisa: And do you think that's because he thinks about adolescents differently than you do?

Dawn: I think it's because he doesn't know how to control them.

Through debriefing discussions such as this, Dawn and I figured out quickly that we could agree implicitly that her language and actions in her classroom communicated certain viewpoints, and this could be plausibly certain. However, we could also agree and disagree to varying extents, and from instant to instant, as to how appropriate and justified these viewpoints were for the benefit of the sixth graders and to what extent these viewpoints reflected, rejected, and/or transformed dominant ideologies about youth, schooling, and literacy. In this way, Dawn and I enjoyed a successful investigation into the highly complex and layered nature of discourses and explored multiplicities of interpretations (Gee, 1996). We developed a "self-consciousness about the rootedness of discourse" (Fairclough, 1989, p. 167). In this sense, the one-page summaries and debriefing conversations never accomplished the goal of triangulating the analysis—a misapplied notion from the irreconcilable viewpoint of quantitative research. Instead these conversations served to textualize my analysis and provide Dawn with a membership role in the research. The conversations also served to incorporate aspects of reconstruction of texts, breaking from a potentially nihilistic cycle consisting only of a particular critical deconstruction of texts. By sharing and talking about the discourse with Dawn, this also created space for different variations on local discourses, more appropriately wrestling with and exploring various hybrid forms of representation and identity (Luke, 2002).

Last, this example also points to the potentially transformative promise of CDA in educational settings. As Dawn and I used a shared metalanguage to discuss the flows between language and ideologies, Dawn showed an impermanent awareness of the connections between some of her language choices and the social relations in her classrooms. Although there is no empirical evidence in this study as to whether this resulted in change in Dawn's practice, such an investigation might be too narrow to allow for the critical realism that discourse demands (Fairclough, 1989). The use of CDA holds great promise as a mediational tactic to be used in educational settings, but should not be saddled with teleological transformative responsibilities because no unilateral and foregone connection exists between discourses and social worlds. Instead public intellectuals can look to CDA as a way to mediate their responsibilities to be an agent of social and political justice (Said, 1996). Because the use of CDA has largely occurred outside of direct contact with the participants, using this framework and methodology in educational settings with participants requires deep consideration of the analyst's responsibilities.

How then should critical discourse analysts proceed in working with research participants? From my experiences with Dawn and other teachers, I have come to believe that the answer to this lies between the explicit self-naming of the analyst's perspectives and subjectivities (reflexivity) and, in a collaborative stance, one that allows for mediation and negotiation of power and knowledge by both the researcher and participant. No small part of this successful investigation and deconstruction/reconstruction cycle was the establishment that Dawn had already enjoyed, under the grant I facilitated, as a teacher-researcher (Cochran-Smith & Lytle, 1999). This collaboration opened the door to collaborative inquiry into teaching and learning, and the discourse analysis was a deepened aspect of this pattern.

However, I must also caution that the conversation we had about Dawn's appropriation of a dominant discourse about adolescents, at first, made me uncomfortable. At the time, I misjudged my discomfort to be from feeling that I needed to objectively justify my analysis. On reflection, I now believe the reason for my uneasiness was a nagging realization that I was perhaps revealing to Dawn an aspect of her discourse and ideology that served a real and possibly justified purpose in her identity kit as a teacher. I was hesitant that I was asking her to question an aspect of her ideology that perhaps she did not want to question. In those moments, I felt uncomfortably like I had somehow stepped into the role of a psychoanalyst rather than a critical discourse analyst working in education. Often discourse analysts avoid this complication by working with the discourse of people far removed from themselves—that of politicians, advertisers, and others who do not participate in weekly interactions about the discourse analysis. However, Dawn and I faced this challenge of using her discourse as a refracted image of her beliefs and practices. Just as I was cautious about exposing aspects of Dawn's discourse and ideology to her, I was equally hesitant about superimposing a false sense of knowledge of what was acceptable to share with her and what was not. Because of Dawn's confidence as a teacher and her experience as a teacher-researcher, I could not arbitrarily decide which discourse analyses to share with her. She needed access to all of them, but she then also assumed the responsibility of determining what she wanted to further understand, what she wanted to question, and what she saw as inconsequential or inaccurate.

Theory of Learning

The exploration of what theory of learning can be used as a lens to understanding the interactions between a critical discourse analyst and participants in an educational setting must first be cautioned with who is doing the learning. As with our previous interactions, Dawn and I enjoyed a dialogic exchange (Freire, 1970), in which roles of teacher and learner were blurred. Although I offered descriptions, interpretations, and analyses of her discourse, she texturized these reactions with reflections from her vantage point.

Also at work in our interactions was a theory of learning about language that differentiates between acquisition and learning (Krashen, 1985; cited in Gee, 1996). Although Dawn had acquired primary and secondary discourses (Gee, 1996) as a teacher, department chairperson, scientist, and middle school educator, our work together engendered a learning situation about language and ideologies. This is not to say that Dawn was learning a discourse. This type of proposition is arguable in terms of plausibility. Rather, Dawn—through her interactions with a critical discourse analyst—was learning a metalanguage for discussing how her practices as a sixth-grade life science teacher shaped and were shaped by ideologies that run amid, between, and inside local, institutional, and societal contexts. This learning is similar to the aspects of critical literacy that are all but missing from traditional educational notions of reading and literacy (Freebody & Luke, 1990). This overall lack of acknowledgment of the highly political, historical, and social nature of language and its role in ideology is part of what made CDA seem at first to Dawn so foreign and then so compelling once she was able to enter into hybridized interpretations.

In a recent article, Turbill (2002) proposed that teachers can and should examine portions of their classroom talk for reflections of language that serve to manage, language that teaches, and language used to respond. This type of inquiry is a good first step—one that could be engaged to move beyond the traditionally stultifying ways in which practitioners are shaped to rugged individualists with little to no time for reflection (Britzman, 1991). However, the role of language analysis should also appropriate dimensions of CDA as invaluable—to push beyond the local layers discourse and also noting the institutional and societal discourses at work in classrooms. In this way, researchers and teachers can further understand the ways in which time and space hybridizations of common societal discourses serve to perpetuate certain types of cultural models of teaching and learning, opening up particular opportunities and closing off many others. Also the use of the tools and social theories behind CDA by end users such as teachers and students would serve the larger and much needed purpose of opening of CDA to the complexly hybridized enactments of power, identity, hegemony, and text used in fast capitalistic, globally mediated new times (Luke, 2002).

Engaging educators in this type of analysis is easily done and facilitated using nonidentified samples of discourse and language. However, engendering on this type of inquiry with a teacher's own discourses requires an altogether different type of relationship. The exchanges between Dawn and I proved to be successful from the standpoint of achieving shared understandings and maintaining respect for divergent opinions because of the high level of trust and forthright conversations. This type of relationship must be cultivated and constantly remediated for the various hegemonic underpinnings of such an inquiry. Ample spaces must be co-negotiated by the discourse analyst and educator. In our situation, Dawn and I achieved those spaces by eventually blurring the lines between who was doing the discourse analyst. As Dawn and I furthered our interactions, she appropriated the language of discourse analysis and was able to at times coincide with my "read" of her discourse and at other times challenge it. This engaged Dawn in a situation that evened the overemphasis on acquisition and automatic appropriate of discourses of adolescents, teaching, and learning that marks educational settings. The process provided myself and Dawn with opportunities to learn about language, opening up spaces for all-too-rare instances of analytic awareness.

This aspect of analytic awareness sheds light on a last but crucial aspect of learning in the interactions between myself and Dawn—that of reflexivity. Dawn and I engaged in many conversations in which we were refracting the discourses used in her classroom, used in teacher education, and used in the school and district. We were in essence looking back on captured moments in time. Rather than characterize these backward looks as reflective of either the participants or the language, it is more appropriate to term them *refractive*, accounting for the altered ways in which the habitus is captured, primarily in print-dominant forms (Scollon, 2001).

This refraction, or altered reflection, is more closely attuned to Chouliarki and Fairclough's (1999) description of reflexivity rather than more commonly understood notions of reflection found in education discourse. It is generally believed that reflection is an essential component of teachers' professional development and is commonly defined as an individual reflecting on their unique practices and beliefs as an educator (Risko, Roskos, & Vukelich, 1999). However, this type of definition, focusing on the sole practitioner and introspection, is contrary to the social situatedness of CDA. Rather, as Chouliarki and Fairclough (1999) discussed, CDA calls for a reckoning of historical and social positioning as crucial aspects and contexts of discourse, ideology, and habitus. However, the interactions between myself and Dawn demonstrate that in negotiating the various contexts, interpretations, and analyses, possible refractions of the discourses were offered with varying degrees of what was plausible. This notion of refraction accounts for the appropriately altered interpretations offered, negotiated, and rejected throughout our discussions.

By situating these teacher-researcher interactions against a larger context, using CDA as a tool to critical language and social critique, and allowing for various refractions of representations, Dawn and I were able to move away from restrictive binaries that dominated educational research: good/bad, what works/what doesn't, teacher/researcher, and, of course, teacher/student. In the end, this also helped us move away from a potentially nihilistic presence of CDA and research in a larger sense in classrooms. In numerous locations around the world, relationships between schools and universities are strained as teachers and administrators have felt the sting of a research article that has characterized their work in negative portrayals. Although a level of reflexivity in the researcher-participant collaboration does not and should not guard against research and discourse analysis that shows damaging aspects of education, it should offer an opportunity for a dialogic process between researcher and participant. This was imminently useful for our particular conversations. It points to a possible way for critical discourse analysts who work in educational settings to consider how blurring the roles of the discourse analyst can help argue against potentially structuralist and overly modernistic interpretations whose analyses are often faits accompli.

Reflection and Action

1. Susan is an assistant professor who teaches preservice courses in a teacher education program with an explicit social justice agenda. Susan has recently begun an ethnographic and discourse analysis in Mark's classroom. Mark is a first-year teacher who was a student of Susan's when he was enrolled in the teacher education program. After a few visits, it is apparent to Susan that Mark's pedagogical choices reflect little of the social justice agenda highlighted in her course. Her initial analysis shows an approach to teaching which privilege dominant middle-class discourses. At the same time, Mark is accustomed to talking about education issues with Susan and has expressed interest in what she has been observing and thinking during her visits in his classroom. In light of this chapter's exploration of the complexities of CDA, reflexivity, and learning/acquisition, how should Susan and Mark collaborate in this educational research project?

2. Reflect on a recent ethnographic or discourse analysis project that you recently conducted. If this is not possible, choose a research article that employed CDA. How might the research have proceeded, developed, or resulted differently if there had been a large amount of sharing of analysis while you (the researcher) were in the research setting? How would the relationship between power and knowledge between you and the participants shifted with this type of exchange? Would this type of interaction have transformed the nature of the research and/or transformed the participants' views of the research, the context, and ideologies?

RECOMMENDED READINGS

Luttrell, W. (2000). "Good enough" methods for ethnographic research. *Harvard Educational Review, 70,* 499–523.
Sullivan, G. B. (2002, September). Reflexivity and subjectivity in qualitative research: The utility of a Wittgenstinian Framework. *Form Qualitative Sozialforschung/Forum: Qualitative Social Research* [On-line Journal], *3*(3). Available at: http://www.qualitative-research.net/fqs/fqs-eng.htm. [Date of Access: September 25, 2002].
Turbill, J. (2002). The language used to teach literacy: An activity for teachers. *Reading Online.* (Available at: http://www.readingonline.org/international/turbill5/index.html.)

REFERENCES

Britzman, D. P. (1991). *Practice makes practice: A critical study of learning to teach.* Albany, NY: State University of New York.

Chouliuaraki, L., & Fairclough, N. (1999). *Discourse in late modernity: Rethinking critical discourse analysis.* Edinburgh: Edinburgh University Press.

Cochran-Smith, M., & Lytle, S. L. (1999). The teacher-researcher movement: A decade later. *Educational Researcher, 28*(7), 15–25.

Fairclough, N. (1989). *Language and power.* New York: Longman.

Fairclough, N. (1992). *Critical language awareness.* New York: Longman.

Finders, M. (1998). Raging hormones. *Journal of Adolescent & Adult Literacy, 42,* 252–263.

Foucault, M. (1982). *The archaeology of knowledge.* New York: Pantheon.

Freebody, P., & Luke, A. (1990). "Literacies" programs: Debates and demands in cultural context. *Prospect: The Australian Journal of TESOL, 5*(5), 7–16.

Freire, P. (1970). *Pedagogy of the oppressed.* New York: Continuum.

Gee, J. P. (1996). *Social linguistics and literacies: Ideology in discourses* (2nd ed.). Bristol, PA: Taylor & Francis.

Halliday, M. A. K. (1985). *An introduction to functional grammar.* London: Edward Arnold.

Krashen, S. (1985). *The input hypothesis: Issues and implications.* London: Longman.

Luke, A. (2002). Beyond science and ideology critique: Developments in critical discourse analysis. *Annual Review of Applied Linguistics, 22,* 96–110.

Luttrell, W. (2000). "Good enough" methods for ethnographic research. *Harvard Educational Review, 70,* 499–523.

Merriam, S. B. (1998). *Case study research in education: A qualitative approach.* San Francisco, CA: Jossey-Bass.

Risko, V., Roskos, K., & Vukelich, C. (1999). Making connections: Preservice teachers' reflection processes and strategies. In T. Shanahan & F. V. Rodriguez-Brown (Eds.), *48th Yearbook of the National Reading Conference.* Chicago, IL: National Reading Conference.

Said, E. W. (1996). *Representations of the intellectual: The 1993 Reith Lectures.* New York: Vintage Books.

Scollon, R. (2001). *Mediated discourse: The nexus of practice.* London: Routledge.

Spradley, J. P. (1980). *Participant observation.* Austin, TX: Holt, Rinehart & Winston.

Turbill, J. (2002). The language used to teach literacy: An activity for teachers. *Reading Online.* (Available at: http://www.readingonline.org/international/turbill5/index.html.)

Chapter 10

Semiotic Aspects of Social Transformation and Learning

Norman Fairclough
University of Lancaster

CENTRAL CONCEPTS

A common critique of CDA is that it has not often attended to matters of learning. Learning, in this chapter, is addressed as a performativity of texts—both spoken and written. Social practices such as teaching and learning are mediated by structures and events and are networked in particular ways through orders of discourse. Orders of discourse are comprised of genres, discourses, and styles or "ways of interacting," "ways of representing," and "ways of being."

This chapter theoretically reflects on semiotic aspects of social transformation and learning. Its particular focus is one gap in my work in Critical Discourse Analysis (CDA), which a number of contributors in this volume have pointed out: It has not addressed questions of learning. So my objective is to incorporate a view of learning into the version of CDA that has been developing in my more recent work (Chiapello & Fairclough, 2002; Chouliaraki & Fairclough, 1999; Fairclough, 2000a, 2000b, 2001, 2003; Fairclough, Jessop, & Sayer, 2003). I approach the question of learning indirectly in terms of the more general and in a sense more fundamental question of the *performativity* of texts or, in critical realist terms (Fairclough, Jessop, & Sayer, forthcoming), their causal effects on nonsemiotic elements of the material, social, and mental worlds and the conditions of possibility for the performativity of texts. I use the term *semiosis* rather than *discourse* to refer in a general way to language and other semiotic modes such as visual image, and the term *text* for semiotic elements of social events, be they written, spoken, or combine different semiotic modes as in the case of TV texts.

SEMIOTIC ASPECTS OF SOCIAL STRUCTURES, SOCIAL PRACTICES, AND SOCIAL EVENTS

Let me begin with the question of social ontology. I assume that both (abstract) social structures and (concrete) social events are real parts of the social world that have to be analyzed separately as well as in terms of their relation to each other—a position of analytical dualism (Archer, 1995, 2000; Fairclough, Jessop, & Sayer, forthcoming).

Social structures are abstract entities. One can think of a social structure (such as an economic structure, a social class or kinship system, or a language) as defining a potential—a set of possibilities. However, the relationship between what is structurally possible and what actually happens, between structures and events, is a complex one. Events are not in any simple or direct way the effects of abstract social structures. Their relationship is mediated—there are intermediate organizational entities between structures and events. Let us call these *social practices*. Examples would be practices of teaching and practices of management in educational institutions. Social practices can be thought of as ways to control the selection of certain structural possibilities and the exclusion of others, and the retention of these selections over time in particular areas of social life. Social practices are networked together in particular and shifting ways. For instance, there has recently been a shift in the way in which practices of teaching and research are networked together with practices of management in institutions of higher education—a *managerialization* (or more generally *marketization*; Fairclough, 1993) of higher education. Semiosis is an element of the social at all levels. Schematically:

  Social structures: languages
  Social practices: orders of discourse
  Social events: texts

Languages can be regarded as among the abstract social structures to which I refer here. A language defines a certain potential, certain possibilities, and excludes others—certain ways of combining linguistic elements are possible, others are not (e.g., *the book* is possible as a phrase in English, *book the* is not). Yet texts as elements of social events are not simply the effects of the potentials defined by languages. We need to recognize intermediate organizational entities of a specifically linguistic sort—the linguistic elements of networks of social practices. I call these *orders of discourse* (see Chouliaraki & Fairclough, 1999; Fairclough, 1992). An order of discourse is a network of social practices in its language aspect. The elements of orders of discourse are not things like nouns and sentences (elements of linguistic structures), but discourses, genres, and styles (I differentiate them shortly). These elements, and particular combinations or articulations of these elements, select certain possibilities defined by languages and exclude others—they control linguistic variability for particular areas of social life. Thus, orders of discourse can be seen as the social organization and control of linguistic variation.

There is a further point to make: As we move from abstract structures toward concrete events, it becomes increasingly difficult to separate language from other social elements. In the terminology of Althusser, language becomes increasingly *overdetermined* by other social elements. At the level of abstract structures, we can talk more or less exclusively about language— more or less because *functional* theories of language see even the grammars of languages as socially shaped (Halliday, 1978). The way I defined orders of discourse makes it clear that at this intermediate level we are dealing with a much greater overdetermination of language by other social elements— orders of discourse are the social organization and control of linguistic variation, and their elements (discourses, genres, styles) are correspondingly not purely linguistic categories, but categories that cut across the division between language and nonlanguage, semiosis and the nonsemiotic. When we come to texts as elements of social events, the overdetermination of language by other social elements becomes massive: Texts are not just effects of linguistic structures and orders of discourse, they are also effects of other social structures and of social practices in all their aspects, so it becomes difficult to separate out the factors shaping texts.

SEMIOSIS AS AN ELEMENT OF SOCIAL PRACTICES: GENRES, DISCOURSES, AND STYLES

Social events and, at a more abstract level, social practices can be seen as articulations of different types of social elements. They articulate semiosis (hence language) together with other nonsemiotic social elements. We might see any social practice as an articulation of the following elements:

Action and interaction
Social relations
Persons (with beliefs, attitudes, histories, etc.)
The material world
Semiosis

For instance, classroom teaching articulates together particular ways of using language (on the part of both teachers and learners) with particular forms of action and interaction, the social relations and persons of the classroom, and the structuring and use of the classroom as a physical space.

We can say that semiosis figures in three main ways in social practices:

Genres (ways of acting)
Discourses (ways of representing)
Styles (ways of being)

One way of acting and interacting is through speaking or writing, so semiosis figures first as part of the action. We can distinguish different genres as different ways of (inter)acting discoursally—interviewing is a genre, for example. Second, semiosis figures in the representations, which are always a part of social practices—representations of the material world, of other social practices, reflexive self-representations of the practice in question. Representation is clearly a semiotic matter, and we can distinguish different discourses, which may represent the same area of the world from different perspectives or positions. An example of a discourse in the latter sense would be the political discourse of New Labour, as opposed to the political discourse old Labour, or the political discourse of Thatcherism (Fairclough, 2000b). Third and finally, semiosis figures alongside bodily behavior in constituting particular ways of being, particular social or personal identities. I call the semiotic aspect of this a *style*. An example would be the style of a particular type of manager—the way a particular type of manager uses language as a resource for self-identifying. Genres, discourses, and styles are realized in features of textual meaning and form, and we can distinguish three main aspects of textual meanings and their formal realizations (similar to the macrofunctions distinguished by Halliday, 1994) corresponding to them: actional, representational, and identificational meanings. These meanings are always simultaneously in play in texts and parts of texts.

Reflection and Action

Using Fairclough's definitions of genre, discourse, and style or "ways of interacting," "ways of representing," and "ways of being," code a classroom interaction. What are the possible configurations of discourse practices in this event? Consult Fairclough's (1992) *Discourse in Social Change*. In chapter 8, Fairclough outlines the particular aspects of grammar to analyze when conducting a CDA. What aspects of grammar would fall under the category of *genre*, *discourse*, or *style*?

SOCIAL EFFECTS OF TEXTS AND ON TEXTS

I have begun to discuss the causal effects of social structures and social practices on texts. We can see texts as shaped by two sets of causal powers and by the tension between them: on the one hand, social structures and social practices; and on the other hand, the agency of people involved in the events of which they are a part. Texts are the situated interactional accomplishments of social agents whose agency is enabled and constrained by social structures and social practices. Neither a broadly interactional perspective nor a broadly structural perspective (the latter now including social practices) on texts can be dispensed with, but neither is sufficient without the other.

We also have to recognize that texts are involved in processes of meaning making and that texts have causal effects (i.e., they bring about changes) that are mediated by meaning making. Most immediately, texts can bring about changes in our knowledge, beliefs, attitudes, values, experience, and so forth. We learn from our involvement with and in texts, and texturing (the process of making texts as a facet of social action and interaction) is integral to learning. Yet texts also have causal effects of a less immediate sort—for instance, one might argue that prolonged experience of advertising and other commercial texts contributes to shaping people's identities as consumers or their gender identities. Texts can also have a range of other social, political, and material effects—texts can start wars, for instance, or contribute to changes in economic processes and structures, or in the shape of cities. In summary, texts have causal effects on, and contribute to changes in, persons (beliefs, attitudes, etc.), actions, social relations, and the material world.

We need to be clear what sort of causality this is. It is not a simple mechanical causality—we cannot, for instance, claim that particular features of texts automatically bring about particular changes in people's knowledge or behavior or particular social, political, or material effects. Nor is causality the same as regularity: There may be no regular cause–effect pattern associated with a particular type of text or particular features of texts, but that does not mean that there are no causal effects.[1] Texts can have causal effects without them necessarily being regular effects because many other factors in the context determine whether particular texts as parts of particular events actually have such effects, and this can lead to a particular text having a variety of effects.

Contemporary social science has been widely influenced by social constructivism—the claim that the (social) world is socially constructed.

---

[1]The reduction of causality to regularity is only one view of causality—what is often referred to as *Humean causality*, the view of causality associated with the philosopher David Hume (Fairclough, Jessop, & Sayer, 2003; Sayer, 2000).

Many theories of social constructivism emphasize the role of texts (language, discourse, semiosis) in the construction of the social world. These theories tend to be idealist rather than realist. A realist would argue that, although aspects of the social world such as social institutions are ultimately socially constructed, once constructed they are realities that affect and limit the textual (or discursive) construction of the social. We need to distinguish *construction* from *construal*, which social constructivists often do not: We may textually construe (represent, imagine, etc.) the social world in particular ways, but whether our representations or construals have the effect of changing its construction depends on various contextual factors, including the way social reality already is, who is construing it, and so forth. So we can accept a moderate version of the claim that the social world is textually constructed, but not an extreme version (Sayer, 2000).

One of the causal effects of texts that has been of major concern for Critical Discourse Analysis is ideological effects—the effects of texts in inculcating and sustaining ideologies. I see ideologies as primarily representations of aspects of the world that can be shown to contribute to establishing and maintaining relations of power, domination, and exploitation—*primarily* because such representations can be enacted in ways of interacting socially and inculcated in ways of being in people's identities. Let us take an example: the pervasive claim that in the new global economy countries must be highly competitive to survive (something like this is presupposed in this extract from a speech by Tony Blair to the Confederation of British Industry: "Competition on quality can't be done by Government alone. The whole nation must put its shoulder to the wheel"). One could see such claims (and the neoliberal discourse with which they are associated) as enacted in new, more businesslike ways of administering organizations like universities and inculcated in new managerial styles. We can only arrive at a judgment about whether such claims are ideological by looking at the causal effects they have in particular areas of social life—for instance, factories or universities, asking whether they contribute to sustaining power relations (e.g., by making employees more amenable to managers' demands).

DIALECTICAL RELATIONS

The relations between elements of a social event or social practice, including the relation between semiosis and nonsemiotic elements, are dialectical relations. We can say that elements are different, cannot be reduced to another, require separate sorts of analysis, and yet are not discrete. In Harvey's (1996) terms, each element internalizes other elements. What I said earlier about overdetermination can be seen in terms of the internalization of nonsemiotic elements in semiotic elements (texts, orders of discourse).

What I said about the causal effects of texts can be seen in terms of the internalization of semiotic elements in nonsemiotic elements.

We can see claims about the socially constructive effects of semiosis, including the moderate social constructivism advocated earlier, as presupposing the dialectical internalization of semiosis in the nonsemiotic—presupposing, for instance, that discourses can be materialized (internalized within the material world) in the design of urban spaces. We can also see claims about how people learn in the course of communicative interaction (such as the claims in the chapters of this volume) as presupposing the dialectical internalization of semiosis in the nonsemiotic. What people learn in and through text and talk, in and through the process of texturing as we might put it (making text and talk within making meaning), is not merely (new) ways of texturing, but also new ways of acting, relating, being, and intervening in the material world, which are not purely semiotic in character. A theory of individual or organizational learning needs to address the questions of retention—of the capacity to recontextualize what is learned, to enact it, inculcate it, and materialize it.

Dialectical relations obtain intrasemiotically as well as between semiotic and nonsemiotic elements. For instance, processes of organizational learning often begin (and especially so in what has been conceived of as the contemporary *information society* or *knowledge society*) with the recontextualization within organizations of discourses from outside—an obvious example these days is the discourse of new public management (Salskov-Iversen et al., 2000). Yet such discourses may (the modality is important in view of the moderate version of social constructivism advocated before) be enacted as new ways of acting and interacting, inculcated as new ways of being, as well as materialized in for instance new buildings and plants. Enactment is both semiotic and nonsemiotic: The discourse of new public management may be enacted as new management procedures, which semiotically include new genres (e.g., new ways of conducting meetings within an organization). Inculcation is also both semiotic and nonsemiotic: The discourse of new public management may be inculcated in new managers, new types of leaders, which is partly a matter of new styles (hence partly semiotic), but also partly a matter of new forms of embodiment. Bodily dispositions are open to semioticization (as indeed are buildings), but that does not mean they have a purely semiotic character—it is precisely a facet of the dialectical internalization of the semiotic in the nonsemiotic. What this example (and the case study by Salskov-Iversen et al.) also points to is the dialectic between colonization and appropriation in processes of social transformation and learning: Recontextualizing the new discourse is both opening an organization (and its individual members) up to a process of colonization (and to ideological effects) and, insofar as the new discourse is transformed, in locally specific ways by being worked into a distinctive relation with other (existing) discourses—a process of appropriation.

Let us come back to the modality of the claim that discourses may be enacted, inculcated, and materialized. There are social conditions of possibility for social transformation and learning, which are in part semiotic conditions of possibility (Fairclough, Jessop, & Sayer, 2003). In the example of new public management discourse, for instance, the semiotic conditions of possibility for the recontextualization and dialectical enactment, inculcation, and materialization of the discourse within particular organizations refer to the order of discourse: the configuration of discourses, genres, and styles, which is in place not only within a particular organization, but in the social field within which it is located and the relations between the orders of discourse of different fields. To cut through the complexities involved here, we can say broadly that the openness of an organization to transformations led by a new discourse, and the openness of the organization and its members to learning, depend on the extent to which there is a discourse or configuration of discourses in place within the organization and the field for which the dialectic of enactment, inculcation, and materialization is fully carried through, and the capacity for autonomy with respect to other fields (not, of course, a purely semiotic matter).

EMERGENCE AND LEARNING

The CDA of texts includes both interdiscursive analysis of the genres, discourses, and styles drawn on and how different genres, discourses, and styles are articulated together (textured together), and analysis of how such mixes of genres, discourses, and styles are realized in the meanings and forms of texts (which entails linguistic analysis and other forms of semiotic analysis, such as analysis of visual images or body language). The chapters in this volume by Rogers (chap. 3) and Lewis and Ketter (chap. 6), for instance, point to the significance in talk of interdiscursivity, discourse hybridity, for learning. In the critical realist frame I have been drawing on, one can see this as the basis for semiotic emergence, the making of new meanings. Yet as Lewis and Ketter (chap. 6) indicate, the possibilities for emergence depend on the relative dialogicality of text and talk—the orientation to difference. We can schematically differentiate five orientations to difference, with the proviso that this is not a typology of texts—individual texts and talk may combine them in various ways (Fairclough, 2003):

(a) an openness to, acceptance of, and recognition of difference; an exploration of difference, as in dialogue in the richest sense of the term

(b) an accentuation of difference, conflict, and polemic—a struggle over meaning, norms, and power

(c) an attempt to resolve or overcome difference

(d) a bracketing of difference, a focus on commonality, solidarity

(e) consensus, a normalization and acceptance of differences of power, which brackets or suppresses differences of meaning and over norms

Scenario (e) in particular is inimical to emergence. Dialogicality and orientation to difference depend on the sort of broadly structural conditions I pointed to in the previous section—conditions to do with social practices, fields, and relations between fields, which have a partly semiotic character (in terms of orders of discourse). However, as suggested earlier, the causal powers that shape texts are the powers of agency as well as of structure—whatever the state of the field and the relations between fields, we can ask about both latitudes for agency and their differential uptake by different agents, including agents involved in the sort of critical educational research reflected in the chapters of this volume.

A relatively high degree of dialogicality and orientation to difference can be seen as favoring the emergence of meaning through interdiscursive hybridity, although to talk about learning there needs to be some evidence of continuity and development (provided by longitudinal aspects of the research reported in this book) and retention (which one might see as requiring evidence of transfer and recontextualization, from one context to others). Learning can be seen as a form of social transformation in itself, but as a necessary but insufficient condition of social transformation on a broader scale. Learning through text and talk can be interpreted as part of what I referred to earlier as the semiotic conditions for social transformation.

CRITICAL RESEARCH, LEARNING, AND SOCIAL TRANSFORMATION

In assessing the possibilities for and limitations of critical educational research motivated by emancipatory (e.g., antiracist) agendas for learning and social transformation, one needs to consider both factors of a broadly structural character and factors to do with agency. With respect to the former, educational research can be seen as part of a network of social practices that constitutes an apparatus of governance (in part semiotically constituted as an order of discourse; Fairclough, 2003)—a network that includes practices of classroom teaching, educational management, educational research, and (national, state, local, etc.), government, and policy making (Bernstein, 1990). The nature and workings of the apparatus are internally as well as externally contested—critical educational researchers are, for instance, often seeking to create more open and equal relations between academic research and classroom teaching. One issue they must consider is what I referred to earlier as the social conditions of possibility for social transformation and learning, which include latitudes for agency within educational research. These issues can be partly addressed from a semiotic perspective in terms of latitudes for agents in social research to develop, recontextualize, and seek to enact and inculcate new discourses. But there are also considerations to do with forms of agency in recontextualizing contexts (e.g., questions of the dialogicality of interactions between educational researchers and teachers). Once again neither a structural nor an interactional perspective can be dispensed with, but neither is sufficient without the other.

Reflection and Action

In educational research, the researcher is often a member of the social practices he or she is studying or have a history of participation within the social practice. Given that we as researchers are often implicated into the practices we study, how do we uncover the networks of discourse patterns that might be natural or invisible to us as researchers?

RECOMMENDED READINGS

Fairclough, N. (1992). *Discourse and social change.* Cambridge: Polity.
Fairclough, N. (2003). *Analysing discourse: Text analysis for social research.* London: Routledge.
Habermas, J. (1987). *The philosophical discourse of modernity.* Cambridge, MA: MIT Press.

REFERENCES

Archer, M. (1995). *Realist social theory; the morphogenetic approach.* Cambridge: Cambridge University Press.
Archer, M. (2000). *Being human: The problem of agency.* Cambridge: Cambridge University Press.
Bernstein, B. (1990). *The structuring of pedagogic discourse.* London: Routledge.
Chiapello, E., & Fairclough, N. (2002). Understanding the new management ideology. A transdisciplinary contribution from critical discourse analysis and the new sociology of capitalism. *Discourse and Society, 13*(2), 185–208.
Chouliaraki, L., & Fairclough, N. (1999). *Discourse in late modernity.* Edinburgh: Edinburgh University Press.
Fairclough, N. (1992). *Discourse and social change.* Cambridge: Polity.
Fairclough, N. (1993). Critical discourse analysis and the marketisation of public discourse: The universities. *Discourse & Society, 4*, 133–168.

Fairclough, N. (2000a). Discourse, social theory and social research: The case of welfare reform. *Journal of Sociolinguistics, 4*(2), 163–195.

Fairclough, N. (2000b). *New labour, new language?* London: Routledge.

Fairclough, N. (2001). The dialectics of discourse *Textus, 14,* 231–242.

Fairclough, N. (2003). *Analysing discourse: Textual analysis for social research.* London: Routledge.

Fairclough, N., Jessop, R., & Sayer, A. (2003). A critical realist interpretation of the effectivity of the production of meaning. In J. Roberts (Ed.), *Critical realism, deconstruction and discourse.* London: Routledge.

Halliday, M. (1978). *Language as social semiotic.* London: Edward Arnold.

Halliday, M. (1994). *Introduction to functional grammar.* London: Edward Arnold.

Harvey, D. (1996). *Justice, nature and the geography of difference.* Oxford: Blackwell.

Salskov-Iversen, D., Hansen, H., & Bislev, S. (2000). Governmentality, globalization and local practice: Transformations of a hegemonic discourse. *Alternatives, 25,* 183–222.

Sayer, A. (2000). *Realism and the social sciences.* London: Sage.

Chapter 11

Setting an Agenda for Critical Discourse Analysis in Education

Rebecca Rogers
Washington University in St. Louis

In this volume, James Gee (chap. 2) positions his work as critical discourse analysis (small cda), and Norman Fairclough (chap. 10) addresses CDA, learning, and social transformation. Working between the two frameworks, each of the chapters in this volume demonstrates the intersections between the two theoretical and methodological frameworks. In this last chapter, I comment explicitly on the intersections between the two CDA frameworks, drawing on each of the chapters. Although there is a great deal of synergy between the two frameworks, there is also tension. I demonstrate how this tension is productive because it allows for the theory and method of CDA to be reformulated and applied to important educational issues.

Reflection and Action

What makes each of the chapters a "Critical" Discourse Analysis?
How do each of the authors engage with the construct of "Discourse"?
How do each of the authors explicate their "analysis"?

FORM AND FUNCTION

Gee and Fairclough present complementary methods for analyzing the relationship between linguistic structure and social structure. Figure 11.1 illustrates the relationships among Gee, Fairclough, and Halliday in terms of

237

A. Halliday (1978)

Contextual Variable	Metafunction (Meaning)	"The Work of Language"
Mode	Textual	Presenting messages as text in context
Tenor	Interpersonal	Enacting social relations
Field	Ideational	Representing experience

B. Gee (1996, 1999)

Contextual Variable	Example	Metafunction	"The Work of Language"
'd'iscourse	Language "bits"; assumes all language bits are social and dialogic	Textual	Presenting messages as texts in contexts
Connection building	Six activity building areas -Meaning and value of material world; Activities; Identities* and Relationships*; Politics; Connections; Semiotics	Textual, Interpersonal, Ideational	Simultaneous construction of "reality"
Discourse	Ways of representing, believing, valuing; includes language bits	Interpersonal, Ideational, Textual	Presenting message as a way of representing and a way of being

C. Fairclough (chap. 10, this volume) Chouliaraki & Fairclough (1999)

Contextual Variable	Example	Metafunction	"The Work of Language"
Genre	Interview, sermon, literacy lesson (turn taking, participant structure, theme, topic control)	Textual	Ways of interacting— Presenting messages as texts in context
Discourse	Teacher as authority Student as passive How the perspective is set forth	Interpersonal	Ways of representing— Enacting social relations from a particular perspective
Style	Affiliation within Discourses: modality, transitivity, pronoun use	Ideational	Ways of being—Enacting experiences of reality

FIG. 11.1.   Language structure.

their views on language structure. This chart includes the constructs they each use to refer to the unit of language under analysis (contextual variable). It also includes the function of the unit of analysis and the work that is done (or the function) by each unit of analysis.

"d"/"D"iscourse

Gee outlined his social theory of Discourse as consisting of "d" and "D" discourse. Little "d" discourse consists of language bits—or the grammatical packaging of language—what Saussure (1959) referred to as "langue." Big "D" discourse includes the ways of representing, being, believing, valuing, and feeling that are connected with what it means to be a competent user of language in a range of discursive communities—from a bar, to the basketball court, to a conference. Saussure referred to this as "parole." Further distinguishing d/Discourse, Gee conceptualized two discursive spaces, primary and secondary Discourses. The primary Discourses are the sets of values, beliefs, ways of acting, and talking that are connected to a child's primary network including their home, family, and immediate community. The secondary Discourses include the network of social practices including both "d" and "D"iscourse that comprise the institutions children and family interact with, including schools, businesses, churches, government agencies, and so on.

The link among language bits, social languages, and situated meanings can be located in the network of connection-building tasks. Figure 11.1, chart B, illustrates the relationship between "d" and "D." Gee (1999) wrote, "discourse analysis focuses on the thread of language (and related semiotic systems) used in the situation network. Any piece of language, oral or written, is composed of a set of grammatical cues or clues (Gumperz, 1982) that help listeners or readers (in negotiation and collaboration with others in an interaction) to build six things" (p. 85). The six tasks that allow the analyst to construct meaning from a network of Discourse patterns include: semiotic building, world building, activity building, socioculturally situated identity building, political building, and connection building. Gee provided a useful list of questions to ask of each "task." The questions consist of various aspects of grammar. For example, within "semiotic building," Gee asked the question: What sign systems are relevant (and irrelevant) in the situation? In "world building," Gee posed the question, "What are the situated meanings of some of the words and phrases that seem important in the situation?" The work of language at each of these levels roughly corresponds to Halliday's systemic functional linguistics. Little "d" discourse corresponds to Hallidays' "mode," which is the way in which messages are presented in contexts. Big "D" discourse corresponds to Halliday's field, tenor, and mode because "D"iscourse includes language bits as well as ways of representing and being while using language. Gee provided connection-building tasks to link the grammatical aspects of language with social languages. He did not, however, specifically address which aspects of language structure map onto each of his connection-building tasks.

Orders of Discourse

Fairclough (1992) borrowed the term *orders of discourse* from Foucault (1972) as a heuristic for describing the relationship among texts, social practices, and social identities. An order of discourse is not a stable system, according to Fairclough. Rather it is an "open system, which is put at risk by what happens in actual interactions" (p. 69). The grammar of language[1] is put to work within each of the meta-functions. Fairclough referred to these configurations as "orders of discourse," which may be thought of as the linguistic analogy of social structure, include genres, Discourses, and styles, and are represented in each and every utterance[2] (see Fig. 11.1, chart C, for an illustration of orders of discourse).

Fairclough (1992) provided a series of text analytic procedures (e.g., turn taking, exchange structure, topic control, modality, politeness, transitivity, etc.). In chapter 8 of *Discourse and Social Change,* Fairclough (1992) specifically broke the linguistic features into text analysis with a corresponding set of questions and social practice analysis. *Text analysis* refers to the description, interpretation, and explanation of interactional and grammatical aspects texts (spoken and written) that includes: turn taking, cohesion, politeness, ethos, grammar, transitivity, theme, modality, word meaning, wording, and metaphor.

More recently, Chouliaraki and Fairclough (1999) moved closer to Halliday's system of mode, tenor, and field and delineated the analytic procedures within each domain of genre (ways of interacting), Discourse (ways of representing), and style (ways of being). Within each domain of genre, Discourse, and style are specific grammatical or interactional dimensions of texts to look for (see Fairclough, chap. 10, this volume, for definitions of genre, Discourse, and style; see Lewis & Ketter, chap. 6, and Rogers, chap. 1, this volume, for a complete breakdown of the grammatical features that accompany genre, Discourse, and style). Figure 11.1, chart C, demonstrates the relationship among genre, Discourse, and style, and the textual, interpersonal, and ideational functions in Halliday's model.

Fairclough and Gee seem to agree on many of the central elements of a Critical Discourse Analysis. The metafunctions of language for both Gee and Fairclough involve textual, interpersonal, and ideational functions, derivative of systemic functional linguistics (discussed in chap. 1). Further, there is a good deal of overlap between Gee and Fairclough's frameworks in the interpersonal and ideational domains of Discourse. This level of analy-

---

[1]Grammar may be thought of as "the level of language that maps experiential, interpersonal, and textual meaning onto the structure of the clause and its parts" (Kress, 1993, p. 250).

[2]Wodak (1996, 1999) questioned whether the construct should be orders of discourse or disorders of discourse. In a reflexive CDA, we must also ask the question: What is an alternative order of discourse?

sis involves the way in which language is represented and the social identities that are carried with such representations.

In this volume, Rogers (chap. 3) uses Gee's theory of Discourse and Fairclough's orders of discourse to analyze how adult literacy students represent their literate selves in three distinct discursive contexts. She analyzes the relationship among "ways of interacting," "ways of representing," and "ways of being" within and across three contexts. Lewis and Ketter attend to genre, Discourse, and style over time and argue that, "form and function constructs and is constructed by the situated identities of the speakers" (p. 17). Both Rogers as well as Lewis and Ketter have included appendixes that highlight the linguistic aspects to code for at each domain of analysis.

Peyton Young (chap. 7) uses pieces of Gee's connection-building activities and Fairclough's analytic tools of local, institutional, and societal. She focuses specifically on cultural models and the microlinguistic aspects of cultural models for different participants. She identifies the linguistic and paralinguistic elements of pace of speaking, animation, reported speech, descriptive nominalizations, and frequency of I-statements as constructing the cultural models of Chavo's teacher, his mother, and Chavo. Peyton Young moves beyond the linguistic in her analysis to include aspects of emotion. She examines, "what she said and listened to how she said it . . . the tone of her voice changed as she told stories about Chavo's literacy. Her voice was warm with the memories of Chavo becoming a reader and a good student. When retelling Chavo's middle school years, her voice reflected the anger and the disappointment she felt about Chavo's experiences with some of his teachers" (p. 157). Peyton Young includes aspects of emotion in her Critical Discourse Analysis—an area often neglected by most critical discourse analysis. This neglect of emotion is troublesome because emotions are the stronghold of ideological relationships.

Rowe uses a combination of Gee and Fairclough's discourse theories and methods. He uses Gee's (1999) three-part terminology of activity, subactivity, and action. Rowe argues for the importance of accounting for activity within a Critical Discourse Analysis framework—an aspect of social interaction that is often overlooked in accounting for learning. He offers a new method of transcribing and analyzing the relationship between form and function that includes activity.

On the analysis of form and function, Sarroub (chap. 5, this volume) writes, "Critical Discourse Analysis refers to how and why people talk and interact the way they do in their everyday lives. It means understanding the relationship between talk, interaction, and power" (pp. 98–99). Her analysis focuses on the interactions during one group meeting, focusing on a discursive pattern, reframing, which serves two local functions within the group of participants. It establishes co-patterns of turn taking and sharing, and it promotes changes in participants' social positioning. Important to

note, reframing is characterized by the use of modal verbs when participants in the group attempt to distribute authority and status.

Woodside-Jiron (chap. 8, this volume), in her critical analysis of reading
policy in California, uses Fairclough's system of texts, discourses, and social
practices at the local, institutional, and societal levels. Like others in the
book (e.g., Rogers, Lewis & Ketter, and Fairclough), she argues that we cannot assume the presence of power, but that the details of power need to be
documented. Each level of Woodside-Jiron's analysis has an accompanying
set of linguistic categories. She argues that the specific analytic tools of CDA
have not been explicated clearly and offers Bernstein's framework of regulative and instructive discourses as a solution to this problem. Woodside-
Jiron argues that the grammar of policy—the authoritative structuring, vocabulary, determiners, and establishment of facts—needs to be attended to
in CDA. She makes the argument for specific links to be made between the
levels and across time to understand the intertextual chaining of discourse
practices.

Stevens analyzes both her own and the teacher's discourse using genre,
discourse, and style (and the accompanying linguistic codes) at the local,
institutional, and societal levels of analysis. She makes the argument that
the same analytic framework used with participants should be turned on
the researcher as well.

Reflection and Action

Reread Peyton Young's analysis of cultural models and Lewis and
Ketter's analysis of the Discourses of liberal humanism and critical multiculturalism. What are the similarities and differences between cultural
models and Discourses? What aspects of linguistic structure are included
in each of their analysis? What others might have been added?

CONTEXT AND DISCOURSE

Both Critical Discourse Analysis models (Gee's and Fairclough's) go beyond describing Discourse practices to explaining the relationship between
language and social structure. Based on a synthesis of the two models, the
framework in Fig. 11.2 attends to both the context of the analysis and the
context in which the analysis is located.

Figure 11.2[3] represents a simplified heuristic of the relationship between
contexts at the local, institutional, and societal levels of analysis. These are
represented on the left-hand side of the heuristic. To draw on examples

---

[3]This diagram was collaboratively constructed during a Critical Discourse Analysis doctoral
seminar that I taught. It appears in Rogers, Berkes, O'Garro, and Hui (in progress).

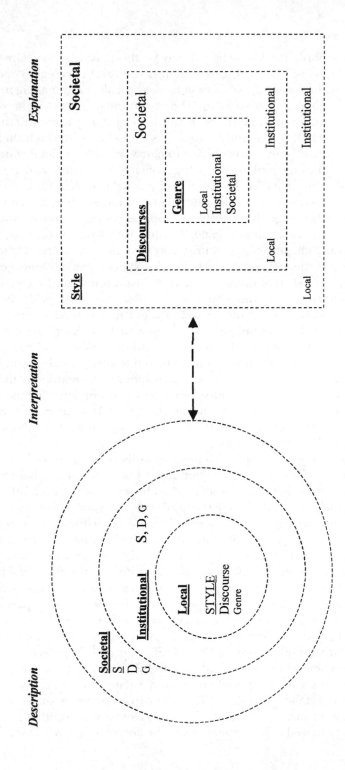

FIG. 11.2. Critical Discourse Analysis heuristic.

243

from the book, the local context may be thought of as the "Great Gravity Race" by Rowe (chap. 4, this volume), the teacher-research meeting by Lewis and Ketter (chap. 6, this volume), or the decision-making meeting by Sarroub (chap. 5, this volume). The institutional context is the social and political institutions that frame the local context. For Rowe it is the science center, for both Lewis and Sarroub it is the schools in which their participating teachers and university researchers work. The societal context is the larger governing bodies, including policies, mandates, and political climates that influence the local and institutional contexts. Each of these contexts is embedded within and informs the other. Further, the language bits and social languages in Gee's terms, and the genre, Discourse, and styles in Fairclough's terms, are embedded within each level of context.

On the right side of the heuristic are orders of discourse. Orders of discourse are the network of Discourse practices that include genre, Discourse, and style that occur within local, institutional, and societal contexts (in Halliday's terms, this would be the *mode, tenor,* and *field*). Genre, Discourse, and style are always linked together in discourse events. The local context of a math lesson, for example, may include the genre of a transmission model math lesson, the discourse of individualism, and a style of negative ability. The institutional context linked to such a math lesson may have similar parameters for the genre (e.g., teacher-proof textbooks and curriculum), but a different Discourse and accompanying style for the teachers. There are many possibilities for how the genre, Discourse, and style might be networked together. There are even more when we add local, institutional, and societal contexts.

Balancing ethnographic contexts and discourse analysis is an ongoing tension played out in each chapter of this book. In Rowe's chapter, context is not only talk, but talk and actions and how they shape each other. Peyton Young includes an analysis of the local (the interview), institutional (school and family), and societal contexts (discourses of schooled literacy and masculinity) in her chapter. Stevens explores the interactions surrounding her ongoing analysis with her participants—turning the CDA frame back on herself as a researcher. Rogers defines context as the three discursive domains (history with schooling, experiences with children's education, and family and community literacy practices) she constructed as part of her in-depth interviews with adult literacy students. Lewis and Ketter provide an exemplary demonstration of balancing Critical Discourse Analysis within a larger ethnographic context. Of their ethnographic context they write, "the ethnographic context included a careful analysis of our own positions within the study group and community related to status, affiliation, and ideological stances" (p. 122). They draw from previous analyses to inform this chapter and argue that this larger context is important because part of how they arrived at interpretations of the changing genres, Discourses, and styles of their middle school teachers and themselves was based on their understanding of them over the course of 4 years. They write, "as we have read and reread Sarah's words, placing them in the context of our historical understanding of Sarah and her position in our group, we have come to see her contribution differently" (p. 136).

The context of Woodside-Jiron's analysis is the 2 years of documents—both spoken and written—that comprise the changes in reading policy in the state of California. She argues that to know not only what changes took place, but how these changes are embedded in the subtleties of linguistic practices, the analyst must look over time and across contexts. Her ethnographic analysis is embedded within her analysis of the history of changes in the documents that unfolded around CA reading policy from 1995 to 1997. To this end, she includes an analysis of policies, speeches, and media documents that constructs the context of the reading policy mandates in California. Woodside-Jiron's chapter contributes significantly to analysis of written documents using CDA. Unlike other analyses of written texts (Downing, 1990; Hastings, 1998; Johnson & Avery, 1999), she asserts that there is an interaction between the text and reader. That is, that neither the text nor the reader is responsible for the cultural models that are constructed.

In her chapter, Sarroub calls CDA an interdisciplinary endeavor and argues for a return to interactional sociolinguistics. Her analysis demonstrates how attention to the "ways of interacting," or what Goffman referred to as "footing," gives us insight into the ways of representing and ways of being embedded in the decision-making process. She demonstrates, making interdisciplinary links between interactional sociolinguistics and contemporary approaches to discourse analysis, including CDA, that concepts such as *footing* and *positioning* fit within a CDA framework. Part of being critical, Sarroub argues, is in the questions one asks. She argues that CDA offers educators insights into learning by providing a lens or frame from which to view change at the personal and institutional levels. Sarroub does not overtly focus on matters of power and privilege. Like others in this volume, she attends closely to linguistic analysis, the cultural models of the participants, and the contexts in which their relationship emerges. She includes herself as a researcher into the analysis and describes and interprets how academic discourse is not always powerful. Sarroub's contribution to CDA is an exemplification of what Gee refers to as the "framing problem." Sarroub identifies and locates her frame at the level of discourse within a 12-minute meeting. She does not make broad interpretations and explanations of how this decision making reinforces or subverts commonsense understandings about power in educational settings. Instead she offers an ethnographic description of the transformation and shifts in ways of interacting, representing, and being inherent in social practices. Her findings reveal that people are using ways of interacting, representing, and being in ways that are subverting and transforming power relations in local ways. Such transformation or learning might be missed without the type of analysis Sarroub provides.

Reflection and Action

What do you see as the relationships between ethnography and CDA in each of the chapters?

CRITICAL DISCOURSE ANALYSIS AND LEARNING IN EDUCATIONAL SETTINGS

Educational research sets out to study what views of learning are important, what counts as important knowledge, what methodologies are worth pursuing, the relationship between the researchers and the researched, and how education is positioned with other disciplines. Lagemann (2001) pointed out how the scientific study of education in the early 20th century was led by psychology and what counted as researchable questions and appropriate methodologies. Indeed Thorndike viewed the scientific study of education as necessary outside of schools in areas of relative specialization. Dewey, in contrast, believed that educational research could become a science only if and when schools as they existed were transformed into communities built on freedom of action and freedom of thought—against the hierarchy that developed between universities and schools. The study of education in the late 20th century focused on asking complex questions that needed qualitative methods to answer research questions that arose from the inside of educational sites. Lagemann (2001) pointed out that, although there have been shifts in the nature of educational study over the past century, the preferred methodology has remained rather stable. However, she also pointed out that educational questions driving diverse methodologies, including CDA, are coming from inside of educational communities and, therefore, hold the possibility to change the face of educational research.

In this volume, we argue that CDA contributes to an understanding of learning, a primary issue in educational research, in two ways. First, analyzing discourse from a critical perspective allows one to understand the processes of learning in more complex ways. Indeed the close analysis of the networking of language allows the analyst insight into aspects of learning that other theories and methods might have missed. Second, in the process of conducting CDA, researchers and participants' learning is shaped (also an aspect of reflexivity addressed later), thus offering possibilities not only for critique, but for social transformation that arises from critique. From a science museum (Rowe) to professional development for inservice middle school teachers (Lewis & Ketter), to interviews with adult literacy students

(Rogers), to an analysis of state policies (Woodside-Jiron), each of the chapters focuses on CDA in various formal and informal educational settings.

In each of these settings, it is clear that matters of learning are closely related to discourse and identity. The authors seem to concur with what Resnick, Saljo, Pontecorvo, and Burge (1991) stated:

> Inherently (and throughout the life space) social activities in which talk and social interactions are not just a means by which people learn to think, but also how they engage in thinking. They might say that discourse is cognition is discourse . . . one is unimaginable without the other. (p. 2)

Learning involves changes in participation and the subsequent shifts in identity. Such changes construct and are constructed by social change or social transformation. In this volume, Fairclough further articulates the relationship between social transformation and learning. He writes, "[l]earning can be seen as a form of social transformation in itself, but as a necessary but not sufficient condition of social transformation on a broader scale" (p. 233). In other words, it is necessary to contextualize the shifts in ways of interacting, representing, and being within the broader institutional and global contexts in which they occur.

Fairclough writes, "I shall approach the question of learning indirectly, in terms of the more general and in a sense more fundamental question of the performativity of texts or, in critical realist terms . . . their causal effects on nonsemiotic elements of the material, social, and mental worlds, and the conditions of possibility for the performativity of texts" (p. 225). For Fairclough, texts refers to, "semiotic elements of social events, be they written, spoken, or combine different semiotic modes" (p. 226). Texts comprise social events that, in turn, construct and are constructed by social practices such as the practices of teaching or the practices of management in an educational institution. As people interact with the texts of social practices, they are involved in a process of meaning making. Fairclough writes,

> . . . texts can bring about changes in our knowledge, our beliefs, our attitudes, values, experience, and so forth. We learn from our involvement with and in texts, and texturing (the process of making texts as a facet of social action and interaction) is integral to learning. Yet texts also have causal effects of a less immediate sort—one might, for instance, argue that prolonged experience of advertising and other commercial texts contributes to shaping people's identities as consumers or their gendered identities. (p. 229)

In other words, as we interact with texts, we acquire the ideological positions associated with such texts. Fairclough continues, "what people learn in and through texts and talk in and through the process of texturing as we might put it . . . is not merely (new) ways of texturing, but also new ways of acting, relating, being, and intervening in the material world" (p. 231). This process involves the reconfiguration of social practices through ways of interacting, ways of representing, and ways of being (genre, Discourse, and style) and construct the basis for what Fairclough refers to as "semiotic emergence"—or the making of new meanings.

Learning, combined with discourse theories, can be seen as a network of social practices that changes over time and varies from place to place. Analyzing the configuration of social practices and the shifts across time and context can help educators describe, interpret, and explain the ways of interacting, representing, and being that accompanies learning. Such configurations of practice often rub up against one another and are not mutually exclusive. Gee (1996) discussed this patterning in terms of "boundary crossing," and Fairclough (1995) showed it in terms of manifest and constitutive intertextuality or interdiscursivity.

The authors in this volume present various perspectives on learning. For example, a central concern Stevens (chap. 9) raises is, "the exploration of what theory of learning can be applied to the interactions between a critical discourse analyst and participants in an educational setting must first be cautioned with who is doing the learning" (p. 220). Rogers views learning as shifts in ways of interacting, representing, and being across contexts and over time. She demonstrates how adult literacy students' sense of literate self shifts across contexts and documents the way in which orders of discourse are configured within each sphere of practice. Rowe defines learning as, "the appropriation of culturally valued mediational means or members' resources as part of participation in active, distributed meaning making" (p. 91). Lewis and Ketter view learning as a social act that involves identities in practice. They define learning as, "the appropriation and reconstruction of one's social world" and as interdiscursivity" (p. 140). As they explain, "Carol did not simply appropriate a way of thinking more associated with Cynthia or Jean. Instead, she reconstructed this world view in her own way, one that centered as much on the individual as it don on the social constitution of the individual" (p. 134). Woodside-Jiron views learning as an interaction between the text and reader. Unlike other analyses of written texts, Woodside-Jiron does not assume that the reader or text has the power to construct cultural models. Rather, it is an interaction between the two. Peyton Young conceptualizes how literacy practices shape and are shaped by the Discourses of masculinity and how a critical discourse frame accounts for the acquisition of problematic gender identities. Sarroub illustrates how discourse analysis can help educators understand the process of teacher decision making that would "eventually transform not only their practice, but also the ways in which they understood themselves in the process" (p. 98). Finally, Fairclough provides a discussion of how learning, seen as social transformation, can be combined with a critical discourse framework.

Reflection and Action

How might teachers and students use CDA as a learning tool in classrooms?

What are other critiques of CDA based on your reading of these chapters?

REFLEXIVITY AND TRUSTWORTHINESS OF CDA

Reflexive intentions vary from building rigor in the research to questioning the authenticity of the researcher (Alvesson & Skoldberg, 2000). The intention of reflexivity depends on whether researchers view their aim as strengthening the rigor of social science research or questioning the epistemological and ontological foundations of the knowledge claims we make. There are varying degrees by which aims are made at increasing the strength or assaulting the strength of social science research as being more or less "scientific." For example, Myerhoff and Ruby (1982) defined *reflexivity* as "structuring communicative products so that the audience assumes the producer, process and product are a coherent whole . . . scientists have also been engaged in reflexive activities . . . scientists continuously test their own assumptions and procedures" (pp. 6–9). This statement implies that being reflexive is synonymous with being scientific. Similarly, for Bourdieu and Wacquant (1992), reflexivity is not a reflection on the subject, but rather entails, "the systematic exploration of the unthought categories of thought which delimit the thinkable and predetermine thought" (p. 40). Although Bourdieu and Wacquant (1992) called into question the ideological nature of monitoring one's own thoughts and actions, their reflexive intention is to "strengthen the epistemological moorings" of the research (p. 46). This intention might be viewed in much the same way as traditional claims to validity that often safeguard researchers from a self-reflexive research paradigm. That is, if we triangulate our data, member check with participants, and establish and maintain a paper trail of our theorizing and analytic moves, we can claim that our CDA is valid or an accurate representation of "reality." Such a view is problematic especially within a CDA framework, which rejects the view of an objective and neutral science.

Reflexivity within a CDA framework arises from a concern about the stabilization of knowledge claims and the slipperiness of language. That is, the fundamental nature of language hinders empirical research that is aimed at establishing the truth. Indeed Chouliaraki and Fairclough (1999) asserted that reflexivity is caught up in social struggle and reflexivity assumes a discursive element—that researchers are part of the language practices they study. Gee concurred and stated, "at one and the same time, an utterance influences what we take the context to be and context influences what we take the utterance to mean." This is further complicated when there is a linguistic and subsequent cultural gap between the researcher and the participants (as was the case in Rogers' chapter or in Young's study of masculinity). The intention of reflexivity is to problematize the epistemological and ontological foundations of the research. The intention of the reflexive stance depends on the claims to knowledge and reality of the researcher and the extent by which they turn these frameworks on themselves either methodologically or theoretically.

Reflexivity is a term often conflated with reflection. Although sharing similar roots, the concepts have marked differences in their intentions. Reflexivity describes the capacity of any system of signification to turn back on itself, to make itself its own object by referring to itself—so that object and subject blur. Reflexivity assumes not just a reflection of self in the research, but a turning inward toward the process of knowledge construction to acknowledge what researchers are positioned to know given their location in the research (see also Stevens, chap. 9, for a clarification of the difference between reflection and reflexivity).

Reflexivity assumes that the self does not merely reflect the social structure, but embodies it through the constitutive nature of language. On the difference between reflexivity and reflection, Alvesson and Skoldberg (2000) wrote, "[S]elf-reflection . . . is more about trying to present research from contributing to dominance and less about directly overcoming it" (p. 129). Reflexivity implies more than introspection. It implies an acknowledgment that the person producing the theory is included in the subject matter she is trying to understand.

If we understand reflexivity to mean not only a reflection, but also a turning inward, then we need to be able to point—through our own constructs—back to ourselves and our locations as researchers. Assuming that the researcher is part of the empirical data gathering, the framework, and the method of analysis, there are consequently different intentions, positions, and reflexive locations. Reflexivity, as it has been outlined here, is crucial in research agendas involving CDA in educational research. Educational researchers are often researchers of familiar educational settings. As members and ex-members of the school communities we study, we bring with us histories of participation within these institutions as students, teachers, and parents. We often bring with us histories of participation with these institutions that have been successful. Thus, we have embodied what Fairclough (1992) referred to as "members resources,"[4] or what Gee (1999) re-

---

[4]Fairclough (1992) referred to such scripts as member resources (MR). He likened members' resources to the social resources individuals bring with them to interpret, consume, produce, and distribute texts. These resources include the internalized social structures, norms,

fers to as "cultural models"[5] around our participation in school, but particular sorts of beliefs, assumptions, and values within these discursive contexts. Thus, the classic tension between distance and closeness in the research setting are often blurry in the educational research we conduct. I suggest this is because we have acquired a set of assumptions that are largely invisible in the work we do—concerning our personhood in relation to texts (Rogers, 2002; see Lewis & Ketter, chap. 6, this volume, for a discussion of their negotiation of boundaries in their teacher-research group).

A reflexive stance in this paradigm assumes working on researching issues that are mutually defined by both the researcher and participants—an ongoing cycle of feedback with the participants and critical workshops around issues that may be ideological and not recognized by the participants. The worth of research in this project is often gauged on the nature of catalytic validity. Each of the chapters have provided a set of action-oriented questions as a means to push their CDA into the public realm.

Reflection and Action

Take the analytic framework used by Stevens (chap. 9) and apply it to the researchers in Sarroub's chapter (chap. 5).

CONCLUSIONS AND WAYS FORWARD

Throughout this book we have argued for a research agenda that focuses on three themes: form and function, context, and learning. In each of the chapters, the authors demonstrated how they see these aspects of CDA in their empirical work. Future research should be conducted with attention to these three themes. Much of the CDA conducted over the past 20 years

---

and conventions, including orders of discourse that people bring with them into each discursive domain. Members' resources shape how texts are produced, consumed, and distributed—both for research participants and researchers. Thus, MR are essential in reflexivity in discourse analysis.

[5]Indeed reflexivity draws on what Gee (1999) referred to as "cultural models." Cultural models serve to define people's beliefs, values, and stances based on achieving desirable outcomes in work, family, relationships, school, and so on (D'Andrade & Strauss, 1992; Holland & Quinn, 1987). Gee (1999) referred to cultural models as the storylines or scripts that people hold in their minds as they participate in situated meaning-making activities. Gee stated, "a cultural model is usually a totally or partially unconscious explanatory theory or "storyline" connected to a word—bits and pieces of which are distributed across different people in a social group—that helps to explain why the word has the different situated meanings and possibilities for the specific social and cultural groups of people it does (p. 44). Cultural models include the social and cultural resources individuals and groups of individuals (this includes both participants and researchers) bring to bear on their understanding or their reading of social situations.

has demonstrated the relationship among power, ideology, and discourse and how people are enabled and constrained by particular sets of discursive arrangements. Working from this empirical basis, part of the agenda for critical discourse analysts is continuing to document such relationships while acknowledging the changing nature of such relationships. This is important because as Chouliaraki and Fairclough (1999) pointed out, it is harder to pinpoint power in texts because of the increasing conversationalization of Discourse. They also argued that we should look for discourses where there is the greatest amount of heterogeneity because these discourse practices are less stable and, thus, more easily changed than those discourse practices that are homogeneous and stable.

CDA represents an interdisciplinary theory and method and, consequently, will continue to be critiqued from various angles. Linguists will critique CDA for not being linguistically oriented enough. Educational researchers may critique CDA for spending too much time on one interaction. This plays out in specific ways in different disciplines depending on which type of CDA is being used. Foucault's work, within the French discourse analytic tradition, foregrounds power–knowledge relationships, but does not attend closely to the linguistic construction of texts. Put to work within a social work perspective that recognizes power imbalances between people and institutions, but not necessarily the linguistic construction of such power imbalances, CDA may be critiqued for not focusing enough on language. When a critical linguistics approach is applied within a second language classroom and analyzes the form and function of code switching and relates this to identity and solidarity in the classroom, the methodology may be critiqued for being too linguistically focused and not attending enough to the social and political contexts in which code switching emerges. The point is that neither the linguistic nor the critical turn in the social sciences has been nor should expected to be equally distributed in all disciplines.

The goal of CDA is to denaturalize ideologies that have been naturalized. However, a great deal of work across disciplines has demonstrated that linguistic interactions (process) and linguistic realizations (meaning) are structured in ways that reproduce dominant ideologies. The future of CDA may mean spending less analytic time on proving that the content and structure of discourse is ideologically laden and more time on how the meaning, structure, and identity are linked together in dynamic ways. Demonstrating that people who hold power make decisions is rather easy. However, it is much more difficult to demonstrate how the decisions made today are a product of a complex chain of Discourse practices that are historically situated. What we want to avoid is a set of loosely grounded analyses of Discourse that are used to support a finding arrived at before any analysis. In other words, future analyses should let ideologies emerge from the data, rather than imposing ideologies onto the data.

Although there are no set rules for conducting CDA, it is important for the analyst to consider each aspect of CDA—the "critical," "discourse," and "analysis." People doing CDA and those interested in CDA might continue to ask, "What is critical about this Critical Discourse Analysis?" This is especially important in educational research because as Threadgold pointed out in an interview with Kamler (1997), educational researchers are not often trained as linguists and often emphasize the critical aspects of research over the linguistic analysis. However, to avoid critiques that CDA is a loosely grounded methodology where the analyst knows his or her conclusions before conducting the analysis, researchers must be committed to studying the relationship between linguistic form and function. For educational researchers, this also means committing to learning more about language structure and analysis.

Educational research is always embedded in a context—whether it is a classroom, an after-school program, or a policy meeting. Further educational research always occurs within a social, political, and cultural context. Researchers using CDA that focuses on different aspects of the local, institutional, and societal domains of analysis might collaborate to bring together research that foregrounds different aspects of CDA with similar research questions and research sites. Little CDA has been conducted on interactional data with different stakeholders in the educational process. The research in this volume is among the exceptions. Further, future work in CDA should attend to the nonlinguistic aspects of ideology such as emotion. Arguably, emotions are the stronghold of ideology, and yet little CDA has described, interpreted, and explained the relationship between affect and ideology. Finally, researchers drawn to CDA are often interested not only in conducting educational research, but in social change stemming from their educational research (either in the process or through the findings). We need to continue to think through the myriad of ways CDA can contribute to social change.

REFERENCES

Alvesson, M., & Skoldberg, K. (2000). *Reflexive methodology. New vistas for qualitative researchers.* London: Sage.
Bourdieu, P., & Wacquant, L. (1992). *An invitation to reflexive sociology.* Chicago, IL: University of Chicago Press.
Chouliaraki, L., & Fairclough, N. (1999). *Discourse in late modernity: Rethinking critical discourse analysis.* Edinburgh, Scotland: Edinburgh University Press.
D'Andrade, R., & Strauss, C. (Eds.). (1992). *Human motives and cultural models.* Cambridge: Cambridge University Press.

Downing, J. (1990). US media discourse on South Africa: The development of a situation model. *Discourse & Society, 1*(1), 39–60.

Fairclough, N. (1995). *Critical discourse analysis. The critical study of language.* New York: Longman.

Fairclough, N. (1992). *Discourse and social change.* Cambridge, England: Polity.

Foucault, M. (1972). *The archeology of knowledge and the discourse on language.* New York: Pantheon Books. (Originally published as *L'Archeologie du Savoir.* Paris: Editions Gallimard, 1969.)

Gee, J. P. (1996). *Social linguistics and literacies: Ideology in discourses* (2nd ed.). London: Taylor & Francis.

Gee, J. P. (1999). *An introduction to discourse analysis.* London: Routledge.

Gumperz, J. (1982). *Discourse strategies.* Cambridge: Cambridge University Press.

Hastings, A. (1998). Connecting linguistic structures and social practices: A discursive approach to social policy analysis. *Journal of Social Policy, 2,* 191–211.

Holland, D., & Quinn, N. (1987). *Cultural models in language and thought.* Cambridge: Cambridge University Press.

Johnson, T., & Avery, P. (1999). The power of the press: A content and discourse analysis of the United States history standards as presented in selected newspapers. *Theory and Research in Social Education, 27*(4), 447–471.

Kamler, B. (1997). An interview with Terry Threadgold on critical discourse analysis. *Discourse: Studies in the Cultural Politics of Education, 18*(3), 437–451.

Kress, G. (1993). Against arbitrariness: The social production of the sign as a foundational issue in critical discourse analysis. *Discourse and Society, 4*(2), 169–191.

Lagemann, E. (2000). *An elusive science. The troubling history of educational research.* Chicago: The University of Chicago Press.

Myerhoff, B., & Ruby, J. (Eds.). (1982). *A crack in the mirror: Reflexive perspectives in anthropology.* Philadelphia: University of Pennsylvania Press.

Resnick, L. B., Saljo, R., Pontecorvo, C., & Burge, B. (Eds.). (1991). *Discourse, tools, and reasoning: Essays on situated cognition.* Berlin, Germany: Springer.

Rogers, R. (2002). Between contexts: A critical analysis of family literacy, discursive practices, and literate subjectivities. *Reading Research Quarterly, 37*(3), 248–277.

Rogers, R., Berkes, E., O-Garro, G., & Hui, D. (in progress). A literature review of critical discourse analysis in education.

Saussure, F. (1959). *Course in general linguistics* (W. Baskin, Trans.). New York: Philosophical Library.

Wodak, R. (1996). *Disorders of discourse.* London: Longman.

Wodak, R. (1999). Critical discourse analysis at the end of the 20th century. *Research in Language and Social Interaction, 32*(1 &2), 185–193.

Author Index

A

Achinstein, B., 120, *141*
Adorno, T., 3, *15*
Allington, R., 193, 196, *203*
Alt, M., 120, *142*
Althusser, L., 20, *48*
Alvermann, D., 122, *141*
Alvesson, M., 249–250, *253*
Antaki, C., 52, *72*
Archer, M., 226, *234*
Atkinson, T., 203
Avery, P., 245, *254*

B

Bakhtin, M. M., 86–88, 93, *95*, 117, 119–120, 124, *141*
Ball, D., 174, *204*
Barrera, R., 121, *141*
Beach, R., 125, *141*
Beaupre, B., 149, *170*
Benveniste, G., 200, *204*
Berkes, E., 242, *254*
Bernstein, B., 89, 174, 176, 192, 201, *204*, *234*

B

Bigum, C., 150, *171*
Bislev, S., 231, *235*
Blakar, R., 10, *17*
Blommaert, J., 10–11, 14, *15*
Bloome, D., 3, *15*
Bonilla-Silva, E., 125, 140, *141*
Bourdieu, P., 199, *204*, 249, *253*
Bower, C., 54, *72*
Briggs, C., 10, *15*
Britzman, D., 221, *223*
Broughman, S., 120, *142*
Brown, G., 4–5, *15*
Brozo, W., 149–150, *170–171*
Bucholtz, M., 14, *15*, 52, *72*
Burge, B., 247, *254*

C

Cai, M., 121, *141*
Cain, C., 45, *49*, 141
Cambourne, B., 69, *72*
Carlos, L., 187, *204*
Carlson, L., 121, 132, *141*
Chafe, W. L., 20, *48*
Chatman, S., 20, *48*
Chen, X., 120, *142*

Subject Index